M000116157

Courage, Passion, and Vision

A Guide to Leading
Systemic School Improvement

Francis M. Duffy

A SCARECROWEDUCATION BOOK.
Published in partnership with the
American Association of School Administrators

The Scarecrow Press, Inc.
Lanham, Maryland, and Oxford
2003

A SCARECROWEDUCATION BOOK
Published in partnership with
the American Association of School Administrators

Published in the United States of America
by Scarecrow Press, Inc.
A Member of the Rowman & Littlefield Publishing Group
4720 Boston Way, Lanham, Maryland 20706
www.scarecroweducation.com

PO Box 317
Oxford
OX2 9RU, UK

British Library Cataloguing in Publication Information Available

Library of Congress Cataloging-in-Publication Data

Duffy, Francis M. (Francis Martin), 1949–
  Courage, passion, and vision : a guide to leading systemic school
improvement / Francis M. Duffy.
      p. cm.
"Published in partnership with the American Association of School
Administrators."
"A ScarecrowEducation book."
  ISBN 0-8108-4609-8 (pbk. : alk. paper)
  1. School improvement programs—United States. 2. Educational
leadership—United States. I. Title.
LB2822.82.D815 2003
371.2'00973—dc21

                                                    2002012345

⊗™ The paper used in this publication meets the minimum requirements of
American National Standard for Information Sciences—Permanence of
Paper for Printed Library Materials, ANSI/NISO Z39.48-1992.
Manufactured in the United States of America.

To those courageous, passionate, and visionary leaders working in school districts who are either engaging their districts in whole-system change or who aspire to that challenge. The challenge is daunting. The emotional costs can be high. They will experience "pain." But the results, the glorious results, are truly worth it—whole school systems providing unparalleled world-class opportunities for student, teacher, and system learning. This book's for them!

Contents

List of Figures and Table

FIGURES

TABLE

Foreword

In past graduate courses that I taught on leadership and schools, I typically began the first class with a video documentary by the Merrow Report entitled, "A Tale of Three Cities: The Minister, The General, The Politician/Businessman." The video is about three individuals from very different backgrounds who have taken the superintendencies of three large, urban school districts in different parts of the United States. The documentary follows each of these leaders over several years with actual footage of meetings around particular crisis events. The documentary goes on to show how each superintendent had to meet challenges of politics, constituents, finances, policies, and other obstacles to eventually change the culture of expectations to improve learning of all students.

After viewing the video, my students and I would analyze the factors around school district improvement, both internal and external, personal and professional, that all school leaders face when serious about trying to coordinate and accelerate the renewal and improvement of an entire district system. In this first class, students who came to the course with an eagerness to right all the wrongs in education immediately became quite somber. It became clear to all of us that driven determination on the part of a single leader will not be sufficient to the task at hand.

Frank Duffy's book *Courage, Passion, and Vision: A Guide to Leading Systemic School Improvement* explains that keeping to a shared district vision of learning for all students takes great planning, collaboration, and the savvy use of influence, expertise, and sometimes power. Duffy points out that schooling is a complex enterprise with the need for constant adjustments, competing demands, and dealing with unpredictable occurrences. He examines how leaders can and do change a district for the better through analytical tools, plans, interpersonal skills, and strategies. This book will help students and practitioners of district leadership, who should be one and the same, lead educational change.

In the collection of chapters, some written by Duffy alone, others with coauthors, and some by current school superintendents, union leaders, and district facilitators, we have an interesting set of intersecting and supplementing theories, concepts, analytical tools, strategies, and practical experiences. Duffy's organization of the book begins with insights about powerful leadership needing courage, passion, and vision with the skills of power, politics, and ethics. This is followed by an explanation of the knowledge needed to help staff, board members, faculty, and community members to "unlearn" and "learn new mental models" of educational success.

The essays from practicing educational leaders, including three current highly successful superintendents, a progressive teacher union leader, and an external facilitator of district change, are refreshingly honest about the realities of strong and successful struggles to improve a school district. These practitioners reflect vast differences in how they approach and prioritize educational accomplishments, yet what they hold in common is an unstinting regard for doing what is right for students and having the fortitude, support, and eventual documentation of learning results to keep the efforts alive. The final chapters by Frank Duffy, alone and with colleagues, draw the roles of leadership and systemic effort together in a pragmatic "step up to excellence" guide with an analysis of finances for school, cluster, and district improvement.

The reader who thinks about, currently serves, or aspires to the superintendency will find much of value in these writings. Duffy weaves together organizational and leadership theories, motivation and cognitive psychology, and change navigation strategies and adds the experiences of practitioners to provide a thoughtful and valuable treatise on guiding superintendents on the most important and basic task of all: improving the educational lives of all our students.

Carl D. Glickman
Roy F. and Joann Cole Mitte Endowed Chair in School Improvement
Southwest Texas State University

Prologue

Leaders cannot know all the obstacles they will encounter, but they certainly need to be aware of the large ones that have stopped reform efforts at other schools. By establishing a framework that anticipates these obstacles, leaders create the conditions that enable their schools to sustain promising reforms and attain their goal—unleashing the power of student learning.

—Carl D. Glickman, "The Courage to Lead"

THE NEED FOR WHOLE-SYSTEM CHANGE

One of the greatest challenges facing school systems in the twenty-first century is their need for effective superintendent leadership for transforming entire school districts into high-performing organizations of learners that provide students and the adults who work with them with unparalleled opportunities to learn. If history offers any guidance for the future, one consequence of not having this kind of leadership at the superintendent's level is that good education change programs that attempt to improve student learning will come and go, largely with mediocre results. When there is success, it will be isolated in "pockets of excellence." Regarding this phenomenon, Michael Fullan says:

> What are the "big problems" facing educational reform? They can be summed up in one sentence: School systems are overloaded with fragmented, ad hoc, episodic initiatives—[with] lots of activity and confusion. Put another way, change, even when successful in pockets, fails to

go to scale. It fails to become systemic. And, of course, it has no chance of becoming sustained. (as cited in Duffy, 2002, p. ix)

Even the best current and past education reform programs are limited in their scope of impact because they focus almost exclusively on changing what happens inside single schools and classrooms. This focus is not misguided. Schools and classrooms are where changes need to happen. School-based reform must continue. But I believe it needs to evolve to a different level because this focus is insufficient for producing widespread, long-lasting, district-wide improvements.

Many of us believe that change in school districts is piecemeal, disconnected, and nonsystemic. Jack Dale, Maryland's Superintendent of the Year for 2000, comments on the problem of incremental, piece-by-piece change. He says piecemeal change occurs as educators respond to demands from a school system's environment. He asks:

> How have we responded? Typically, we design a new program to meet each emerging need as it is identified and validated. . . . The continual addition of discrete educational programs does not work. . . . Each of the specialty programs developed have [*sic*], in fact, shifted the responsibility (burden) from the whole system to expecting a specific program to solve the problem. (as cited in Duffy, 2002, p. 34)

Another person who comments on the ineffectiveness of piecemeal change is Scott Thompson, assistant executive director of the Panasonic Foundation, a sponsor of district-wide change. In talking about piecemeal change, Thompson (2001) says, "The challenge [of school improvement], however, cannot be met through isolated programs; it requires a systemic response. Tackling it will require fundamental changes in the policies, roles, practices, finances, culture, and structure of the school system" (p. 2).

Focusing school improvement on individual school buildings within a district leaves some teachers and children behind in average and low-performing schools. Leaving teachers and students behind in average or low-performing schools is a subtle, but powerful, form of discrimination. School-aged children and their teachers, families, and communities deserve better. It is morally unconscionable, I believe, to allow some schools in a district to excel while others celebrate their mediocrity or languish in their desperation. Entire school districts must improve, not just parts of them.

There are two consequences of piecemeal change within school systems. First, piecemeal improvements are not and never will be *widespread*; second, piecemeal improvements are not and cannot be *long lasting*. Widespread and long-lasting improvements require district-wide change led by courageous, passionate, and visionary leaders who recognize the inherent limitations of piecemeal change and who recognize that a child's educational experience is the cumulative effect of his or her "education career" in a school district.

Leading systemic school improvement, although challenging, is not an impossible task for school superintendents, teachers, and support staff. It is, however, a leadership task requiring courage, passion, and vision. Brenegar (2001) comments on the courage needed to lead when he says:

> What leaders need to learn is not so much just how to be courageous. You can go sky dive or bungee jump off a bridge to learn that. . . . The most important thing to learn is the courage to do the right thing at the right time, despite all pressures to the contrary. . . . Confidence for leaders comes from knowing what is the right thing to do, and taking the risk to do it. It is learned in the day-to-day decisions that require us to be courageous on a small scale. It is the heroism of doing the right thing in daily, unexpected challenges that prepares leaders for the courageous risk-taking that extraordinary circumstances sometimes demand. This is the lesson that successful leaders learn and practice every day. (n.p.)

Thompson (1999) also captures the enormous challenges faced by superintendents who want to lead district-level change. He says:

> There is no question that those who are leading school districts in systemwide reform face enormous challenges. They must be skilled at maneuvering political shoals, untangling intermingled problems, building consensus among divergent groups, motivating the "the troops" in the face of demoralizing setbacks, managing media, sorting through educational innovations and fads, and redesigning the human systems through which students are educated. (p. 1)

Courage, passion, and vision, however, are not enough. Change-leaders also need real-life superintendent role models who are engaging or who have tried to engage their districts in systemic change. They also need a methodology and change tools designed to create whole-system improvement, which brings me to the purpose of this book.

THE PURPOSE OF THIS BOOK

I have a clear vision of the purpose of this book. It offers an artful and compelling blend of practical, theoretical, and philosophical perspectives on leading systemic school improvement. These perspectives are supplemented with essays by three real-life superintendents and two other education leaders who share their views on the courage, passion, and vision needed to lead district-wide change. Not only will you learn what it takes to be an effective change-leader, you will also discover an innovative methodology and a set of tools for producing and sustaining systemic school improvement. Given the preceding vision, the book is written to help aspiring and practicing superintendents learn what it takes to lead systemic school improvement.

DOMINANT AND SHADOW
PARADIGMS FOR SCHOOL IMPROVEMENT

Ever since John Goodlad proposed the idea that individual school buildings should be the unit of change for improving teaching and learning, that advice has served as the dominant paradigm for school improvement. Paralleling the school-based improvement paradigm, however, has been another important and powerful paradigm—a paradigm advocated by people such as Seymour Sarason and Michael Fullan—the shadow paradigm of systemic school improvement.

The dominant paradigm—school-based improvement—caught on, I think, because it made intuitive sense. After all, where else can improvements occur except in schools and classrooms? Yet, so little has really changed in our school districts after all these years of using this approach. Why?

In my opinion, an important part of the answer is that school-based improvement is important and necessary, but by itself, it is insufficient for producing widespread and sustained improvements throughout school districts. It is insufficient because as Wimpelberg (1987) suggests, "Schools can develop as places for excellent teaching and learning, but left to their own devices many of them will not" (p. 100).

If the school-based improvement approach is insufficient, what approach is sufficient? I think that the shadow paradigm of systemic school improvement is. But, why hasn't it caught on? Why don't more school districts use this approach?

Part of the answer, I believe, lies in the fact that many people do not understand what whole-system change means and they do not have a methodology or the tools to create and sustain it. Contributing to the mystical nature of systemic improvement are the numerous and often conflicting definitions of the term *system,* which can make people's heads spin.

Some people think of the "system" as the children, classrooms, schools, district, colleges and universities, state and federal departments of education, communities, regions, nation, world, and ultimately, the universe. Sometimes this definition is modified by the adjective *nested,* as in "nested systems." Although it is theoretically correct, how in the world can educators working in a school district create changes in a system defined that broadly? Given this definition, eyes roll and then glaze over as people mentally walk away from the idea. That concept is much too broad to wrap a mind around.

There is a more pragmatic and ultimately more manageable definition of a system. It's provided by Merrelyn Emery, who, along with her deceased husband, Fred Emery, was one of the pioneers of systemic change in organizations. She says (as cited in Emery & Purser, 1996) to identify the system to be improved practitioners temporarily draw a circle around those buildings, units, teams, and people who need to collaborate to create a "whole" service or product. In the case of school districts, the circle goes around everything that goes on inside the district. The "whole service" is a child's total education within a district (e.g., in many cases, this is organized as a K–12 experience). Everything *not inside* that circle is considered part of the district's external environment. The focus of improvement, then, is on making three simultaneous improvements. The first two sets of improvements happen inside the circle: improve the district's work processes and improve the internal social architecture (culture, communication, job descriptions, policies, organization design, and so on). The third set of improvements focuses on improving the district's relationship with who and what is outside the circle. This definition makes whole-system change imminently more doable.

LEADERSHIP FOR WHOLE-DISTRICT CHANGE

The courage to do the right thing when others say it's wrong; a passion that focuses energy like a laser and drives a person forward; a crystal-clear vision of a future for a school district that others may not yet be able to see—these are, I believe, the characteristics of superintendents who are or who will be leading systemic improvement in their districts. This book is written to help them move their districts toward higher levels of performance and to create unparalleled opportunities for improving student, teacher, and system learning in their districts.

Leadership for successful systemic school improvement, I believe, must be unambiguously provided by a superintendent of schools. Certainly, leadership for change can and must come from many quarters: from outside the district (e.g., from a state department of education or from the community), from a farsighted school board, from a coalition of change-minded building principals, from a group of influential and motivated teachers, or from teachers union leadership. The ultimate success of systemic school improvement will be unequivocally connected to leadership from all these quarters. But, without unambiguous change-leadership from the superintendent, I believe that a whole-district improvement effort is predestined to fail. This presumption is supported in the literature, too. For example, Massell (2000) comments on the role of district-level leadership for change when she says:

> School districts strongly influence the strategic choices that schools make to improve teaching and learning. Districts—composed of local school boards, superintendents, and central office staff—act as gate-keepers for federal and state policy by translating, interpreting, supporting, or blocking actions on their schools' behalf. In fact, the efforts of districts to build the capacity of students, teachers, and schools are often the major, and sometimes only, source of external assistance that schools receive. (p. 1)

Others have also documented the need for effective district-level leadership in bringing about change and improvement (Coleman & LaRocque, 1990; Hill, Wise, & Shapiro, 1989; Jacobson, 1986; Muller, 1989; Murphy, Hallinger, & Peterson, 1985; Paulu, 1988).

WHAT THIS BOOK HOPES TO PROVIDE

Given the need for whole-district change and given the challenges of leading systemic school improvement, this book was written to provide readers with the following:

- Highlights of the challenges that you will face while trying to lead systemic school improvement (found in part 1)
- Role models and inspiration from three practicing superintendents who are leading or who attempted to lead whole-district change and two nonsuperintendents who are also deeply involved in helping districts with whole-district change (found in part 2)
- A methodology and tools to create and sustain systemic school improvement (found in part 3)

Audiences and Uses

The *primary audience* for the book is practicing superintendents who want to lead their districts to higher levels of organization performance. This book will provide these superintendents with the inspiration to exercise their own personal courage, passion, and vision while simultaneously providing them with a methodology and tools for bringing to reality the visions they have for their districts.

A *secondary audience* is found in educators aspiring to become superintendents. To reach this audience, the book could be incorporated into the curriculum of university superintendent training programs, like those of Harvard, Stanford, and the University of Pennsylvania. I also anticipate that the book will be of interest to nonprofit education organizations like New Leaders and New American Schools, both of which are implementing leadership-training programs for education professionals, from principals to superintendents. In this training context, I see the book as a primary resource for courses on change management for superintendents-in-training.

A *tertiary audience* includes state department of education policymakers, school board members, and politicians interested in improving whole-school systems. These people will be able to use the information in the book to develop policies for leading systemic school improvement and criteria for selecting new superintendents to lead school districts in their states and communities.

How the Book Is Organized

The book has three parts and seven chapters. Part 1 is titled "Critical Issues and Challenges for Leading Systemic School Improvement." In chapter 1, you will read about the courage, passion, and vision that change-leaders need to lead the redesign of their school systems. These leadership traits are linked to power, politics, and ethics. I believe these two leadership pillars (courage-passion-vision and power-politics-ethics) can provide superintendents with a solid foundation upon which they can lead the redesign of their school districts.

One of the most challenging aspects of leading systemic change is establishing an internal organizational climate marked by trust, commitment, and collaboration. Chapter 2 highlights the challenges of creating this kind of climate and talks about the benefits of having these elements in place.

People have an uncanny and natural ability to construct mental models that represent what they think works and doesn't work in both their personal and professional lives. When people come together in organizations, they also develop a collective mental model of what their organizations stand for and can do. These personal and organizational mental models can either support or constrain efforts to improve a school district. In almost all cases, mental models need to be exposed, examined, and either changed or reinforced. Chapter 3 presents a discussion about the nature of mental models and how to unlearn old ones and learn new ones.

We used to say we managed change. Now we say we navigate change. This is not an insignificant difference. Managing change implied that we could plan for change, implement goals and objectives, suppress or eliminate unexpected events, and arrive at our desired future. As many of us have so painfully learned, this is usually not the case; or, as the French so eloquently state in their ancient folk wisdom, "The more things change, the more they stay the same." Now we are beginning to see that the course of change is rather like a river with class-5 rapids. Instead of managing our way down that "river," we have to navigate our way down it. Navigating change requires us to learn new concepts and principles for creating and sustaining change. Chapter 4, coauthored by Edward Hampton, presents and discusses these new concepts and principles.

Part 2, titled "Role Models and Inspiration," has one chapter, chapter 5, which is a collection of essays written by practitioners: three superintendents, one education agency assistant executive director, and one leader of a teachers union. Scott Thompson, the assistant executive director of the Panasonic Foundation, leads off in essay 1 with an essay describing research on "critical success factors" associated with high-performing school systems. This essay provides a context for those that follow.

Next, in essay 2, Richard DeLorenzo shares his views on leading whole-system change that resulted in his small, rural district in Alaska becoming one of the first two school districts to win the prestigious Baldrige National Quality Award. Essay 3 was written by Diana Lam, superintendent of the Providence Public Schools in Rhode Island. Diana speaks to the issues of class, race, and gender and how these issues affect efforts to create reform in urban school districts.

In essay 4, Jack Dale, the award-winning superintendent of Frederick County Public Schools in Maryland, shares his views on leading whole-system change in his district. Finally, in essay 5, Louise Sundin, president of the Minneapolis Federation of Teachers and a ten-term national vice president of the American Federation of Teachers, speaks about whole-system change from her perspective as a leader of a teachers union. Combined, these wonderful essays from practitioners offer what I think are important role models and inspiration to those of you who might be thinking about or who are in the beginning stages of whole-district improvement.

Finally, part 3, titled "A Methodology and a Set of Tools to Create and Sustain Systemic School Improvement," has two chapters. Chapter

6 presents an innovative methodology for creating and sustaining systemic school improvement called *Step-Up-To-Excellence*. The principles that underlie this methodology and the tools that are part of it are not new. What's innovative about the method is that it combines these principles and tools for the first time to create a comprehensive, systemic, systematic, and strategic approach to redesigning entire school systems. Further, this methodology *is not an education reform* like outcomes-based education, or extending a school year, or charter schools. It is a systemic, strategic, systematic, and comprehensive process that can help you scale up any reform idea you have to create whole-district improvements.

In Anticipation of "Yes, buts . . ."

One of the most frequent objections to the idea of leading whole-district change is found in the question, "Yes, but . . . how will we pay for this?" In chapter 7, you will find ideas for how to pay for whole-system improvement. These ideas are a combination of practical, tested financing strategies combined with some innovative thinking about how to find the money, and other resources, needed to fund systemic school improvement.

Some of the ideas in chapters 6 and 7 are innovative. One of the greatest "innovation killers" in the history of humankind is captured in the question, "Yes, but . . . where is this being used?" or its corollary, "Yes, but . . . who else is using this?" I can imagine Peter Senge being asked these questions when he first proposed his 5th Discipline ideas. Or perhaps Morris Cogan, when he first described the principles of Clinical Supervision back in the late 1960s. New ideas, by definition, are not being used anywhere, but they want to be used. However, being the first at doing anything, especially doing something that requires deep and broad change, demands a high degree of courage, passion, and vision on the part of school district leaders.

The methodology presented in chapter 6 is new and, therefore, not perfect. Some of you will read about how it works and may find glitches in the processes and logical flaws in the reasoning. But I am confident that the underlying principles of systemic improvement are valid and time-tested. So, if and when you find flaws in the methodology, think about how you might correct the flaws to make the method work for you and your district. If you find flaws, please let me know so I can continuously improve the methodology.

Some of you will read about this methodology and say, "Impossible!" The methodology not only "is possible," but many of its principles, tools, and processes (not the methodology itself) are already being used effectively in school systems throughout the United States; for example, in the Baldrige Award-winning Chugach Public Schools in Anchorage, Alaska, and in the Frederick County Public Schools in Maryland. So, if you read something that seems impossible, ask yourself, "If other school districts are using ideas like these, why can't we?"

Some of you will read about this new methodology and say, "Impractical." Not only are the core principles and tools that comprise the methodology practical, they are proven to work, with more than forty years of experience behind them. Even some of the "outside-the-box" ideas are being applied. So, if and when you think the methodology seems impractical, ask yourself, "If other school districts have used these tools effectively, why can't we?"

Some of you will read about this new methodology and say, "Wow, this guy is really far out with his thinking. He is way outside the box." It is my hope that you will say this. If you do, this means I have succeeded in offering you some innovative ideas to think about and apply. And, if and when you see something that seems "way outside the box," ask yourself, "If this idea is outside the box, what box are we in?" and "Do we want to stay inside this box of ours?"

The methodology presented in chapter 6 will also never produce perfect results. Perfect results are impossible when trying to improve a complex human system. Instead, improvement in a living system is evolutionary, sometimes punctuated with spikes of rapid and breathtaking change. Achieving higher levels of performance is a lifelong journey for a school district.

As you read about the methodology and tools in chapter 6, please remember that the processes, tools, and principles that you see have been used successfully for more than forty years in changing all kinds of organizations. What makes this methodology innovative is that it combines these methods for the first time to create a unified, comprehensive, strategic, and systemic set of blueprints and tools for creating and maintaining successful school systems.

CONCLUSION

Leading whole-system change is not for the timid, the uninspired, or the perceptually nearsighted. It requires personal courage, passion, and vision. It is my hope that you will find in these pages the key that unlocks or reinforces your personal courage, passion, and vision to lead this kind of large-scale effort. If you do step forward toward that vision, please know that you step forward into a world that is not fully illuminated by research findings, into a minefield of politics and turf battles, and into a place where you will often suffer emotional pain and feelings of betrayal by those you thought loyal. You may even lose your job. But, with courage, passion, and vision, I believe you can create a coalition of like-minded change-leaders within and outside your district, and in collaboration with this coalition, together, you can endure pain and betrayal, move forward toward your collective vision, and ultimately succeed in creating and sustaining heretofore unheard-of opportunities for improving student, teacher, and system learning.

It is my desire that this book will provide you with the inspiration, motivation, methodology, and tools to do all that needs doing. But I know that some of you will think, "How can a person who has never been a superintendent give us advice about leading whole-district change?" Let me answer this with a short story.

I do not know if you are a sports fan—football fan, in particular. I am. There are three men in the United States who are considered *the* absolute best kicking coaches in professional football. One of these three coaches suffers from severe cerebral palsy and has been wheelchair-bound all his life. He has never once walked without assistance, never mind kicked a football through a goalpost. Yet, he is one of the top three kicking coaches in professional football.

Why is he one of the three best kicking coaches? Because he has studied the process. He knows it inside out. He knows the subtleties of it. He knows the angles. And he is skilled at communicating what he knows.

In much the same way, I am "handicapped" by never having served as a superintendent, but I know the process of systemic school improvement inside out. I know the methods. I know the tools. I know how to do it. And I can explain to others how to do it. In this respect, I am like the wheelchair-bound coach.

I hope that you will see me in this way and perceive this book as your "playbook." As a "coach," I know whole-system change is doable. The risks are high. The costs can be stiff. But the outcome is truly desirable and important: a school district offering world-class opportunities for improved student, teacher, and system learning.

So, the question I ask of you as you prepare to read this book is this: "Do you have the courage, passion, and vision to lead your entire school system toward higher levels of performance, thereby, as Glickman says, 'unleashing the power of student learning'?" I think you do, and I know you can!

Francis M. Duffy
7404 Bucks Haven Lane
Highland, MD 20777
Phone: (301) 854-9800
Fax: (202) 651-5749
Email: fmduffy@juno.com

REFERENCES

Brenegar, E. (2001). The lesson of leadership courage. Available: www.morrisinstitute.com/weekly/mihv_pc_bren_01.html

Coleman, P., & LaRocque, L. (1990). Struggling to be good enough: Administrative practices and school district ethos. London: Falmer Press.

Deal, T. E. (1990). In T. Sergiovanni (Ed.), *Value-added leadership: How to get extraordinary performance in schools* (pp. v–ix). Orlando, FL: Harcourt Brace Jovanovich.

Duffy, F. M. (2002). *Step-Up-To-Excellence: An innovative approach to managing and rewarding performance in school systems*. Lanham, MD: Scarecrow Education.

Emery, M., & Purser, R. E. (1996). *The Search conference: A powerful method for planning organizational change and community action*. San Francisco: Jossey-Bass.

Glickman, C. D. (2002, May). The courage to lead. *Educational Leadership*, 59(8), 41–44.

Hill, P. T., Wise, A. E., & Shapiro, L. (1989). *Educational progress: Cities mobilize to improve their schools*. Santa Monica, CA: Rand Center for the Study of the Teaching Profession.

Jacobson, S. L. (1986). *Administrative leadership and effective small-rural schools: A comparative case study*. Ithaca, NY: Cornell University, State University of New York, and Ithaca College of Agriculture Life Sciences.

Massell, D. (2000, September). *The district role in building capacity: Four strategies*. Philadelphia: Consortium for Policy Research in Education at the University of Pennsylvania.

Muller, R. W. (1989). *Instructional leadership superintendent competencies related to student achievement*. Unpublished doctoral dissertation, University of Texas, Austin.

Murphy, J., Hallinger, P., & Peterson, K. D. (1985). Supervising and evaluating principals: Lessons from effective districts. *Educational Leadership*, 43(2), 78–82.

Paulu, N. (1988). *Experiences in school improvement: The story of 16 American districts*. Washington, DC: U.S. Department of Education, Office of Educational Research and Improvement.

Thompson, S. (1999, July). Systems thinking: Untangling the Gordian Knots of systemic change. *Strategies for School System Leaders on District-Level Change*, 6(1). Available: American Association of School Administrators Web site, at www.aasa.org/publications/strategies/Strategies7_99.pdf

Thompson, S. (2001, November). Taking on the "all means all" challenge. *Strategies for School System Leaders on District-Level Change*, 8(2). Available: American Association of School Administrators Web site, www.aasa.org/publications/strategies/Strategies_11-01.pdf

Wimpelberg, R. K. (1987). The dilemma of instructional leadership and a central role for central office. In W. Greenfield (Ed.), *Instructional leadership: Concepts, issues, and controversies* (pp. 10–117). Newton, MA: Allyn & Bacon.

Acknowledgments

It astounds and humbles me to see how generous extraordinarily busy people can be with their time. Take, for example, the five practitioners who wrote essays for this book. Two of them are nonsuperintendents. Scott Thompson, the assistant executive director of the Panasonic Foundation (which collaborates with school districts to create whole-district change), and Louise Sundin, the president of the Minneapolis Federation of Teachers, Local 59, Minnesota's largest local; and the ten-term national vice president of the American Federation of Teachers. Scott and Louise wrote two of the essays that you will read in part 2 of this book. Both of these practitioners are deeply engaged in the affairs of their daily work lives, yet they found precious time to write two outstanding essays for you to enjoy.

And then there are the superintendents: one from an urban district; another from a small rural district; and the third from a relatively affluent suburban/rural district. All of them are up to their ears in the all-too-well-known busy-ness of a superintendent's job. Yet, Diana Lam, the superintendent of Providence Public Schools in Rhode Island; Richard DeLorenzo, superintendent of the Baldrige Award-winning Chugach School District in Anchorage, Alaska; and Jack Dale, superintendent of the Frederick County Public Schools in Maryland, each found time in their hectic work lives to write an essay expressing their personal views on the courage, passion, and vision needed to lead systemic school improvement.

I am so grateful to these practitioners. They made a promise to me to write an essay for the book. They kept the promise and kept it well.

John Anderson, the retired president and now vice chairman of New American Schools, Inc. (one of the foremost advocates of comprehensive school reform in the United States), introduced me to several superintendents who he thought might be able to contribute an essay to this book. One of those introductions led me to Diana Lam, whose essay is included in chapter 5. Thank you, John, for your gracious willingness to make those introductions.

Next, I would like to say thank you to the three colleagues who coauthored two of the chapters you will read. Edward Hampton coauthored chapter 4, which focuses on the challenges of leading systemic change. Ed is the president and managing member of Performance Perspectives, a consulting firm specializing in helping organizations and individuals realize their performance potential, and he is a professor of leadership in the Department of Industrial Engineering and Management Systems at the University of Central Florida. Together, in chapter 4, we discuss principles derived from the "new sciences" that shed light on how to navigate rapid, nonlinear change.

Chris Henson and Jason Cascarino helped me write chapter 7, which talks about how to finance whole-system change. Chris is the assistant superintendent for business and facility services, Metro Nashville Public Schools, Nashville, Tennessee, and the former assistant director for finance and administration for the Franklin Special School District, Franklin, Tennessee, where he helped finance the complete redesign of that K–8 district. Jason is a private consultant who is affiliated with New American Schools, one of the leading sponsors of comprehensive school reform in the United States. Jason has authored articles on financing comprehensive school reform. Together, the three of us scaled up our thinking about how to finance change from the level of individual school buildings to the level of an entire district, and you'll read about that in chapter 7.

Carl Glickman wrote the foreword for this book. Carl is also an extraordinarily busy professional. He is professor emeritus of education at the University of Georgia and the Roy F. and Joann Cole Mitte Endowed Chair in School Improvement at Southwest Texas State University. He is also the president of the Institute for Schools, Education, and Democracy, an independent and nonpartisan organization devoted to strengthening education, civic engagement, and the promise of a fully functioning democracy. Additionally, while a professor at the University of Georgia in Athens, he founded and chaired The Program for School Improvement and the nationally recognized K–12 school renewal network, League of Professional Schools.

In my professional life I have felt God's blessings in so many different ways and from so many different people. But I have never felt as blessed as I feel now, having received the generous and kind "gifts" of these people's essays and coauthorships. Thank you so much—each of you—for these gifts.

Thomas Koerner. This is a name I have come to admire and respect. Tom is the editorial director for ScarecrowEducation. He is the person who said "yes" to my proposal to write this book, my second book under his leadership and the fifth in my career. Thank you, Tom, for the confidence you have in me as an author. I really, really appreciate that.

Sometimes it seems like a cliché for authors to thank their spouses for their support. I'm going to do it anyway. My wife, Marcia, has been my biggest fan since the day I met her, more than twenty-nine years ago. Her most famous questions when I'm writing are, "Are you done with that book yet? You're not starting another one soon, are you?" I always answer "no" and "no," but I always think "almost" and "well, maybe." Thank you, Marcia, for the emotional space and time you give me to write—which is my passion. I love you for that (among other things).

Finally, I want to say thank you to all the practitioners I've met over the past several years as I've talked about my approach to creating and sustaining systemic school improvement. The feedback and encouragement I have received from such people as Janice Shelby (the retired superintendent of Franklin Special School District in Tennessee), Tony Lancaster (the executive director of the Tennessee Organization of School Superintendents), and Edward Pajak (chairman of the Department of Teacher Development and Leadership at The Johns Hopkins University) have helped me significantly to improve the whole-district redesign methodology that you will read about in part 3.

Critical Issues and Challenges
for Leading Systemic School Improvement

Leadership for creating and sustaining systemic school improvement requires extraordinary courage, passion, and vision. It also requires a foundation of power, politics, and ethics. These two foundational pillars—courage-passion-vision and power-politics-ethics—are explored in chapter 1.

A superintendent's leadership for creating systemic change is like a tree. But effective, sustainable whole-district change requires a forest of courageous, passionate, and visionary leaders—leaders found among the teacher ranks, in the teachers union, among building principals, in supervisors, and in school board members. If superintendents want to propagate their leadership "trees" into "forests," the "soil" (the internal social architecture of a school system) must be enriched with trust, commitment, and collaboration. Chapter 2 explores these dynamics.

People and organizations have mental models that guide their thoughts and actions. Often, existing mental models are incomplete or they conflict with desirable new mental models. People and organizations are also very reluctant to change their mental models because so much of who they are is woven into those models. Chapter 3 presents a discussion of what mental models are and how they can be unlearned.

Once upon a time, a path from the present to the future was conceived of as relatively linear and sequential. Managers were advised to develop a vision for their organizations, compare that to their present situation, determine the differences (the gaps) between what they have and what they want, set goals, establish objectives, and march straight forward toward a future that was sitting out there waiting for them.

1

That once-upon-a-time advice is not exactly what current realities allow for change-leaders in organizations. Today, change-paths are more like a winding river with class-5 rapids than a straight shot forward to the future. Learning how to navigate these nonlinear, rapidly changing pathways is a twenty-first-century competence for senior leaders in all organizations. Thanks to the "new sciences," metaphors, analogies, concepts, and principles have emerged that inform how we think about and practice change management in school districts. Chapter 4 examines the nature of rapid, nonlinear change within the context of school systems and offers advice on how to navigate that kind of change to create and sustain systemic school improvement.

CHAPTER 1

Courage, Passion, and Vision: Leading Systemic School Improvement

> There is nothing more difficult, more perilous, or more uncertain of success, than to take the lead in introducing a new order of things.
>
> — Machiavelli

There is a resurgence of interest in redesigning entire school systems. Michael Fullan (as cited in Duffy, 2002) comments on this revival. He says:

> Most of the reform work of the present focuses on how to go to scale, and additionally, how to sustain large-scale reform once you get it underway. In our work, and that of others, for example, we are working with entire school districts, and in one case with an entire national system. (pp. ix–x)

Redesigning whole systems is a daunting task that requires a special breed of leader. This chapter describes what I believe are two pillars of effective change leadership for systemic school improvement: courage-passion-vision and power-politics-ethics.

There are voices in the field of education, in our universities, and in our communities that are speaking loudly and clearly about their views of what it will take to redesign entire school systems for the third millennium (e.g., as cited in Duffy & Dale, 2001). These voices speak of leading-edge views on systemic school improvement and cutting-edge methodologies for redesigning entire school systems in ways that have the potential to make significant and positive differences in the lives of school-aged children and the adults who work with them. Most of these voices also deliver the same message even if in different words and images; that is, school systems can and must be transformed into high-performing organizations of learners that create student, teacher, and system learning; and leading systemic transformation requires the unambiguous leadership of a district's superintendent.

Systemic redesign is not for the timid, the emotionally indifferent, or the perceptually nearsighted. Systemic redesign requires change-leaders who possess unwavering courage to do the right thing, a burning passion to educate all children, and a grand vision of what schooling can become for children, teachers, and communities. This leadership also must be rooted in a culture of trust, commitment, and collaboration. The question, therefore, for those who dream of leading systemic school improvement is, "Do you have the courage, passion, and vision it takes to lead this kind of transformation?"

THE COURAGE, PASSION, AND VISION TO LEAD SYSTEMIC SCHOOL IMPROVEMENT

There are many folks, some of them my friends, who argue that leadership for systemic school improvement can come from anywhere in a school system. I say this belief is only partially true. The "motivation" to change may come from anywhere in a school system, and eventually leadership for systemic school improvement must permeate all levels of a school system. But the key leadership for system-wide change *must begin* at the level of a school board and the superintendent. Here's an example of why.

Recently, I had coffee with two school principals. We met to talk about how they might transform a school improvement tool they created into a system-wide improvement method. Their idea is brilliant. It combines innovative ideas from the business world with proven curriculum design and project management methodologies. It's a method that could be used by an entire school system. We started talking about scaling up their method to the system. I asked them about their superintendent's support for systemic school improvement. They said they really couldn't use their tool throughout the system because there was no district-level support for systemic improvement. They were not even sure they could get other schools in their K–12 cluster to use their idea. So, here are two motivated school principals with a brilliant idea that has produced extraordinary improvements in their building, and they have no support to scale it up to improve the entire district. Why? Because there is no leadership for this kind of improvement from the superintendent or from any other key system-level administrator.

Leadership for systemic school improvement must exist at all levels, but most importantly it must first exist at the school board and superintendent's leadership team level. Leadership for systemic school improvement at this level is somewhat like a tree. This kind of leadership has roots, a trunk, and a canopy. Its roots are made of unwavering courage. The trunk is a burning passion to educate children—all children. The canopy is a grand vision of a school district that creates excellent student, teacher, and system learning. Like a healthy tree, this kind of leadership must also be rooted in rich and fertile "soil"—a school district's internal social architecture marked by trust, commitment, and collaboration.

This kind of leadership will not, by itself, result in systemic school improvement. Only when the tree becomes a forest will systemic improvement occur. It is only when courage, passion, and vision are replicated throughout a system like the fractals we read about in the new sciences (see Wheatley, 1992) that systemic school improvement will spread like a contagion (see Gladwell, 2000).

Unwavering Courage

Members of elite military units like Army Green Berets and Rangers and the Navy Seals have a reputation for being intelligent and fierce warriors. One thing that makes them fierce is their unwavering courage. What gives a person unwavering courage?

Being courageous does not mean being without fear. Being courageous means facing fear and doing what has to be done in spite of it. The most courageous Green Berets, Rangers, and Seals are those who face death, accept it, and fight ferociously anyway. And in fighting ferociously, they often prevail and live.

In the movie *Gladiator*, the fictional character Maximus Decimus Meridius, the heroic Roman general who was betrayed, enslaved, and later becomes a victorious gladiator, faces his betrayer Commodus (portrayed in the movie as the son, murderer, and successor of his father, Caesar Marcus Aurelius). They are talking about Maximus's fate, which seems like certain death. Maximus (the good guy) looks Commodus (the bad guy) in the eye and says, "A wise leader once told me that death smiles every man in the face and all that a man can do is smile back." Commodus sneers at Maximus and asks, "And did this man smile at his death?" To which Maximus replies, "You should know, he was your father" (who was murdered by Commodus). Again, facing fear with courage.

It's also important to point out that another reason male and female warriors sometimes prevail and live is their intelligence. They don't take unnecessary risks. They don't make stupid moves that leave them vulnerable to more deadly countermoves.

Leading systemic school improvement also requires this kind of intelligent, strategic, and tactical thinking and acting. Like the metaphorical war of chess, courageous men and women have to think two or three moves ahead of the current move, and then move intelligently, strategically, and tactically.

Superintendents and school board members, of course, don't face physical death in trying to lead systemic school improvement. Some do, however, face the fear of losing their jobs as superintendents or their elected positions as board members. Marc Fisher in the May 18, 2000, edition of *The Washington Post* (p. B1) says the national average job tenure for superintendents is 7 years, and 2.3 years for urban school superintendents. Natkin et al. (2002) challenged the validity of the 2.3-year figure. In their study of superintendents' tenure, they suggested that the 2.3-year tenure was not representative of the true length of service of superintendents. Instead, they calculated the median superintendent tenure during the period covered by their study as 6.5 years.

Whatever the length of service for superintendents really is, the fact is that for some superintendents, thinking about redesigning their entire school district is scary—they don't want to do anything to jeopardize their jobs. I don't have any data about the average term of office of school board members, but many of these boards are elected and members must "please" the electorate to keep their positions. So, the thought of redesigning their school systems is also scary for them, I would guess.

Systemic redesign is not for the timid. It requires a great deal of courage. School board members and superintendents who want to lead their districts onto this dangerous ground must accept the "death" of their school board or superintendent positions as probable, and do what has to be done anyway. They must smile back at this metaphorical death and fight ferociously for what they believe. Unwavering courage serves as the roots of the leadership tree. This courage is what anchors brave leaders to their ground and gives them the strength and courage to prevail.

Burning Passion

Have you ever believed in something so deeply, with such conviction, that no one and no event could stop you from acting on that belief? Bennis and Nanus (1985) in their famous book *Leaders* talk about how leaders "do the right things" while managers "do things right." Have you ever felt the unquenchable desire to do what you think is right? Have you ever been in a situation where people say, "you can't do that," and you did it anyway because you knew you had to do it since it was the right thing to do? Acting in this way is acting with passion. The passion needed to lead systemic school improvement is an absolutely burning desire to do what's right for children, teachers, and school systems.

In the martial art of Aikido, the center of the universe is in each individual. It is located in each of us about three fingers below the navel. This spot is called "one point." The center of a school system is in individuals, too. According to Lew Rhodes, the former assistant executive director of the American Association of School Administrators and the president of Sabu, Inc., a consulting practice in Silver Spring, Maryland, the true center of a school system is in the mind of each child. Thus, like the "one point," the center of a school system is the mind of each child. *Doing what's right* for children means recognizing that each of their minds is the true center of a school system.

There are many adults working in school systems. Those adults who are closest to children are the most important adults in a school system. *Doing what's right* for those adults—especially teachers—means recognizing how important these people are to a child's educational experience and then doing everything possible to help these people to be knowledgeable and skilled.

In our society, organized, large-scale, and free public education would not occur without the organization called a "school district." These organizations of learners must be made more flexible, speedier in responding to change, and more effective in delivering top-quality educational services. *Doing what's right* for school systems means taking the necessary steps to redesign those districts to make them more flexible, speedy, and effective.

It is not enough to hold these beliefs in your head. Passion is not a "head thing"—it's a "heart thing." Rational, logical goals and plans won't do it. You have to possess a burning desire—and I do mean "burning"—to do what's right for children, teachers, and school systems. Leadership for systemic school improvement is from the heart.

Passion is the trunk of the leadership tree. This is what gives courageous leaders the will and strength to persevere despite the odds. This trait helps these leaders bear the pain that will be inflicted upon them—and it will be inflicted in large doses—as leaders of systemic change.

Compelling Vision

Courageous leaders with passion must have a compelling mental picture of what they want to achieve. It doesn't have to be a perfect picture with every detail finely painted into it, but it has to have sufficient detail to make the picture recognizable. It is not enough for a superintendent or a school board to have that vision. Teachers, union leaders, building principals, support staff, children, parents, and the community must "own" the vision. A powerful and motivating vision is one held by a district's internal and external stakeholders. Bennis and Nanus (1985) say that the first task of effective leaders is "managing meaning." In the context of systemic school improvement, managing meaning is the act of envisioning a desirable future for a district and then engaging stakeholders in the development of that vision. This kind of involvement often creates feelings of ownership. Then, once a vision is created and owned, leaders must keep that vision in front of people.

Bennis and Nanus call this "managing attention." Leaders must keep people's attention focused on the canopy of their leadership tree.

THE FERTILE SOIL OF TRUST, COMMITMENT, AND COLLABORATION

Trust

Trust is a scarce commodity in modern-day organizations, school systems included. In an era when people are "downsized," "rightsized," "reengineered," or "restructured" out of jobs, it's no wonder that proposals for redesigning organizations are met with massive distrust. In school systems where educators endure rapid-fire "flavor of the month" changes, it's no wonder they are suspicious of a call for more change.

Yet, in a trust-filled organization culture, many people will commit and collaborate to create desirable changes. It is trust that is so desperately needed if you want to improve the quality of education for children, the quality of work life for teachers, and the quality of your district's relationship with its environment. Without mutual trust (your trust in your colleagues and their trust in you), ideas for change will be viewed skeptically at best and outright destroyed at worst.

Commitment

You can order people to change. Many of them will comply with your order; but compliance results in people meeting expectations and requirements at a minimal level—just enough to avoid punishment. If you want to create a high-performing school system, minimal levels of performance won't do it. With commitment, on the other hand, people willingly and enthusiastically support change and perform. If you want to transform your whole district into a high-performing organization of learners, you need commitment.

Collaboration

Almost every book you read and every journal article you scan about improving the performance of contemporary organizations speaks to the need for and power of employees collaborating to improve their work and their organizations. High-performing organizations throughout the world are making this kind of collaboration happen. It must also happen in school systems. It takes a courageous, passionate, and visionary leader to allow collaboration to happen because when you increase opportunities for genuine collaboration, you decrease centralized authority and power. This decrease is scary to superintendents steeped in authoritarian philosophy and principles of command and control. Contrast this fear of losing power to Jack Dale's philosophy for serving as a superintendent (he is Maryland's Superintendent of the Year for 2000 and superintendent of Frederick County Public Schools). He says, quite profoundly, "I have challenged my cabinet to create an organizational culture and organizational system where there is *no need* [emphasis added] for a CEO. I wonder if we can truly become a self-directed, high performing learning organization" (Duffy, 2002, p. 118). Jack's got it. He understands the power of participation—the power of creating a web of networked teams with the authority to manage their own work and to seize opportunities at the intersection of anticipatory planning and unanticipated events.

By enriching the "soil" within which your change leadership grows with trust, commitment, and collaboration (these three elements are discussed in detail in chapter 2) prior to beginning a district redesign effort, you instill the nutrients needed to transform your single leadership tree (your personal courage, passion, and vision) into a forest of courageous, passionate, and visionary change leaders. All these leaders will be energized to move as one toward a common goal of delivering to children the best quality education possible, providing teachers and staff with state-of-the-art working conditions, and relating to their community in more effective ways. An impossible dream? I don't think so.

POWER, POLITICS, AND ETHICS

Part of being a courageous, passionate, and visionary leader is your willingness to exercise power and political behavior that are anchored in a solid code of ethics. Leadership during times of extraordinary change is particularly challenging. Thus, you must learn to use power effectively, exercise positive political behavior, and act from a firm code of ethics.

Whether or not they are willing to admit it, effective leaders are excellent politicians in the most positive sense. They recognize that an organization is at least as nonrational as it is rational. They know that managers who naively assume that rational management behavior is what works best (planning, organizing, staffing, directing, controlling, budgeting, and reporting) are often losers in the interplay between organizational power and politics.

Leaders know that power must be used with masterful skill and within the bounds of ethical decision making. They see power being used like a laser, targeted precisely to achieve a specific purpose. The leader-politician views power as a Promethean gesture, while political behavior is seen as a Daedalian gesture.[1]

Despite the fact that effective leaders are also effective politicians, many managers and others in organizations eschew political behavior, denigrate those who demonstrate it, and sometimes punish that behavior when they see it in others. However, even those managers who deny they are political and who scorn those who are political often are, in fact, very political themselves—an interesting irony.

Here are a few insights into the dynamic trio of power, politics, and ethics.

The Paradoxical Blend of Power, Politics, and Ethics

Whenever power, politics, and ethics are discussed simultaneously, a paradox is created in the minds of some people. "How," they ask, "can a leader use power in a political way and be ethical at the same time?" Yet, effective leadership in a school district, I believe, results from the skillful interplay of power, politics, and ethics. This section presents an argument in support of this belief. Let's explore each element of this triad.

Power

Power is a pervasive part of the fabric of organizational life. It is possible to interpret every interaction and every social relationship in an organization as involving power (Mintzberg, 1984). Leaders and followers use it. They use it to accomplish goals and, in some cases, to strengthen their own positions (Cornelius & Love, 1984). The understanding of power, knowing how and when to use it, and being able to anticipate its probable effects significantly influence a leader's success or failure in using power. Power used within the framework of an organization's structures (job descriptions, policies, procedures, and so forth) is basically nonpolitical in nature. Power used outside the framework of these structures is basically political and will often present ethical dilemmas.

Power also helps a school district to adapt to its environment. Individuals and groups that assist in this adaptation have power, too (Ivancevich & Matteson, 1990). Power is derived from interpersonal, structural, and situational sources.

Interpersonal Power

French and Raven (1959) provide the classic topology of interpersonal power. They describe five kinds of power:

- Legitimate power: This is power gained because of one's position in the organizational hierarchy.
- Reward power: This type of power is connected to a person's ability to reward others for compliance.
- Coercive power: This is the opposite of reward power—it is the power to punish.
- Expert power: This type of power is when a person possesses special expertise that is highly valued.
- Referent power: This is power derived from one's personality or behavioral style. It is often referred to as charisma.

Structural Power

Power is frequently prescribed by structure within an organization (Pfeffer, 1981; Tjosvold, 1985). Structure is a control mechanism for governing an organization. Structure creates formal power and authority by assigning certain individuals specific tasks and giving them the right to make certain decisions. Structure also encourages the development of informal power by affecting information and communication within the organization. Ivancevich and Matteson (1990, pp. 353–354) describe three sources of structural power:

- Resource power—access to and control of resources.
- Decision-making power—degree to which a person or unit affects the decision-making process in the school district.
- Information power—having access to relevant and important information.

Situational Power

A number of organizational situations can serve as a source of either power or powerlessness. The powerful manager exists because he or she

- allocates required resources,
- makes crucial decisions, and
- has access to important information.

The powerless manager, however, lacks the resources, information, and decision-making prerogatives needed to be effective. Structural and situational power bases are significantly interconnected.

Politics

Politics is also an integral part of organizational life. Individuals and subunits of an organization engage in politically oriented behavior (Velasquez, Moberg, & Cavanaugh, 1983; Yoffie & Bergenstein, 1985). Block (1987) writes about the positive use of power and politics in organizations. Political behavior, at its most positive, is all about influencing others to join with you to achieve worthy goals and dreams.

Ethics

The study of ethics is an ancient tradition, rooted in religious, cultural, and philosophical beliefs (Lewis, 1985). My understanding of ethics tells me that it focuses on a critical analysis of human behavior to judge its rightness or wrongness in relation to two major criteria: truth and justice.

Daft and Noe (2001, p. 437) offer a set of criteria for determining whether power and political behavior are used ethically. "Yes" answers suggest ethical behavior. "No" answers suggest unethical behavior. These criteria are as follows:

- Is the behavior consistent with the organization's goals?
- Does the behavior preserve the rights of groups affected by it?
- Does the behavior preserve the rights of individuals affected by it?
- Does the behavior meet standards of fairness?
- Would you wish others to behave in the same way, if that behavior affected you?

EFFECTIVE LEADERSHIP: THE SKILLFUL INTERPLAY OF POWER, POLITICS, AND ETHICS

To make a real difference, leaders in school districts must be able to affect decisions and events. This is what power and politics are all about; and there is nothing inherently wrong or evil with power and politics. Power and politics are neutral dynamics. Problems arise in the way they are practiced; either for selfish, negative reasons or for the good of the whole. Therefore, the exercise of power and politics must, I believe, be done in an ethical manner. Macher (1988) reinforces this belief in his discussion of a concept called ethical influence. Ethical influence (which I interpret to mean the ethical use of power and politics) is based on the premise that straightforward, nonmanipulative politics is an effective approach to power and self-respect.

Effective leadership in organizations results from the skillful interplay of power, politics, and ethics. Power and political behavior are like two edges of a single sword blade, while ethical behavior is like the conscience of the swordsman using the blade as an instrument of his or her intentions—whether they are evil or good. Manley-Casimir (1989) indirectly reinforces this interplay when he says (the bracketed terms are mine):

The school administrator occupies and works in a context with inherent tensions [politics?], which give rise to the need to reconcile competing claims [the use of power and political behavior?], which in some cases involve the voices of conscience [ethics?] and require their recognition and affirmation. . . . Administrative success . . . depends upon the way the administrator handles these tensions in the everyday world of administrative life [the skillful interplay of power, politics, and ethics?]. (p. 3)

A graphic display of the arena for effective leadership formed by the skillful interplay of power, politics, and ethics (Duffy, 1991) is shown in figure 1.1. It is my hope that this figure will help to dispel the myth that power and politics are evil, immoral denizens of flagrant egotistical psyches; or, as Kipnis (1976) observes, activities engaged in by dark, pernicious figures. Also, I would like to make a

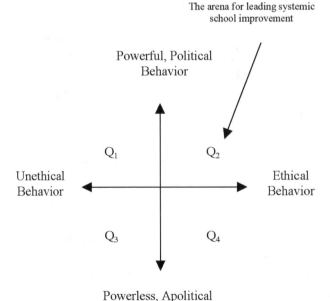

Figure 1.1. Q_2—the arena for powerful, political, and ethical leadership. © 1991 by Francis M. Duffy, Ph.D.

case for the position that administrators need to admit (not suppress or repress) that they do use power and political behavior to achieve desirable goals for their school districts. As Fisher (1984) notes, "Power is a subject about which leaders are seldom candid. The current style has been to apologize for using the authority of position and to speak of the terrible burdens. The secret seems to be to contrive a pose of refined disinterest and modesty behind which one wields all the power possible" (p. 11). This masquerade is not authentic leadership behavior, and, therefore, it can have a deleterious effect on a leader's professional effectiveness as people begin to see through the facade of contrived disinterest and modesty.

Figure 1.1 is constructed using a y-axis, representing the inseparable forces of power and political behavior, and an x-axis, representing ethical behavior. Both axes represent a continuum where the poles of the y-axis are powerful, political behavior versus powerless, apolitical behavior; and the poles of the x-axis are unethical behavior versus ethical behavior. The intersection of the two axes creates four quadrants. Quadrant 1 (Q_1) represents leader behavior that is powerful, political, but unethical. Quadrant 2 (Q_2) represents leader behavior that is powerful, political, and ethical. Quadrant 3 (Q_3) is for leader behavior that is powerless, apolitical, but unethical. And, finally, quadrant 4 (Q_4) represents leader behavior that is powerless, apolitical, and ethical. Let me now provide examples of behaviors within each quadrant.

Q_1: Powerful, political, but unethical behaviors:

- a superintendent using his position to attack a principal who is outspoken
- a superintendent having sexual relations with an intern working in his or her office
- a director of human resources punishing people who disagree with her during a meeting
- an assistant superintendent leaking sensitive information to influence underhandedly a future decision by the superintendent

Q_2: Powerful, political, and ethical behaviors:

- a superintendent using her position to serve as a mentor to a subordinate, even though there is no formal requirement to do so
- an assistant superintendent for curriculum and instruction resolving conflict among several internal constituencies by bending some rules so that the organization does not suffer
- a department chair building support for a major change that will benefit multiple constituencies

Q_3: Powerless, apolitical, but unethical behaviors:

- an assistant superintendent for business and administration lying about involvement in a nonproblematic situation
- a supervisor cheating on a travel voucher
- a superintendent using district funds to install a cruise-control device on his personal automobile
- an assistant superintendent using district funds to pay her way to a professional conference, but never attending any sessions at the conference

Q_4: Powerless, apolitical, and ethical behaviors:

- a director of pupil personnel services minding her job by following the job description to the letter and never doing more than is necessary
- a department chair showing up for meetings with other chairs, but participating minimally in the meetings
- a principal complying with unquestioning obedience to directives from his superiors

From my understanding of the literature on effective leadership, I must conclude that effective leadership occurs in Q_2. For example,

Bennis and Nanus (1985) identified common traits among "super-leaders." The traits were (questions in parentheses are mine):

- The capacity to create a compelling picture of the desired state of affairs that inspires performance (is this political behavior?).
- The ability to portray the vision clearly and in a way that enlists the support of followers (is this political behavior?).
- The ability to persistently move ahead regardless of obstacles (is this use of power?).
- The ability to create a structure that effectively uses others' talents to achieve objectives (is this the interplay of power, politics, and ethics?).
- The capacity to monitor followers, learn from mistakes, and, consequently, improve performance (is this, also, the interplay of power, politics, and ethics?).

CONCLUSION

I believe courageous, passionate, and visionary leaders in school districts need to recognize that their effectiveness as change-leaders is the result of the skillful interplay of power, politics, and ethics; that is, they need to be Q_2 leaders. I do not believe that Q_1 leaders can become or stay effective if they continuously exercise power and political behavior unethically. In fact, I think that the most dangerous and potentially destructive leaders are the Q_1s, and they ought to be fired outright. Q_3 leaders should also be removed from their positions for obvious reasons. Q_4 leaders function in a powerless, apolitical, yet ethical way and do just enough to get by in an aboveboard fashion. They have and wield little influence, yet they somehow remain in their jobs. These people must either move into Q_2 or be asked to step aside.

In my heart I know most people who move into leadership positions want to be Q_2 leaders. But something happens to them when they actually make the move to the administrator's office. Somehow some of them lose their sense of moral direction, their notions of rightness and wrongness, their definitions of truth and justice, and they frequently seek expedient solutions to problems without regard to underlying ethical principles. Then, before long, they change into Q_1s, Q_3s, or Q_4s. This presents a management development problem for school districts: how do they recruit leaders who are capable of and willing to be Q_2 leaders, and how do they restructure their district's reward system to help leaders stay within the Q_2 arena? The solution to this puzzle is, I believe, important to the future of leadership for systemic school improvement.

REFERENCES

Bennis, W., & Nanus, B. (1985). *Leaders: The strategies for taking charge.* New York: Harper & Row Publishers.

Block, P. (1987). *The empowered manager: Positive political skills at work.* San Francisco: Jossey-Bass.

Cornelius, E., & Love, F. (1984, February). The power motive and managerial success in a professionally oriented service industry organization. *Journal of Applied Psychology,* 2–39.

Daft, R. L., & Noe, R. A. (2001). *Organizational behavior.* Orlando, FL: Harcourt College Publishers.

Duffy, F. M. (1991, fall). Q_2—Power, politics, and ethics: The arena for effective leadership in higher education. *College and University Personnel Association Journal,* 42(3), 1–6.

Duffy, F. M. (2002). *Step-Up-To-Excellence: An innovative approach to managing and rewarding performance in school systems.* Lanham, MD: Scarecrow Education.

Duffy, F. M., & Dale, J. D. (Eds.). (2001). *Creating successful school systems: Voices from the university, the field, and the community.* Norwood, MA: Christopher-Gordon Publishers.

Fisher, J. L. (1984). *Power of the presidency.* New York: Macmillan Publishing Company and the American Council on Education.

Fisher, M. (2000, May 18). Editorial. *The Washington Post,* p. B1.

French, J. R. P., & Raven, B. (1959). The basis of social power. In D. Cartwright (Ed.), *Studies in social power* (pp. 150–167). Ann Arbor: Institute for Social Research, University of Michigan.

Gladwell, M. (2000). *The tipping point: How little things can make a big difference.* Boston: Little, Brown.

Ivancevich, J. M., & Matteson, M. T. (1990). *Organizational behavior and management* (2nd ed.). Homewood, IL: Richard D. Irwin.

Kipnis, D. (1976). *The powerholders.* Chicago: University of Chicago Press.

Lewis, P. V. (1985). Defining "business ethics": Like nailing jello to a wall. *Journal of Business Ethics*, 4, 377–383.

Macher, K. (1988, September). Empowerment and the bureaucracy. *Training and Development*, 41–50.

Manley-Casimir, M. (1989). Conscience, community mores and administrative responsibility: A prologue. *Administrator's Notebook*, XXXIII(4), 3.

Mintzberg, H. (1984, October). Power and organizational life cycles. *Academy of Management Review*, 207–224.

Natkin, G., Cooper, B., Fusarelli, L., Alborano, J., Padilla, A., & Ghosh, S. (2002, May). Myth of the revolving-door superintendency. *The School Administrator Web Edition*. Available: American Association of School Administrators Web site, www.aasa.org

Pfeffer, J. (1981). *Power in organizations*. Marshfield, MA: Pitman Publishing.

Tjosvold, D. (1985, summer). Power and social context in superior-subordinate interaction. *Organizational Behavior and Human Decision Process*, 281–293.

Velasquez, M., Moberg, D. J., & Cavanaugh, G. F. (1983, autumn). Organizational statesmanship and dirty politics: Ethical guidelines for the organizational politician. *Organizational Dynamics*, 65–79.

Wheatley, M. J. (1992). *Leadership and the new science: Learning about organization from an orderly universe*. San Francisco: Berrett-Koehler.

Yoffie, D., & Bergenstein, S. (1985, fall). Creating political advantage: The rise of corporate entrepreneurs. *California Management Review*, 124–139.

NOTE

1. Prometheus was a figure in Greek mythology who stole fire from heaven, gave it to humankind, and was consequently put to extreme torture by Zeus. Daedalus, another Greek mythical character, was the legendary builder of the Cretan labyrinth and the maker of wings, which he and his son Icarus used to escape imprisonment. However, they flew too close to the sun and fell back to earth. Leader–politicians know that power is a gift given to them (i.e., a Promethean gesture) and that politics is a process they can use to soar to extreme heights, but which can also make them plummet (i.e., a Daedalian gesture).

CHAPTER 2

The Rich Soil of Trust, Commitment, and Collaboration

In a hierarchy, it is natural for people with less power to be extremely cautious about disclosing weaknesses, mistakes, and failings—especially when the more powerful party is also in a position to evaluate and punish. Trust flees authority, and, above all, trust flees a judge.

—Fernando Bartolom,
"Nobody Trusts the Boss Completely—Now What?"

Courageous, passionate, and visionary change-leadership is like a "leadership tree" (courage as roots, passion as trunk, and vision as canopy). This leadership tree is critical for launching systemic school improvement, but it is insufficient for sustaining it. To sustain a district transformation process, the tree must grow into a forest full of leadership at all levels of a school district. Propagating the leadership tree into a leadership forest requires soil enriched with trust, commitment, and collaboration. Let's explore each of these elements in turn.

TRUST

One thing's for sure . . . if you have the courage, passion, and vision to lead systemic school improvement, you will get nowhere if your teachers and professional staff don't trust you. Trust is the foundation for respect. Respect is a cornerstone of professional influence. Influence is the essence of leadership. No trust + no respect + no influence = less-than-effective change-leadership.

Mistrust in senior leaders in organizations of all kinds is as widespread and contagious as the common cold in wintertime. Someone gets it, and then it spreads through the whole population like a wildfire. Unlike the common cold, however, once mistrust spreads, there is almost no chance of recovering from it quickly, if at all. What makes trust even more difficult to understand is that it takes a very long time to build and only a moment to destroy.

Given the complexities of trust and mistrust, what can you do to ensure that your faculty and staff trust you enough to lead them and your district through the challenging endeavor called whole-system transformation (also known as systemic school improvement)? Let's take a walk through the literature on this topic to see what we can learn together about managing trust.

Over the past thirty years, research in applied psychology and leadership has suggested that the level of trust in a leader affects organizational performance (e.g., Bennis & Nanus, 1985; Fairholm, 1994; Golembiewski & McConkie, 1975; Kouzes & Posner, 1987; Likert, 1967; McGregor, 1967; Zand, 1997). Within this literature, trust is defined in many different ways, but the one common thread among the definitions is that trust is based on an expectation or belief that a person can depend on another person to act in predictable ways and with good intentions (e.g., Cook & Wall, 1980; Cummings & Bromiley, 1996; Dirks, 1999; McAllister, 1995; Robinson, 1996). Thus, the concept of trust is simple. It is built on a person's confidence in you as a change-leader, and it is enhanced and deepened in a work climate where fear is eliminated.

The perception of trust has two components. The first component is affective, and the second is behavioral. The affective component is influenced by a person's perception of your leadership, truthfulness, and reliability. If they "feel" good about you in these areas, and if they do not fear you, then they have a feeling of trust. But the feeling of trust is not all that matters. Those feelings must be validated by your behavior as a change-leader.

Feelings of trust are validated by observing your behavior. People observe what you do and how you do it. What makes trust building challenging is that there is sometimes a difference between what a superintendent says he or she believes and how he or she actually behaves. Argyris and Schön (1978) call this the difference between an espoused theory of action and a theory of action in use.

If there is a difference between what you say your values are and the values actually expressed in your behavior, people will believe what they see, not what they hear come out of your mouth or see in your written memoranda. This is why you have to, as they say, "walk your talk," "practice what you preach," and "do as you say."[1]

Dirks (2000) reports the effects of trust on team and organization performance. He defines trust as an expectation or belief that people can rely on a leader's actions or words and that the leader has good intentions toward those people. His research focused on two related hypotheses related to trust. Hypothesis 1 was "Trust in leadership has a positive effect on team performance." Hypothesis 2 was "Trust in leadership mediates the relationship between past team performance and future team performance." He was interested in testing these hypotheses because there was very little empirical research to support all of the popular literature about the importance of trust in the workplace.

Dirks's findings validate much of what the popular literature says about the importance of trust. First, trust in a leader *does* have an effect on team performance. Second, trust *is* an important factor for leaders and their leadership because it increases people's willingness to accept a leader's decisions and actions and helps leaders achieve organization or team goals.

Bennis and Nanus (1985) describe the four main characteristics of the effective leaders who participated in their research. The effective leaders in their study, they say, shared the following behaviors. They manage

- meaning (by developing a powerful and attainable vision for the future of their organizations)
- attention (which means they help everyone stay focused on the vision)
- trust (which is discussed in this chapter)
- self (which means that if a manager cannot manage him- or herself, there is no way he or she can manage others)

In speaking about managing trust, Bennis and Nanus (1985) say that trust is "the emotional glue that binds followers and leaders together.

The accumulation of trust is a measure of the legitimacy of leadership. It cannot be mandated or purchased; it must be earned. Trust is the basic ingredient of all organizations, the lubrication that maintains the organization and . . . it is as elusive a concept as leadership—and as important" (p. 153).

According to Bennis and Nanus (1985), trust is managed through positioning. This principle is explained as follows: "The leader's positions must be clear. We tend to trust leaders when we know where they stand in relation to the organization and how they position the organization relative to the environment" (p. 154). Superintendents position their school districts by designing, establishing, and sustaining a place for their districts in the external environment. Positioning also focuses on aligning a district's internal social architecture and work processes with the district's external environment.[2]

Despite popular metaphors for viewing organizations as living systems, the environments for organizations are different from the environments for living organisms. The environments for organizations are more complex than natural environments because they are composed of manmade components, some of which are irregular, nonrecurring, irrational, and unpredictable (e.g., school board elections that unexpectedly result in members being voted out of office, societal whims and fancies, and other unanticipated events).

Human organizations, like other living systems, also move along a time dimension—past, present, and future. Movement along this dimension only goes in one direction—toward the future. In contemporary organizations this movement along the time dimension happens rapidly and in a rather nonlinear way (this kind of change path, and how to navigate it, is discussed in greater detail in chapter 4). Because change is rapid and nonlinear, change leadership is one of the key competencies for senior-level leaders in all kinds of organizations.

Human organizations also change as a function of choice. People in organizations make specific choices that influence the direction their organization moves along the time dimension. Often, these choices produce unintended consequences, and they are frequently affected by unanticipated events. The impact of these unintended consequences and unanticipated events bends the change-path they are trying to follow into an irregular, nonlinear path leading from the present to the future.

Bennis and Nanus tell us that environmental complexity, time horizon, and choice are the three key factors that change-leaders must focus on when positioning their organizations within the external environment (please remember that positioning is a way to manage trust).

A corollary of trust is trustworthiness. Verderber and Verderber (1995) discuss the importance of trustworthiness in interpersonal relations. They say, "Persuasive messages are likely to be stronger when we perceive the source as trustworthy. Trustworthiness includes a person's mental and ethical traits. People are more likely to trust and believe in a person whom they perceive as honest, industrious, dependable, strong and steadfast" (p. 270).

Calabrese (2002) notes, "Trust within the organization creates the conditions for honesty. . . . Trust, although built by integrity, requires the leader to treat people as if they were trustworthy" (p. 56). Continuing with his discussion of trustworthiness, Calabrese (2002) says, "Each member of the school organization is responsible for contributing to a trust-filled environment. To the extent that each member makes a commitment to creating this environment, members will trust each other. Conversely, a single member can disrupt and destroy a trust-filled environment" (p. 57).

Olgivy (1995) also comments on the effects of mistrust in business organizations. He says, "In organizations, a lack of trust translates into the need for greater hierarchy and vertical integration. In Germany, where there is greater trust than in France, the average foreman can handle 25 blue-collar workers. In France . . . the average foreman supervises only 16 workers" (p. 47).

Trust is the foundation for high-performing organizations. Within the context of whole-district improvement, trust as a foundation for high performance means that everything you do in the name of transformation must be anchored to trusting relationships. If there is no trust, you can order people to change, and you may get them to comply with the order, but you will not get their emotional commitment. Without emotional commitment to your district's vision and strategic direction, you will not see permanent improvements in schools and classrooms, which is where real district-wide transformation in teaching and learning must ultimately occur.

COMMITMENT

Commitment follows from trust. Commitment is like glue. It holds people together so they can collaborate to achieve an organization's vision and strategic direction. Beer (1980) says commitment is a "human output" that is part of a sociotechnical system; that is, an organization. Human outputs are psychological and emotional responses to the design of an organization and how it functions. If your school district has an internal social architecture that is motivating and satisfying to people, if the district has a work process that people perceive as well designed and supportive of personal effectiveness, and if the district has positive relationships with stakeholders in its external environment, your people should have positive "human outputs," according to Beer. Further, Beer suggests that if human outputs (which also include, for example, motivation, job satisfaction, levels of emotional energy, and clarity of goals) are positive, then it can be predicted that an organization will be effective in achieving its goals and objectives.

Commitment is a consequence of leadership, not an antecedent of it. In other words, commitment comes *as the result* of your change-leadership and trust building. Commitment, like trust, must be earned and nurtured because it is easily lost.

Commitment and Motivation

Commitment and motivation are connected. The literature on motivation provides two broad categories of theory: content theories and process theories. Content theories are those that focus on psychological needs as stimuli of motivation (e.g., Maslow, 1954; Herzberg, Mausner, & Snyderman, 1959). These theories are difficult to use in practice because they imply a leader's ability to diagnose a follower's psychological needs. And, since each person has a different constellation of personal psychological needs, the task of trying to identify these needs in each person you work with would be next to impossible. This brings us to the second category of motivation theory—the process theories.

Process theories of motivation focus on the process, or method, managers use to create those conditions that can stimulate motivation in people (managers don't motivate others, they can only create conditions under which people can motivate themselves—this applies to the content theories as well). Perhaps the best-known process theory is Vroom's (1964) expectancy theory, which is discussed later. In simple terms, expectancy theory suggests that if people know what to expect as the result of their performance, that knowledge is motivating.

Eade (1996) comments on an important technique for helping people become motivated. She says,

> Perhaps the single most important technique for motivating the people you supervise is to treat them the same way you wish to be treated: as responsible professionals. It sounds simple; just strike the right balance of respect, dignity, fairness, incentive, and guidance, and you will create a motivated, productive, satisfying, and secure work environment. (online document, n.p.)

Revamp Your District's Reward System to Promote Commitment

Improving motivation to gain commitment suggests the need for a new reward system within your district that will reward people for behavior that supports your district's transformation efforts, and once transformed, will reward them for learning and using new knowledge and skill. Your district's reward system is part of its internal social architecture, and, therefore, it should be examined and revamped when you focus on redesigning the internal social architecture of your district (as described in chapter 6).

Burke (1982) comments on the power of rewards when he says, "There are no laws of behavior, or we simply have not yet discovered them. One type of behavior that comes close to being a law, in that it is highly predictive, is that people will continue to do what they have been rewarded for doing" (p. 105). In some organizations, the reward system is not well articulated, and sometimes the wrong behaviors are rewarded. Risher and Fay (1995) underscore the consequences of rewarding wrong behaviors when they say, "Too often, employees resist change because they continue to be rewarded for old work patterns. If we want them to change, their rewards must be realigned with new work patterns" (p. 442).

Organizations look for ways to encourage their workers and tap their knowledge and skills. We also know that "people are motivated not only by their individual needs . . . but by the way they are viewed and treated by others in an organization" (Daft, 2001, p. 192). Recent research on reward systems also indicates that rewards are viewed as an integral part of organizations (Lawler, 2000). Rewards, therefore, must be "congruent with other organizational systems and practices, such as the organization's structure, top management's human relations philosophy, and work designs. Many features of reward systems contribute to both employee fulfillment and organizational effectiveness" (Cummings & Worley, 2001, p. 394).

Considerable research has been done on the effects of rewards on individual and team performance. This research indicates that one of the most popular models for explaining the relationship between rewards and motivation is value expectancy theory (Vroom, 1964; Campbell, Dunnette, Lawler, & Weick, 1970). According to this theory, "people will expend effort to achieve performance goals that they believe will lead to outcomes that they value. This effort will result in desired performance goals if the goals are realistic, if employees fully understand what is expected of them, and if they have the necessary skills and resources" (Cummings & Worley, 2001, p. 394).

Principles for Designing an Effective Reward System

The literature on reward systems is pretty clear about what makes an effective reward system. Daft (2001, pp. 193–208) discusses in depth the principles that underlie effective reward systems. Here, I present a short summary of these characteristics. Remember that the core purpose of a reward system is to motivate people to perform beyond expectations, not to meet minimal expectations.

1. *Motivation is based on perceptions of fairness.* People are predictable in many ways when it comes to rewards. One of their predictable behaviors is that they will compare what they receive as a reward to what others receive for similar achievements. If they perceive an inequity between what they receive and what others receive for the same kind of performance, that perception

of inequity will be demotivating. Perceptions of equity fall under a broad theory called "equity theory" (Adams, 1965).

2. *Motivation is based on expectations and rewards.* Greenberg (1990) suggests that in addition to viewing how fairly rewards are distributed (distributive justice) and how fairly the reward process is managed (procedural justice), people also judge their own abilities and expectations. Expectancy theory, which was briefly described earlier, suggests that motivation is also partly influenced by a person's expectations about his or her ability to perform in ways that earn rewards.

3. *Motivation is based on learned consequences of behavior.* Learning is how we develop attitudes, concepts, and skills. Learning theory tells us that what we learn depends on what is reinforced and internalized. Reinforcement theory, although eschewed by some people as manipulative, is a very powerful tool for influencing behavior. This theory tells us that there is a relationship between acting in a certain way and the consequences that follow. If you don't think reinforcement theory works, think about what you do when you're driving down the highway at or below the speed limit and you see a police car parked on the shoulder ahead of you. I know how I react and it has nothing to do with stepping on the gas.

A competing learning theory is the social learning theory (Bandura, 1977). This theory proposes that individuals learn to behave by observing others called role models. Individuals will be motivated to adopt the role model's behavior if they believe that the role model's behavior is being rewarded by others. Thus, motivation is based on "observing others, understanding their behaviors, and interpreting their actions" (Daft, 2001, p. 204). Social learning theory also suggests that motivation is influenced by a person's self-perception of whether or not he or she can successfully behave in certain ways. This is called self-efficacy. Research has demonstrated a strong relationship between self-efficacy, learning, and performance (e.g., see Gist & Mitchell, 1992). A person with higher levels of self-efficacy will work harder and will persist longer toward goal achievement. Conversely, people with low self-efficacy are more likely to quit trying.

4. *Motivation is based on a desired future state.* This principle is all about the motivational power of goals. Goal-setting theory suggests that an individual's behavior will be influenced by a future state that the person wants to achieve. This future state is called a goal. This theory posits that motivation is connected to conscious goals and intentions and a desire to fulfill them.

Extrinsic versus Intrinsic Motivation

An effective reward system uses a combination of extrinsic and intrinsic rewards (Lawler, 2000). Intrinsic rewards are linked to the satisfaction people feel while performing in certain ways. It has been demonstrated that certain conditions within an organization's internal social architecture will stimulate intrinsic motivation. These conditions are the six psychological criteria of effective work (Emery & Thorsrud, 1976). The first three criteria measure how well individual needs are met by the content of their jobs. These are:

- Elbow room for decision making
- Opportunities to learn on the job by setting their own goals and getting feedback
- Optimal variety of work experiences

The second set of criteria measures the social climate of the workplace. These are:

- Mutual support and respect
- Meaningfulness of the job
- Desirable career path

In the whole-district change methodology you will read about in chapter 6, teachers and staff participate in *redesign workshops* where they diagnose their work life using the preceding criteria, and then they create innovative ways to redesign their internal social architecture to create and nurture the preceding conditions.

Extrinsic rewards are given to people by others as the result of a person behaving in a certain way. Classic examples of extrinsic rewards include

- Merit pay and other incentive compensation plans
- Fringe benefit plans
- Promotions
- Status symbols
- Certificates
- Plaques
- Award ceremonies
- Special parking places

COLLABORATION

Collaboration is the great multiplier. It works like compound interest. Through collaboration, courageous, passionate, and visionary leadership is propagated throughout an organization. To create and support increased collaboration in your school districts you will need to redesign your district's internal social "architecture." (Your district's social architecture is one of three "big ticket" targets of change if you want to transform your school system into a high-performing organization of learners.)

When you redesign your school district to move toward higher levels of performance, you must create a new internal social architecture for your district that facilitates collaboration among your faculty and staff. This new social architecture should have three distinguishing characteristics. First, it should favor skill-based work, the creation of district-wide professional knowledge, and peer relationships. Second, it should be anchored to the collective knowledge, talent, and resources of a network of redesign teams and Organizational Learning Networks (described later in chapter 6). The link pin that holds all these teams and networks together is a Knowledge Work Coordinator (this role is also described in chapter 6). Third, the new social architecture should facilitate collaboration that is deep and wide.

The goal of creating this kind of networked social architecture is to create, as much as possible, a school system that is self-regulating and self-optimizing (as opposed to being externally regulated and externally forced to improve). This kind of social architecture produces superior performance in a turbulent environment (Daft, 2001). When a school system's external environment is turbulent and things start happening fast and furiously, if it has teams and networks with the resources they need to succeed, then a web of accountabilities is woven that collectively keeps the district on course toward a higher performance peak.

Creating a new social architecture using a web of teams and learning networks doesn't mean that you surrender your authority and control to a networked "mob." Your voice of leadership must still be present and heard. Without some element of governance and leadership from the top of a school district, bottom-up action freezes in place when there are too many options to be considered. Without some element of leadership at the top, the many at the bottom will be paralyzed by an overabundance of choices. The creation of a social architecture in your district that honors and uses formal leadership roles while simultaneously creating and sustaining networked teams will provide strange and wonderful moments for seizing opportunities at the intersection of anticipatory planning and unanticipated events.

Despite the continuing need for formal leadership in school districts, you can gain a lot more by pushing the boundaries of what teams can do than by focusing on what you can do alone. "When it comes to control, there is plenty of room at the bottom. What we are discovering is that peer-based networks . . . can do more than any one ever expected. We don't yet know what the limits of decentralization are" (Kelly, 1998, p. 8).

When improvements are made within a networked social architecture, small efforts yield large results. This is because of the curious mathematics of group size (Kephart, 1950). As the number of people in a networked social architecture increases, the value of that "web" increases exponentially (a term used in the vernacular to mean explosive compounded growth; mathematically, however, the value increases in polynomial patterns). For example, if there are four people in a network, there are twenty-five possible relationships among those people. If just one person is added, the number of relationships increases to 90. Here's a mathematical formula for making this calculation:

$x = \frac{1}{2}(3^n - 2^n + 1) + 1$, where

x = total number of possible relationships in a group

n = number of individuals in a group

For instance, what is the total number of relationships in a group with 7 members?

$$x = \frac{1}{2}(3^7 - 2^7 + 1) + 1$$
$$= \frac{1}{2}(2,187 - 256) + 1$$
$$= \frac{1}{2}(1,931) + 1$$
$$= 966 \text{ possible relationships}$$

Stunning, isn't it? And this is just for real-time, face-to-face groups. This calculation, however, doesn't begin to capture the power of teams and learning networks connected using technology where people can have complex many-way relationships simultaneously.

A networked social architecture also stimulates creativity and innovation by using principles of participative work design (see Emery & Purser, 1996). Creativity and innovation present opportunities for breathtaking district-wide improvement. The more opportunities created and taken, the faster new opportunities will arise. This is called compounded learning—the more we create something, the easier it becomes to create more of it. Therefore, as a change-leader you need to allow people to build their success around the success of others, which, in turn, creates compounded organizational learning.

Protect Voices of Leadership from Below

Nothing will kill trust, commitment, and collaboration quicker than punishing people for expressing their opinions. Let me digress for a moment to tell you a story about this.

Many years ago, I was hired to spend a week with a superintendent of schools for a private residential school and his management team, which consisted of three principals and a business manager. The superintendent hired me to help him improve the performance of his management team.

During the week, I interviewed each member of the management team and I observed team meetings. As the week progressed, an interesting and disturbing pattern of behavior began to emerge from the superintendent. Whenever the superintendent asked for a team member's opinion, if the opinion was supportive of the superintendent's views, he was flattering and supportive of the person giving the opinion. But when someone expressed a negative opinion or one that disagreed with the superintendent, he would publicly humiliate and criticize the person.

When I shared my diagnostic data with the whole team on the last day, the superintendent's jaw literally dropped open. He was not aware of his behavior and was stunned by the data. He then challenged the validity of it by claiming that I was mistaken. Then, one of the principals who was a victim of his humiliation spoke up and began to describe what he did to her when she disagreed with him. Her feelings were so powerful that she began to cry. Then, she said something that reinforces the point I'm making about what happens when you punish people for expressing opinions that disagree with your views. She said, "Because you [the superintendent] criticize people for expressing opinions you don't like, we are reluctant to tell you the truth and we don't want to share our views in meetings for fear of being humiliated and criticized."

Heifetz and Laurie (1997) capture another thing that makes it difficult for superintendents to "listen" to the voices of leadership from below. They say:

> Giving a voice to all people is the foundation of an organization that is willing to experiment and learn. . . . The voices from below are usually not as articulate as one would wish. People speaking beyond their authority usually feel self-conscious and sometimes have to generate "too much" passion to get themselves geared up for speaking out. . . . But buried inside the poorly packaged interjection may lie an important intuition that needs to be teased out and considered. (pp. 129–130)

This observation presents you with a leadership challenge. How will you help give "voice" to people in ways that will (1) allow them to speak up before they "explode" because of pent-up emotions and (2) allow you to uncover ideas and suggestions that may be buried in their statements? There is no one right way to do this. Each of you will need to find a way that works for you and your people.

CONCLUSION

"Organizational trust . . . rests both on the constancy of purpose modeled by the leader and others in the organization and on the constancy of the 'process,' which comprises problem solving, decision making, and implementation styles. A breakdown in these areas could spell failure" (Napier & Gershenfeld, 1993, pp. 262–263).

Collaborative team-based problem solving, as required by contemporary approaches to improving whole systems, may increase trust within the whole organization. Napier and Gershenfeld (1993) suggest this when they say, "The level of trust within the group may increase and be transferred to the organization because mutually agreed-upon solutions require sacrificing of personal self-interest or gain. The giving up of one's personal vested interest often increases one's stake in the organization itself" (p. 431).

As individuals and teams share responsibility for achieving organizational goals and as they exercise personal accountability within a web of accountabilities, their efforts may in turn increase trust and support personal risk taking. Napier and Gershenfeld (1993) support this conclusion when they say, "Shared responsibility as well as personal accountability . . . will increase trust and insure more individual risk taking as well as a willingness to devote the necessary time to resolve working issues of both a substantive and personal nature" (p. 485).

Increasing participation and collaboration is challenging for leaders. One of the most important reasons that it is challenging is related to human psychology. In organizations, people are accustomed to being dependent on others to make decisions for them. This dependency, in turn, motivates them to demand leadership behaviors that ensure their dependence (Napier & Gershenfeld, 1993, p. 501). Thus, a simple directive to become more collaborative often is insufficient for causing these new behaviors to emerge. What's required to increase participation and collaboration are (1) organization structures that support that behavior (e.g., policies and procedures), (2) a reward system that reinforces desirable behaviors, and (3) an organizational culture that supports and encourages collaboration.

If trust, commitment, and collaboration are the foundation for creating and sustaining high performance, then these elements must be in place before you engage your district in a deep and wide change effort. If you try to initiate systemic change before trust, commitment, and collaboration issues are resolved, you will probably fail in your efforts to lead your district to higher ground.

REFERENCES

Adams, J. S. (1965). Injustice in social exchange. In L. Berkowitz (Ed.), *Advances in experimental social psychology*. New York: Academic.

Argyris, C., & Schön, D. (1978). *Organizational learning*. Reading, MA: Addison-Wesley.

Bandura, A. (1977). *Social learning theory*. Englewood Cliffs, NJ: Prentice Hall.

Bartolom, F. (1989, March–April). Nobody trusts the boss completely—now what? *Harvard Business Review* (reprint #89212), 5–11.

Beer, M. (1980). *Organization change and development: A systems view*. Santa Monica, CA: Goodyear.

Bennis, W., & Nanus, B. (1985). *Leaders: The strategies for taking charge*. New York: Harper & Row.

Burke, W. W. (1982). *Organization development: Principles and practices*. Boston: Little, Brown.

Calabrese, R. L. (2002). *The leadership assignment: Creating change*. Boston: Allyn & Bacon.

Campbell, J., Dunnette, M., Lawler, E., III, & Weick, K. (1970). *Managerial behavior, performance, and effectiveness*. New York: McGraw-Hill.

Cook, J., & Wall, T. (1980). New work attitude measures of trust, organizational commitment, and personal need fulfillment. *Journal of Occupational Psychology*, 53, 39–52.

Cummings, L., & Bromiley, P. (1996). The Organizational Trust Inventory (OTI): Development and validation. In R. Kramer & T. Tyler (Eds.), *Trust in organizations* (pp. 302–330). Thousand Oaks, CA: Sage.

Cummings, T. G., & Worley, C. G. (2001). *Organization development and change* (7th ed.). Cincinnati: South-Western College Publishing.

Daft, R. L. (2001). *Organization theory and design* (7th ed.). Cincinnati, OH: South-Western College Publishing.

Dirks, K. T. (1999). The effects of interpersonal trust on work group performance. *Journal of Applied Psychology*, 84, 445–455.

Dirks, K. T. (2000, December). Trust in leadership and team performance: Evidence from NCAA basketball. *Journal of Applied Psychology*, 85(6), 1004–1012.

Eade, D. M. (1996). Motivational management: Developing leadership skills. Available: www.adv-leadership-grp.com/articles/motivate.htm

Emery, F. E., & Thorsrud, E. (1976). *Democracy at work: The report of the Norwegian industrial democracy program*. Leiden, Holland: Martinus Nijhoff.

Emery, M., & Purser, R. E. (1996). *The search conference: A powerful method for planning organizational change and community action*. San Francisco: Jossey-Bass.

Fairholm, G. (1994). *Leadership and the culture of trust*. Westport, CT: Praeger.

Gist, M. E., & Mitchell, T. R. (1992). Self-efficacy: A theoretical analysis of its determinants and malleability. *Academy of Management Review, 17*, 183–211.

Golembiewski, R., & McConkie, M. (1975). The centrality of interpersonal trust in group process. In C. Cooper (Ed.), *Theories of group process* (pp. 131–185). New York: Wiley.

Greenberg, J. (1990). Organizational justice: Yesterday, today, and tomorrow. *Journal of Management, 16*, 399–432.

Heifetz, R. A., & Laurie, D. L. (1997, January–February). The work of leadership. *Harvard Business Review, 75*(1), 124–134.

Herzberg, F., Mausner, B., & Snyderman, B. (1959). *The motivation to work*. New York: Wiley.

Kelly, K. (1998). *New rules for the new economy: 10 radical strategies for a connected world*. New York: Penguin.

Kephart, W. M. (1950). A quantitative analysis of intragroup relationships. *American Journal of Sociology, 60*, 544–549.

Kouzes, J., & Posner, B. (1987). *The leadership challenge: How to get extraordinary things done in organizations*. San Francisco: Jossey-Bass.

Lawler, E., III. (2000). *Rewarding excellence: Pay strategies for the new economy*. San Francisco: Jossey-Bass.

Likert, R. (1967). *The human organization*. New York: McGraw-Hill.

Maslow, A. H. (1954). *Motivation and personality*. New York: Harper & Row.

McAllister, D. (1995). Affect- and cognition-based trust as foundations for interpersonal cooperation in organizations. *Academy of Management Journal, 38*, 24–59.

McGregor, D. (1967). *The professional manager*. New York: McGraw-Hill.

Napier, R. W., & Gershenfeld, M. K. (1993). *Groups: Theory and practice* (5th ed.). Boston: Houghton Mifflin.

Olgivy, J. (1995, November–December). The economics of trust. *Harvard Business Review, 73*(6), 46–47.

Risher, H., & Fay, C. (1995). Managing employees as a source of competitive advantage. In H. Risher & C. Fay (Eds.), *The performance imperative: Strategies for enhancing workforce effectiveness*. San Francisco: Jossey-Bass.

Robinson, S. (1996). Trust and the breach of the psychological contract. *Administrative Science Quarterly*, 41, 574–599.

Verderber, R. F., & Verderber, K. S. (1995). *Inter-Act: Using interpersonal communication skills* (7th ed.). Belmont, CA: Wadsworth.

Vroom, V. (1964). *Work and motivation*. New York: Wiley.

Zand, D. (1997). *The leadership triad: Knowledge, trust, and power*. New York: Oxford.

NOTES

1. I once worked for a dean who knew the language of participatory management. He would talk about involving faculty in decision making. But he rarely involved faculty in decision making. His behavior betrayed his real values. People could see it, and it was his behavior they believed—not his words. And to make it worse, he didn't realize the difference.

2. The sociotechnical design principle of making simultaneous improvements in an organization's work processes, social architecture, and external environmental relationships represents three paths you must follow to transform your school district into a high-performing organization of learners. Each of these paths is explored in depth in chapter 6.

CHAPTER 3

Unlearning and Learning Mental Models: A Leadership Challenge for Creating and Sustaining Whole-District Change

> If we want deeper understanding of the prospect of change, we must pay closer attention to our own powerful inclinations *not* to change. This attention may help us discover within ourselves the force and beauty of a hidden immune system, the dynamic process by which we tend to prevent change, by which we manufacture continuously the antigens of change. If we can unlock this system, we release new energies on behalf of new ways of seeing and being.
>
> —Robert Kegan and Lisa Laskow Lahey,
> *How the Way We Talk Can Change the Way We Work*

One of your central leadership challenges for creating and sustaining systemic school improvement is the daunting task of helping individuals, teams, and your districts unlearn old mental models and learn new ones. Unlearning and learning mental models are extraordinarily difficult, yet extraordinarily crucial to the success of any school district improvement effort. You must also be willing to examine and unlearn your personal mental models because they may stand in the way of whole-district improvement. In this chapter, I highlight aspects of this challenge and offer tips for helping individuals, teams, and systems unlearn and learn mental models.

MENTAL MODELS DEFINE REALITY

People construct cognitive representations of what they learn. These representations are commonly called *mental models* (e.g., Johnson-Laird,

1983). Ann Bradford (1995–1996) reflects the important influence of mental models on thinking and behaving when she says,

> The way we think and receive stimuli are [sic] governed by unspoken assumptions and inherent modes of thought. If we can break free of these confines, we can see patterns and combinations that previously were not apparent to us. How we see is important because it so strongly influences our attitudes and behaviors. (online document, n.p.)

There are two kinds of mental models: personal and organizational. Personal mental models are internal paradigms that help professionals know and understand their worlds. An organizational mental model (often called a "vision statement" and frequently reflected in an organization's culture) is a collective representation of what an organization stands for and how it accomplishes its goals. An organizational mental model is embodied in its internal social "architecture" and in its relationships with the outside world. Neither kind of mental model is easily described in words because some of what the mental model represents is at an intuitive level.

An example of a personal mental model for teachers is found in a teacher's response to the statement "Effective classroom teaching is . . ." Every teacher should have a personal mental model that defines effective classroom teaching. Elements of this mental model might include "communication skills," "classroom management," and "learning styles." A teacher's mental model of effective classroom teaching guides his or her work. When asked to describe his or her mental model for effective teaching, a teacher may not be able to provide a detailed description of that model and will focus instead on its general features. The more abstract and vague the mental model is, the less likely it is that the teacher's work will be effective.

An example of an organizational mental model for a school district is "Our school district is a learning community." Elements of this mental model might include "collective decision making" and "workers as stakeholders." When asked to describe in words their district's mental model, educators may not be able to provide a complete and accurate description of the details of that model and will focus instead on its general features. As with the personal models, the more abstract and vague the mental model is, the less likely it is that the mental model will be effective in guiding thought and action.

HOW MENTAL MODELS AFFECT YOUR CHANGE-LEADERSHIP

When attempting to lead systemic change, you will be faced with a set of intimidating insights into the limitations of your change-leadership. Kegan and Lahey (2001), two developmental psychologists from Harvard University, identify these insights as follows:

- Leading inevitably involves trying to effect significant changes.
- It is very hard to bring about significant changes in any human group without changes in individual behavior.
- It is very hard to sustain significant changes in behavior without significant changes in individuals' underlying meanings [their mental models] that may give rise to their behaviors.
- It is very hard to lead on behalf of other people's changes in their [mental models] without considering the possibility that [you] must also change [your mental models]. (p. 3)

Most change-leaders are not specifically aware of the preceding insights. Instead, these insights often manifest themselves as one big disappointing experience; that is, despite everything you do to lead change, often very little significant change actually occurs (Kegan & Lahey, 2001, p. 3).

Why Mental Models Are Difficult to Change

According to Kegan and Leahy, people have a built-in, antichange "immune system." This immune system is dynamic and provides us with powerful inclinations not to change. If this immune system can be unlocked and modified, people can then release new energy on behalf of new ways of seeing and being. New ways of seeing and being serve as the foundation for unlearning and learning mental models, and, therefore, exist at the critical core of leadership for systemic change. Our internal antichange immune systems are powered by three significant forces: entropy, negentropy, and dynamic equilibrium. Each of these is highlighted in the following sections and is explored more deeply in chapter 4.

Entropy

One of the most widely studied forces in nature is entropy. Entropy is the process by which dynamic systems (such as people, organizations, mechanical systems, or solar systems) gradually fall apart. Entropy is movement toward increasing disorder, decreasing complexity, randomness, and dissipation of energy (Kegan & Lahey, 2001, p. 3).

Negentropy

Mechanical and natural systems cannot slow entropy. People and their organizations, however, do have the potential to slow entropy. They do this by increasing complexity, becoming more ordered, acquiring and using greater energy, and creating extraordinary solutions to their problems. Increasing energy like this is the opposite of entropy and physicists call it negentropy. "It is a distinguishing and heroic feature of living things that they participate not only in deteriorative processes of declining complexity, order, choice, concentration, and power but also in processes that lead to greater complexity, order, choice, concentration, and power" (Kegan & Lahey, 2001, pp. 4–5).

Dynamic Equilibrium

The most powerful force blocking your district's path toward high performance is dynamic equilibrium. Dynamic equilibrium is a force that tends to keep things pretty much the way they are. The forces of dynamic equilibrium play a large role in blocking change in individuals and organizations.

Dynamic equilibrium is not about standing in place or lack of motion. Dynamic equilibrium is motion—the motion of positive and negative forces working against each other, balancing each other, and keeping everything basically locked in place. The consequences of dynamic equilibrium are reflected in the French adage, "The more things change, the more they stay the same." As most of us have experienced in our lives, we produce change only to find ourselves reverting back to prechange conditions. We lose ten pounds, and gain it back. We create a new vision for our school districts, and we march to the tune of the old vision. The competing forces for and against change often balance each other and keep us and our organizations in a relatively stable state of being.

Dynamic equilibrium creates something in us and our school districts that functions like an immune system in our bodies. Just as our bodily immune systems fight off foreign substances inside of us, this metaphorical antichange immune system powered by dynamic equilibrium fights off change in ourselves and in our organizations (Kegan & Lahey, 2001, p. 6). These immune systems are difficult to change because we live inside these systems and they hold us captive; or as Kegan and Lahey say, "We do not have them; they have us."

CHANGING MENTAL MODELS

The performance of school districts is influenced by the forces of entropy and negentropy. Mental models are held in place by antichange "immune systems" (both personal and systemic) that are powered by the forces of dynamic equilibrium. So, if you want to change personal and organizational mental models, how in the world do you do it?

> Because mental models are usually tacit, existing below the level of awareness, they are often untested and unexamined. They are generally invisible to us—until we look for them. The core task [for changing them] is bringing mental models to the surface, to explore and talk about them with minimal defensiveness—to help us see the pane of glass, see its impact on our lives, and find ways to re-form the glass by creating new mental models that serve us better in the world. (Senge, Kleiner, Roberts, Ross, & Smith, 1994, p. 236)

Before people can learn a new mental model they have to unlearn what they think they already know. In some way or fashion, they have to come to the realization that they can no longer rely on their current knowledge, beliefs, and methods (i.e., their current mental models).

What We Know Prevents Us from Seeing What We Don't Know

Unlearning begins when people can no longer rely on their current knowledge, beliefs, and methods. Current knowledge, beliefs, and methods influence our perceptions and, as such, they blind us to other ways of interpreting events around us (Starbuck, 1996). People do not and will not cast aside their current mental models as long as these models *seem* to produce reasonable results (Kuhn, 1962). As Petroski (1992) puts it, people "tend to hold onto their theories until incontrovertible evidence, usually in the form of failures, convinces them to accept new paradigms" (pp. 180–181). However, people are notorious for sticking with their current beliefs and methods despite very poor and even disastrous results. Even after abject failure, some people will attribute their failures to some external event or person instead of recognizing the inadequacies of their own personal mental models.

Starbuck (1996) observes that professionals are among the most resistant to new ideas and to evidence that contradicts their current mental models. This kind of resistance has several sources. Professionals must specialize, and their specialized niches can lock people in place (Beyer, 1981). Because professionals accrue social status in organizations and, in some cases, earn high incomes, they have much to lose if there are significant changes in their fields of expertise. This state of being "blinds" them from seeing opportunities to create change in their mental models (Armstrong, 1985).

An Organization's Social Architecture Blocks Unlearning

An organization's internal social "architecture" is that collection of policies, procedures, organizational culture, climate, communication patterns, among other things, that supports life in an organization. People in organizations hold certain beliefs and values that are collectively built into that architecture. People then create and justify policies, procedures, decisions, and behaviors that support and reinforce their beliefs and values. Further, as people interact, all of these beliefs and values are woven together to create an organizational mental model (the vision and the organization's culture) that reflects what people *think* their organization stands for and how they *think* it should function as an organization. This organization-wide mental model then takes on a degree of rigidity that makes it very difficult for people to think and act in ways that don't fit that model. People, therefore, often find it difficult to accommodate new and innovative ideas, and they find it challenging to change (which is one of the key reasons why people resist innovative, "outside-the-box" ideas).

Tushman, Newman, and Romanelli (1986) discuss how organizations change. They say that an organization develops over long periods of convergent, incremental change that are interrupted by brief periods of "frame-breaking change." They suggest that frame-breaking change occurs in response to or in anticipation of major changes in an organization's environment. Starbuck (1996), however, believes that frame-breaking change happens differently. He thinks that big changes happen when people and organizations unlearn their old mental models and then undertake breathtaking change to enact their new mental models (i.e., change is in response to a dramatic and sudden internal paradigm shift).

Political Pressure Can Stimulate Unlearning

Unlearning by people in organizations is also influenced by political pressure. People and groups with power and political influence affect what people think and how they act (Hedberg, 1981). The political influence of school administrators, building principals, supervisors, and teachers union leaders is especially potent because these people can either block or support proposed actions. Having the political support of these people is absolutely crucial for helping teachers and support staff unlearn old and learn new mental models for teaching, learning, and school improvement.

HELPING PEOPLE UNLEARN

Starbuck (1996) offers some insights into possible ways to help people unlearn mental models that prevent them from seeing the opportunities before them. Although his insights focus on changing individual mental models, I think the ideas very easily apply to changing organizational mental models.

Starbuck suggests that the foundation for unlearning mental models is doubt. Any person, event, or information that raises doubt about current beliefs and methods can become a stimulus for unlearning. Starbuck (1996) says there are several ways to raise doubt and use it to stimulate unlearning. Each one is summarized in the following sections.

It Isn't Good Enough

Dissatisfaction is probably the most common reason for doubting something. Dissatisfaction, however, takes a long time to work. Often, when people fail or something doesn't work right for them, they come up with all kinds of reasons to explain their failures; but none of the reasons focus on a person's mental models. These mental models are quite resistant to change and it takes a lot of painful failures to become dissatisfied with them.

It's Only an Experiment

If people believe a new method they are trying or a new idea they are considering is just an experiment, they are more likely to allow themselves to act outside the box of their existing mental model. When they step outside their "box," they find opportunities to be surprised. Because these new ways of acting and thinking are just "experiments," the risks associated with failure are substantially reduced. Because attendant risks are reduced, people become more willing and able to consider feedback with an open mind and they are more likely to evaluate results more objectively. Experimentation allows them to modify their mental models to allow new ways of seeing, understanding, and doing.

Surprises Should Be Question Marks

Unexpected events or results, both positive and negative, can stimulate unlearning. If people are in an experimental mode, the results of their experiments can be surprising. Faced with a surprise result or outcome, people can then question what happened and why it happened. Answers to these questions can help people unlearn their old mental models as their answers point to new ways of thinking and doing.

All Dissents and Warnings Have Some Validity

When bad news is announced or when warnings about impending failure are given, you have to take this information seriously. Of course, not every person who disagrees with a course of action or a decision should be taken seriously. But, as Starbuck suggests, there are many sensible, well-intentioned people who see things going wrong and will try to alert you about that. Therefore, it is usually a mistake to hastily reject bad news or innovative, outside-the-box ideas that seem to oppose your current personal and organizational mental models.

An organization's internal social architecture can block dissenting messages and warnings. Porter and Roberts (1976) analyzed why people in hierarchies talk upward and listen upward. Their analysis indicates that people send more messages up the hierarchy than down and pay more attention to information they receive from their supervisors than from their subordinates or peers. They also try harder to establish positive working relationships with their supervisors rather than with their subordinates. Messages that get passed up to superiors tend to play up good news and minimize or hide bad news (Janis 1972; Nystrom & Starbuck, 1984). This censoring is particularly problematic for superintendents and other senior administrators, who find themselves receiving filtered information that may or may not be valid. Censoring of information is a serious problem because bad news is much more likely to motivate people to change than good news (Hedberg, 1981). When information is censored, you don't get the bad news you need to hear.

Collaborators Who Disagree Are Both Right

If you have two qualified people working together who have different beliefs about the same issue, each sets of beliefs is nearly always based in some degree of truth. The challenge in situations like this is not to prove one set of beliefs wrong, but to try to reconcile the differences to show that there are commonalities and complementarity. Efforts to illustrate common and complementary features can help people see that their current mental model can expand to accommodate different ways of thinking and doing.

What Does the "Outsider" Think Strange?

Many people cannot and do not accept the views of outsiders. It is so much easier to listen to and respect the views of people who work in the trenches with us. After all, they are familiar with our work. Because outsiders supposedly do not know us or do not understand our "situation" their observations and suggestions may appear naive, foolish, impractical, or impossible (as in "Your idea will never work in this district. You are a professor. You don't understand what it's like to be a practitioner."). Yet, outsiders often see things without the bias of insiders. Although outsiders may be less experienced in the reality of the battle-scarred insiders, they are also free of the biases and the dominant organizational mental models that shape behavior in organizations. Thus, outsiders may see opportunities and possibilities that insiders cannot see; and, therefore, they may be able to offer breakthrough ideas or methodologies.

All Problems Have Multidirectional Causes and Effects

A structured way to analyze the causes and effects of problems is to use a systems dynamics model that illustrates multidirectional cause-and-effect relationships. This kind of analysis can help people challenge their tacit mental models as they begin to see multiple reasons for the problems they are experiencing and the multiple effects of those problems. Identifying and then examining these multidirectional relationships can lead to some breakthrough thinking about how to change personal and organizational mental models as people see the multiple connections the arrows suggest.

What You Know Is Not Optimal

Starbuck (1996) asserts that no one should be confident that his or her current mental models are uniquely optimal. You can count on the fact that if your beliefs about a particular person, method, or event seem valid to you, there are other equally valid, but different, perceptions about that same person, method, or event. For example, if your preferred method for school district improvement seems excellent to you, others will have an equally excellent, but different, method. You can count on it. The problem is that once you have a well-formed mental model about what works for you, you don't want to abandon it. You shut yourself off from outside-the-box (the box is your personal or district's mental model) thinking and doing. Thus, to break free of the constraints of your current mental models, it is helpful to become skeptical about the effectiveness of your personal and organizational mental models.

The preceding tools proposed by Starbuck are useful for helping people become skeptical. "It isn't good enough" and "It's only an experiment" are mental tools you can use to help yourself and your faculty and staff stay alert for opportunities to improve. You need to be on the lookout for new ways of thinking about and practicing school improvement.

Your personal and your district's mental models will always influence how you and your faculty think about district, cluster, school, team, and individual performance. This means that knowingly or unknowingly your existing mental models will filter information you receive and the filtering will tend to select information supporting your existing personal and organizational mental models and reject data and information that contradict them (the problem of filtering was discussed earlier). However, it is the contradictory data, the critic's voice, the warnings from afar, the "outsider's" views that may offer you astounding ways to improve the performance of your district. Thus, when you are surprised by what you see or hear about your district, turn the surprises into question marks, respond to disagreements and warnings as if they have some validity, and act as if outsiders' ideas are as valid as your own.

Tools for Unlearning Mental Models

Chris Argyris and Donald Schön (1974) tell us about theories of action—personal theories that guide one's behavior. They suggest that there are two kinds of theories of action: espoused theories and theories in use. They also teach us that there is often a difference between the two and people don't realize the difference. These theories of action are mental models.

Back in 1980, I had the wonderful opportunity to be appointed by Chris Argyris to an honorary faculty position in the Harvard Graduate School of Education. The purpose of that postdoctoral appointment was to study Argyris and Schön's ideas about theories of action. In a seminar I took with Professor Argyris, I learned about the following two tools that are helpful for unlearning mental models. Senge et al. (1994) describe these tools in their book, *The Fifth Discipline Fieldbook* (pp. 242–259). The tools are the "Ladder of Inference" and the "Left-Hand Column." Both of these tools require an intense effort on everyone's part to use them effectively. It is challenging for people to examine their espoused theories of action (mental models) in relation to their theories in use (the "real" mental models).

A third tool, developed by Kegan and Lahey (2001), two developmental psychologists from Harvard, that seems useful for unlearning and learning mental models is how the way we talk affects the way we work. Their tool, which uses a small-group discussion format, is described in detail in their book *How the Way We Talk Can Change the Way We Work*. When I read their book I was struck by the power of their methodology and by the apparent ease of using it with large numbers of people organized into small groups. To me, it seemed to have great potential for helping educators unlearn and learn their mental models.

CREATING PROFESSIONAL KNOWLEDGE

Learning new mental models is greatly facilitated by using a knowledge-creation process that surfaces personal knowledge and mental models, makes that knowledge and those models explicit, and then converts the best of those into organization-wide knowledge and mental models (Nonaka & Takeuchi, 1995). So, let's explore this idea a bit further.

Individuals create their own personal mental models to represent their knowledge. Theories of knowledge creation, which are generally classified as "constructivist" theories, describe psychological processes people use to build their own understanding of information.

We begin to understand information as we reconcile what we already know and what we already believe with new information or with old information that is being reconsidered from a different perspective. Each of us brings to our personal learning a unique combination of prior experiences and understanding, as well as a set of learning aptitudes and beliefs about learning. Thus, knowledge creation, to a large degree, is idiosyncratic. To what degree does the idiosyncratic nature of knowledge matter when it comes to developing professional knowledge and mental models?

All educators have a different understanding of the world around them, and those personal mental models vary considerably from person to person. Thus, it can be argued that all knowledge is subjective to some degree (e.g., Bednar, 1993). The individual subjectivity of knowledge suggests, therefore, that educators have a wide range of idiosyncratic mental models that guide their work. If educators' personal mental models are at odds with how your school district wants to improve, it can be predicted that those educators will resist your district's movement toward high performance because their personal mental models are powerful and difficult to change (as in "I don't care what the district wants to do. I know I'm right and I'm not going to change.").

The subjectivity of knowledge and educators' resistance to other mental models may not matter in some cases. For example, in situations where there are no "right answers," it doesn't make much difference if people have different views, perspectives, or opinions. In fact, I think in these situations educators should be encouraged to develop unique ideas about what's right or what's effective. For example, I do not believe there is one "right" way to teach effectively. I believe teachers should develop their own personal understandings of effective teaching and then use that knowledge to teach what their district expects (however, I do not believe that teachers should have the same degree of autonomy in deciding *what* to teach).

There are situations, however, where it is important for everyone to be working from the same mental model. For example, many times there are right answers and correct procedures that teachers must teach. I don't think you would want children learning geometry from teachers who construct idiosyncratic theorems. In situations requiring right answers and correct procedures, a school district's goal must be to develop a certain degree of uniformity among teachers' mental models.

Situated Cognition and Learning

Professional knowledge and mental models must be developed within a meaningful context. When educators work with information that is devoid of context, what they try to learn can appear meaningless and may be difficult to learn. For example, my wife is an insurance agent who needed to become licensed to sell financial instruments. She knew nothing about this world of finance, and as she studied the texts she couldn't make sense of what she was reading because she had no context to help her understand those new ideas, principles, and rules. Without the context, all that information was meaningless to her and she struggled to learn it. But, once she started applying those ideas in practice, thereby creating a context, all that information became "situated" and therefore meaningful and understandable. Context is powerful.

Theories of situated cognition (e.g., Lave, 1988; Suchman, 1987) tell us the context within which particular knowledge is required determines how that knowledge is used. Theories of situated learning (e.g., Brown, Collins, & Duguid, 1989) tell us that people develop knowledge by connecting new information to what they already know, and they do this in ways that make the learning meaningful. Traditional staff development and training sometimes do not provide educators with context and meaningful connections; and, therefore, participants see no relevance between what they are trying to learn and their work.

The Social Dimension of Learning

There are three factors comprising the social dimension of learning. First is the social construction of knowledge itself. Second is the social nature of situated learning. The third factor is composed of educators' beliefs about other educators and about themselves, and the reasons they use to explain their own and others' behavior. Each of these dimensions is discussed briefly here.

Organization-wide professional knowledge and mental models are constructed socially. Although educators construct personal and idiosyncratic knowledge and mental models, there has to be a shared or common understanding among educators so they can communicate with each other about what they know and what they are doing. In other words, there has to be organizational learning.

Meaning is shared and negotiated when people have common knowledge (Vygotsky, 1978). Within a school district, this common understanding can be developed through conversations about what people know and can do so that insights and perspectives can be shared among all educators participating in those conversations. The need to reach consensus about the meaning and value of new knowledge and mental models has the advantage of requiring educators to at least consider others' perspectives, even if they disagree with them. Important side effects of these conversations are the abilities to communicate with others about new knowledge and mental models, to cooperatively create a context for the new knowledge (i.e., to situate it), and to apply that knowledge for the benefit of your district.

The social dimension of learning, as implied previously, suggests consensus. Methods for developing this kind of consensual district-wide professional knowledge and mental models include seminars, formal discussions, Organizational Learning Networks (discussed in chapter 6), and informal interactions among teachers and others. Pava (1983) calls all these different kinds of learning places "forums." Achieving this level of consensus increases the likelihood of district-wide professional knowledge being used.

Consistent with constructivist theory, educators construct meaning from information based on what they *think* the information means. Educators' professional knowledge and mental models, therefore, are influenced by their beliefs about the information they receive, about the people who provide that information, and about their own ability to deal with the information (Bandura, 1977, 1978; Salomon, 1982). In almost all cases, professional knowledge and mental models are influenced by perceptions of the source of information (e.g., "I like this speaker. I think I'll use those ideas.") and perceptions of the medium used to deliver it (e.g., "I really like role playing. It helps me learn."). When information is perceived negatively, people have even been known to construct meaning that is in total opposition to the presented information (e.g., "I think that woman is wacko. I am going to do just the opposite of what she is advising us to do.")

Educators not only make attributions about the value and completeness of information they receive, but they also make attributions about their own abilities to use that information. These kinds of attributions are collectively called *self-efficacy*. Self-efficacy is a powerful determinant of how well educators learn new knowledge and whether they enjoy doing so. Low self-efficacy becomes a self-fulfilling prophecy (e.g., the thought, "I'm no good at dealing with disruptive students" leads to poor performance in dealing with disruptive students); whereas unusually high self-efficacy results in reduced effort to succeed (e.g., the thought, "I already know this stuff inside and out. They can't teach me anything I don't already know" leads to reduced effort to study and learn, which leads to low performance in a training situation).

CONCLUSION

Mental models are powerful because they frame the way people perceive, understand, interpret, and act upon their world. However, not all mental models are accurate or complete enough to be effective. An additional problem for school districts is that sometimes personal mental models do not complement, or may even conflict with, a district's desired organizational mental model as represented in its vision and strategic direction.

Mental models can be serious roadblocks to systemic school improvement. Helping educators surface, examine, evaluate, and change their personal and your district's organizational mental models, therefore, is a key step toward effective systemic school improvement. In my opinion, the best time to begin unlearning and learning mental models is *before* you launch a whole-district improvement effort. You need personal and organizational mental models that are evolving in support of your district's grand vision and strategic direction. Of course, this evolution continues throughout the redesign of your district, but it must, I think, start early and often. Your efforts to move your district toward higher levels of performance will most certainly fail if you do not engage your colleagues in a process of unlearning and learning mental models.

REFERENCES

Argyris, C., & Schön, D. A. (1974). *Theory in practice: Increasing professional effectiveness.* San Francisco: Jossey-Bass.

Armstrong, J. S. (1985). *Long-range forecasting: From crystal ball to computer* (2nd ed.). New York: Wiley-Interscience.

Bandura, A. (1977, March). Self-efficacy: Toward a unifying theory of behavioral change. *Psychological Review*, 84(2), 191–215. (ERIC Document Reproduction Service, No. EJ161632).

Bandura, A. (1978, summer). Social learning theory of aggression. *Journal of Communication*, 28(3), 12–29. (ERIC Document Reproduction Service No. EJ195900).

Bednar, M. R (1993). Teachers' beliefs and practices: Dissonance or contextual reality? Paper presented at the annual meeting of the National Reading Conference. (ERIC Document Reproduction Service No. ED374397).

Beyer, J. M. (1981). Ideologies, values, and decision making in organizations. In P. C. Nystrom & W. H. Starbuck (Eds.), *Handbook of organizational design, Volume 2: Remodelling organizations and their environments* (pp. 166–202). New York: Oxford University Press.

Bradford, A. (1995–1996, December/January). It's all in your frame of mind—changing mental models. *Marketer.* Available: www.smps.org/mrc/articleshtml/frameofmind.htm

Brown, J. S., Collins, A., & Duguid, P. (1989). Situated cognition and the culture of learning. *Education Researcher*, 18(1), 32–42.

Hedberg, B. (1981). How organizations learn and unlearn. In P. C. Nystrom & W. H. Starbuck (Eds.), *Handbook of organizational design, Volume 1: Adapting organizations to their environments* (pp. 3–27). New York: Oxford University Press.

Janis, I. L. (1972). *Victims of group-think.* Boston: Houghton Mifflin.

Johnson-Laird, P. N. (1983). *Mental models: Towards a cognitive science of language, inference and consciousness.* Cambridge, England: Cambridge University Press.

Kegan, R., & Lahey, L. L. (2001). *How the way we talk can change the way we work.* San Francisco: Jossey-Bass.

Kuhn, T. S. (1962). *The structure of scientific revolutions.* Chicago: University of Chicago Press.

Lave, J. (1988). *Cognition in practice: Mind, mathematics, and culture in everyday life*. New York: Cambridge University Press.

Nonaka, I., & Takeuchi, H. (1995). *The knowledge-creating company: How Japanese companies create the dynamics of innovation*. New York: Oxford University Press.

Nystrom, P. C., & Starbuck, W. H. (1984). To avoid organizational crises, unlearn. *Organizational Dynamics*, 12(4), 53–65.

Pava, C. H. P. (1983). *Managing new office technology: An organizational strategy*. New York: The New Press.

Petroski, H. (1992). *To engineer is human*. New York: Vintage.

Porter, L. W., & Roberts, K. H. (1976). Communication in organizations. In M. D. Dunnette (Ed.), *Handbook of industrial and organizational psychology* (pp. 1553–1589). Chicago: Rand McNally.

Salomon, G. (1982). *Communication and education: Social and psychological interactions*. Beverly Hills, CA: Sage.

Senge, P. M., Kleiner, A., Roberts, C., Ross, R. B., & Smith, B. J. (1994). *The fifth discipline fieldbook: Strategies and tools for building a learning organization*. New York: Doubleday.

Starbuck, W. H. (1996). Unlearning ineffective or obsolete technologies. *International Journal of Technology Management*, 11, 725–737.

Suchman, L. (1987). Common sense in interface design. *Techné*, 1(1), 38–40.

Tushman, M. L., Newman, W. H., & Romanelli, E. (1986). Convergence and upheaval: Managing the unsteady pace of organizational evolution. *California Management Review*, 29(1), 29–44.

Vygotsky, L. S. (1978). (M. Cole, V. John-Steiner, S. Scribner, & E. Souberman, Eds.). *Mind in society: The development of higher psychological processes*. Cambridge, MA: Harvard University Press.

CHAPTER 4

Dancing on Ice: Navigating Rapid, Complex, Nonlinear Change to Create and Sustain Systemic School Improvement

Francis M. Duffy and Edward E. Hampton, Jr.

The traditional structures that have given us a feeling of solidity and predictability have vanished. This shift has placed a greater emphasis on the need for fluid processes that can change as an organization and its members' needs change. . . . Tomorrow's jobs will be built on establishing networks of relationships.

—Hallie S. Preskill and Rosalie T. Torres,
Evaluative Inquiry for Learning in Organizations

PART 1: THE TRUE NATURE OF CHANGE IN SCHOOL SYSTEMS

The Puzzle

Many contemporary school systems find themselves in amazingly complex and puzzling environments. Educators in these districts are increasingly expected to turn direction quickly in response to changes in their environments, but they can't change direction because they are bound by the arthritic bureaucratic designs of their systems, by the old mental models of hierarchical power and control, or they don't know how to change direction. Combine this observation with the fact that systemic change is sometimes serpentine, sometimes circular, and sometimes spiral, but never purely linear and sequential. This puzzle requires a new way of thinking about and practicing change management. This chapter focuses on this challenge and offers some ideas for what we call "navigating change" (as contrasted with the traditional term, *managing change*).

Seizing Opportunities at the Intersection of Anticipatory Intentions (Planning) and Unanticipated Events (Reality)[1]

The traditional approach to managing change was developed by Kurt Lewin (1951). It is illustrated in figure 4.1. What Lewin said is that to change a system, first you envision a desired future. Then, you assess the current situation and compare the present to the future, looking for gaps between what you have and what you want. Next, you develop a transition plan composed of long-range goals and short-term objectives that will move your system straight forward toward its desired future. Along the way there would be some unanticipated events that might blindside you, but the "pressure" of all your anticipatory intentions (goals, objectives, plans) would keep those unexpected things under control and thereby keep your system on a relatively straight change-path toward the future. But, as many of us have learned from experience, this is not the way organizational change happens.

The complexities of contemporary society and the pressures for rapid change combined with an increasing number of unanticipated events and unintended consequences during change have created a change-path that is nonlinear, as illustrated in figure 4.2.

In figure 4.2, you see a change-path leading from the present to the future that is nonlinear. That change-path moves from the present through the near future (NF) and into the distant future (DF) and brings you, hopefully, to the place you and your colleagues envisioned for your district. As with the traditional approach to change management, you will use strategic planning methods and tools to anticipate desir-

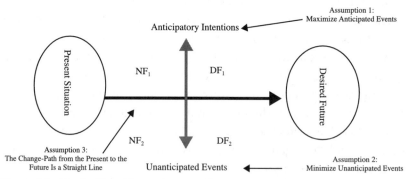

Figure 4.1. The traditional linear change-path.

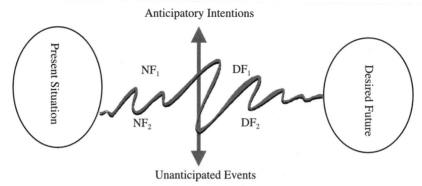

Figure 4.2. The nonlinear change-path in today's complex school districts.

able events, but there will be unanticipated events that emerge along the way that will affect your district's movement toward a future place.

However, if you assume that the strategic path from the present to the future is relatively straightforward (as shown in figure 4.1) when the actual path is really serpentine (as shown in figure 4.2), then you and your people will soon find yourselves off the true path and lost. Being off the path and lost is illustrated in figure 4.3.

To see how you would be off the true path (the nonlinear path), trace your finger along the assumed straight path in figure 4.3. Wherever the straight path leaves the nonlinear path, you're lost. When lost, people revert back to their old ways, thereby enacting the old French adage, "The more things change, the more they stay the same." To get back on

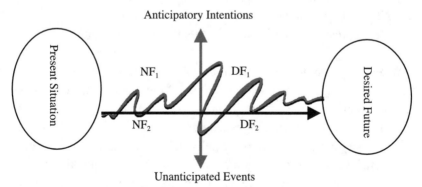

Figure 4.3. Assuming a linear change-path means being off the true path toward a desired future.

course you need a map, compass, and landmarks to help you navigate your way toward a desirable future. This chapter, in conjunction with the whole-district redesign methodology presented in chapter 6, provides you with a map, compass, and landmarks to find and navigate your way along a winding change-path toward higher student, teacher, and system learning.

The Intersection between
Anticipatory Intentions and Unanticipated Events

Unanticipated events (reality) occur in nonlinear, chaotic ways. Their appearance requires an extraordinarily speedy response if school districts are to survive and thrive. The nature of this nonlinear and chaotic reality is diametrically opposed to school improvement and strategic planning models built on the foundation of anticipatory intentions (planned change) that assume change is mostly linear and sequential.

It's possible to illustrate graphically the intersection between anticipatory intentions (planned change) and unanticipated events (reality). This intersection was illustrated in figure 4.2. In that figure you see a vertical line with anticipatory intentions at one end and unanticipated events at the other. You also see a serpentine horizontal line representing a time line that starts in the near future and moves into the distant future. The intersection of these two lines creates four irregular quadrants:

- NF_1 represents anticipated events in the near future.
- DF_1 represents anticipated events in the distant future.
- NF_2 represents unanticipated events in the near future.
- DF_2 represents unanticipated events in the distant future.

Where anticipatory planning and unanticipated events meet at the serpentine change-path shown in figure 4.2 there is an intersection. At this intersection, there will be many innovative and unparalleled opportunities to improve student, teacher, and system learning. There will also be many dangerous and potentially debilitating threats. Therefore, your district needs to develop the capacity to respond quickly and effectively to unanticipated events that push against all of your good strategic planning. You want to create the capacity to seize the golden opportunities and to reject or minimize the dangerous threats. None of the current approaches to school district improvement or strategic planning in school systems seem to be able to do this.

Although the path toward systemic school improvement will continue to be serpentine, circular, and spiral, school districts will continue to need tools for anticipating the future. Even though the journey of systemic school improvement is frequently nonlinear, there still must be beginning and end points and recognizable milestones along the way to help your district stay on the path, its nonlinear nature notwithstanding. So, how do you build your district's capacity to navigate this kind of change-path, fraught with unexpected events and unintended outcomes?

Building Capacity to Anticipate the
Future and Respond to Unanticipated Events

One of the factors contributing to the rapid expansion of nonlinear change-paths is the nature of the environment within which school districts find themselves. This environment is increasingly complex and unstable. In complex and unstable environments organizations need to be able to plan for the future while also being able to respond quickly to unanticipated events (Daft, 2001). The capacity to anticipate the future *and* respond quickly to unanticipated events is a significant function of a school district's internal social "architecture," which includes its culture, communication patterns, reward system, policies and procedures, and organization design. This dual competence (anticipating and responding quickly to events) is also facilitated by the use of tools and structures specifically designed to seize opportunities at the intersection of anticipatory intentions and unanticipated events.

The Illusion of Peak Performance

In nature, successful organisms adapt to their environments by evolving to a peak of success at which the organism is maximally adapted to its environment (as cited in Duffy & Dale, 2001). School districts are like this, too, because they evolve to their current performance peaks. In the twenty-first-century environment for school districts, however, there are multiple peaks that evoke images of the

Figure 4.4 . The route to higher performance—first down, then up. © 2002 by Francis M. Duffy. All rights reserved.

Rocky Mountains, where some peaks are lower than others. This image is illustrated in figure 4.4.

What if the peak a district sits atop is low compared to others, but folks inside the district don't realize it? Wouldn't this lack of perspective create a false sense of success? Is it possible, therefore, for a school district to be at peak performance, but to be on a suboptimal peak? Educators in this kind of school district would cheer themselves silly as they sat atop a peak of mediocrity.

Another problem for school districts is not too much success, but too little perspective. Success creates a wall that obstructs the view of opportunities to move toward higher levels of performance. If educators in a district can't see the next-higher performance peak, how can they go there? They can't go to what they can't see.

A third problem for school districts is that successful districts become remarkably creative in defending their status quo. They argue against the need to improve because they see themselves already at their peak. But sitting too long on any performance peak when there are higher peaks to climb won't be tolerated by our twenty-first-century society.

When a school district is successful, it sits atop a performance peak. The path to the next-higher performance peak is not a straight "as the crow flies" line. A clear view of the next-higher level of performance should not be misconstrued as a straight change-path, forward and upward. There is only one way to get to the next-higher peak—a district has to go downhill before it can go back up. This is depicted in figure 4.4 and discussed in part 2 of this chapter when we talk about Hans Seyle's (1956) General Adaptation Syndrome. You have to move toward the edge of chaos by becoming temporarily less effective, less skilled, and less successful.

"First down, then up" is a basic principle of learning theory. When people first learn a new skill, they are not good at using it. Their performance level declines along the familiar learning curve. As they learn and develop new skills, they move back up the learning curve. This principle applies to organizational learning, too—first down, then up. The problem is, however, that the more successful a school district is, the less inclined it is to let go of what it is doing to move downward toward the edge of chaos. This capacity to let go has to be built into a school system.

The "first down, then up" journey requires educators to question their district's success. Not everything they do well has to be abandoned completely, but everything they do needs to be questioned completely. During this questioning, it is also imperative to search continuously for opportunities for innovation. Searching allows educators not only to anticipate future events but also to respond quickly to unanticipated ones.

From Change to Flux

Organization improvement theory is moving away from the concept of change to the concept of flux (Kelly, 1998). While change focuses on creating differences, flux is about creative destruction followed by nascence. Flux disrupts the status quo while creating a temporary foundation for innovation. The quest for innovation is amaranthine, and robust innovation sustains itself within the context of flux.

Innovation driven by systemic flux is a dangerous and thrilling ride to the edge of chaos in a school system. Yet, I believe there is a need to sustain this kind of innovation so school districts can move continuously toward higher performance peaks. By poising repeatedly at the edge of chaos, school systems can find stunningly creative solutions to the puzzles they are trying to solve—puzzles like, "How do we provide children with world-class instruction?" "How do we provide our teachers and support staff with a motivating and satisfying work life?" and "How do we establish positive and productive relationships with our community?"

Sustaining innovation is particularly tricky because it is inextricably linked to a system being out of balance (i.e., in a constant state of controlled disequilibrium). Thus, a school district wanting to sustain innovative thinking and puzzle solving must create for itself a state of controlled disequilibrium in much the same way that people who skillfully dance on ice remain on the verge of falling, but repeatedly catch themselves and never fall down. To be innovative, to move to the next-higher peak of performance, a school system cannot anchor itself to its past or current performance peak. Instead, the system must perform like a surfer perched atop a wave of uninterruptedly disintegrating water (Morgan, 1988, created the wave metaphor to explain the nature of change). Skilled surfers harness the turbulence of the wave to move forward. Skillful change-leaders help their organizations do the same thing. To create high-performing school systems educators must allow their districts to move to the edge of chaos, to dance on ice, to ride the waves of flux. They need to build into their districts the capacity to exploit flux, not outlaw it.

A New Mental Model for Anticipatory Planning

Don't Solve Problems, Seek Opportunities

The power of compounded results (e.g., compounded interest) is extraordinary. Compounded results can be gained during change and innovation. Each opportunity seized by a school district can be compounded if it becomes a platform to launch yet other innovations. Like a chain reaction, one well-placed innovation can trigger dozens of progeny. New opportunities are created in a combinatorial fashion just as people combine and recombine the twenty-six letters of the alphabet to write an infinite number of books.

A whole-district change process should not be conceived of as a reform to be installed in a school district. It must be conceived of and designed as a comprehensive set of change navigation and change-leadership tools, structures, and processes that can help a school district move to a higher performance peak. And, most importantly, it must be built into the internal social architecture of a school district; that is, it must become part of a district's core operations.

Whole-system change also requires educators to make sure their school districts create and maintain strategic alignment; or, in homely terms, to ensure that all the horses are pulling the wagon in the same direction. The work of individuals must be aligned with the goals of their teams, the work of teams must be aligned with the goals of their schools, the work of schools must be aligned with the goals of their clusters, and the work of clusters must be aligned with a district's strategic goals and grand vision for the future. With strategic alignment, even though the path to the next-higher performance peak is nonlinear, educators inside an improving school district will all move together along that path.

Old change theory was linear, expected stable equilibrium, was piecemeal, installed improvements rather than created innovations, and emerged out of centralized, hierarchical control that viewed school systems as mechanistic entities. New change theory is based on the concept of flux. It is nonlinear and requires educators to seek controlled disequilibrium that provides the energy needed to create innovative opportunities for improvement. New change theory tells us that to improve the performance level of a school district the system must first move downhill before it can move up to a higher level of performance. New change theory requires school districts to use a networked social architecture where innovations are grown from within and used to create systemic change. New change theory requires a simultaneous ability to anticipate the future and to respond quickly to unanticipated events.

PART 2: NAVIGATING RAPID, COMPLEX, NONLINEAR CHANGE

There are many innovative and exciting concepts and principles emerging from the science of physics that serve as metaphors for navigating rapid, complex, and nonlinear change in school districts. Some of these concepts and principles are showcased in this part of the chapter.

Chaos

"Chaos is the absence of patterns." These simple words by Margaret Wheatley (1992) in her book, *Leadership and the New Sciences*, provide a wonderful starting point for understanding how change-leaders in school systems can convert chaos from a foe to a friend. To make this conversion, two questions need to be asked and answered:

- Why should change-leaders care about chaos? After all, isn't chaos a bad thing—something school district leaders get paid to get rid of or prevent?
- What does it matter if patterns are absent? When patterns are absent, we have empty space—nothing. Of what use is empty space?

Why Should Change-Leaders Care about the Meaning of Chaos?

First, let's assume that chaos is a necessary precursor to change. Think of gardening. If you want to plant a new azalea bush, you must first dig a hole. Right? All of the grass and dirt you removed to create the hole represent preexisting patterns. By digging the hole, you removed the preexisting patterns and created an empty space in the ground. That empty space is the absence of patterns, which in a way represents chaos. The empty space in the hole is now ready to accept new patterns—the root ball and "life" in your ready-to-grow azalea bush. If you did not create chaos (by creating the empty hole), you would not be able to plant the azalea. No chaos, no planting. If you failed to recognize the need to create the empty, chaotic space called a hole, and if you simply set the azalea root ball on the surface of the ground, you would be putting new patterns over old, and you know what would happen next—you'd soon have a dead azalea.

Yet, in the field of school improvement over the past thirty or so years, we've been putting new patterns over old, which is sometimes euphemistically referred to as "pancaking." Consider, for example, what Keltner (1998) says about this tendency to put new patterns over old:

Traditional school reform efforts have focused on improving specific and isolated educational performance gaps. To address reading problems, for example, a primary school may adopt a whole language or phonics program. To raise math scores, the same school may introduce a new, technology-supported math curriculum. Often these reform initiatives are adopted by only one or two grade levels or by a few teachers, creating a patchwork of reforms within a school, or what critics have dubbed the "Christmas tree effect." (online document, n.p.)

Given the ineffectiveness of this approach to school improvement that "pancakes" new programs, ideas, and innovations on top of old ones, you might wonder about the origins of this approach. The genesis of this approach lies in traditional management theory and practice; in particular, in management's preoccupation with maintaining stability (i.e., maintaining patterns). The dominant management models of the twentieth century were built on old, outmoded industrial templates or constructs influenced by the thinking of Frederick Taylor and others. Most of these models were designed to create and maintain constancy and stability in organizations that would ensure that a given process or subsystem would behave predictably and, thereby, always consistently produce a desired product or output.

The industrial roots of these traditional management models, especially those with an assembly line focus, supported the creation of management models that were linear and sequentially structured. This happened because linear models were assumed to be easy to structure, operate, and control. Some theorists call such linear modeling mechanistic or Newtonian. Mechanistic management models based on such modeling essentially rest upon salient premises such as:

- Actions result from force; that is, a given action creates an opposite and equal reaction.
- A given result represents additive (as in 1 + 1 = 2) versus synergistic (as in the whole is greater than the sum of its parts) actions.
- Outcomes are predictable, given specific factors and activities.
- The most efficient path to a desired outcome is a progressive, linear path; that is, there is one "true" path consisting of narrowly defined and controlled sequential steps.

The performance of mechanistic systems was used to understand and manage human behavior in organizations. Managers influenced by mechanistic principles assumed that human behavior could respond to the same principles that governed mechanical systems. If a manager could apply just the right pressure or force or define clearly a particular set of steps, then human behavior, much like a machine, would be both predictable and desirable.

Within the mechanistic approach to management, there was an implicit and pervasive belief that if managers could "control" human behavior to produce a desired outcome, then people would function like cogs in a gear wheel and they would perfectly fit the system or process being used. So, although never explicitly stated, management behavior within the mechanistic worldview always sought the holy grail of perfect human involvement, where perfection meant that all nonessential human behaviors and attitudes were removed to create ultimate organizational efficiency. This management fantasy fueled many of the command-and-control and carrot-stick models that pervade management today.

The field of education administration has not escaped the influence of mechanistic management principles. In early education models, when one-room classrooms and schools were structured and operated like assembly lines, such mechanistic, command-and-control modeling had utility. Yet, while one might argue that schooling is linear since students progress sequentially through a preschool through twelfth-grade instructional program, the core work of school districts and their component schools (i.e., classroom teaching and learning) is and has always been rather nonlinear.

Schooling is also becoming increasingly nonlinear as teachers and staff create and perform within webs of teams and Organizational Learning Networks (described later in chapter 6). These various teams and networks include teachers, administrators, supervisors, education specialists, parents, government officials, businesspeople, and other stakeholders. This kind of interactivity is increasing in complexity as more people in more formal and complex roles are engaged and as the frequency of change introduced into school systems increases.

Other variables affecting the complexity of school systems are the changing cultural norms of American society. A key force driving these new norms is a growing interest in democracy in the workplace that is often characterized as empowerment. Although the concept of empowerment is overused and misused to the point that it is almost trite, it is a real and important phenomenon. Understanding what empowerment really is, we think, is central to understanding and using chaos effectively.

Empowerment

Empowerment centers on the concept of locus of control. Locus of control is based in one's belief as to where the controlling authority in a given situation is located. If you believe that I must give you permission to make a choice, then you believe the locus of control is outside of you (an external locus of control). If, on the other hand, you believe you can make choices freely, then the locus of control is within you (an internal locus of control). The operative word in these two examples is *believe*. Where the controlling influence or power actually resides is not as important as where a person *believes* it exists.

Empowerment occurs when people believe they have an internal locus of control and, therefore, they have the power to make choices. In true empowerment, leaders must also trust people to exercise their choices wisely even though those choices may not be what a leader expects or wants. Thus, empowerment is risky from a leader's perspective.

What makes empowerment worth the risk, however, is that empowered people tend to interact synergistically, whereby what they do collectively is so much more than what they do individually. But, in linear, mechanistic, command-and-control situations, people are managed by managerial "gates." Their potential to act is constrained and "managed" by others who control the gates to allow the ebb and flow of ideas, behaviors, decisions, and so on. In an empowered situation, however, people control those gates and they are free to unleash their potential in ways that support an organization's grand vision and strategic direction.

In school districts, as in other kinds of organizations, leadership is needed to create the environment for empowerment to flourish. Managers preoccupied with command and control and with maintaining old patterns of behavior and practice cannot and will not allow empowerment to create and sustain whole-district change. The key to gaining maximum advantage from empowerment while minimizing risk lies in creating change-leaders throughout your district who recognize the inherent benefits of empowerment and who are able to manage it in productive and meaningful ways.

Empowerment of people also creates the conditions your district will need to move toward higher levels of performance. Empowerment helps people move to the edge of chaos, recognize and seize opportunities for improvement, and then move upward toward new levels of individual, team, and system performance. Empowerment helps create and sustain systemic school improvement.

Leadership Concepts for Navigating Complex, Nonlinear Change

The new sciences, as described by Meg Wheatley and others, offer concepts, principles, and metaphors for managing and leading complex, nonlinear change in school districts. Specific concepts derived from the New Sciences that are relevant to the field of education leadership in general and change-leadership in particular are as follows:

- Making chaos a useful tool
- Using chaos for productive change navigation
- New mental models for change-leadership
- Models for creating agile and adaptive organizations

Let's examine each of these concepts in turn.

Making Chaos a Useful Tool

We use a silly metaphor to explain the usefulness of chaos for navigating complex, nonlinear change. Although the metaphor is silly, please bear with it because the principles of chaos, complexity, and nonlinearity will become clearer as we proceed.

Imagine a bowl of cooked, sauce-covered spaghetti. If your imagination works like ours, what you see is this:

- The tangled mess of red spaghetti has no apparent organizational pattern.
- If you try to grab a few strands of spaghetti, it slips through your fingers, and when it falls back in the bowl, the strands readjust themselves into different, yet still unrecognizable patterns as the whole delectable mess regains stability.

- There is no clear point at which to reach in and grab some of the spaghetti—any point of entry is as good as another.
- There is no right or wrong way for the spaghetti to look and act; there is only a state of being that "is."
- This steaming bowl of spaghetti is inviting and demands to be eaten. It is so inviting, we have no reluctance to change what we see.
- Although the whole mess appears chaotic, at a certain level there is some degree of order; that is, we see something we recognize as a "bowl of spaghetti" and not as a bowl of cereal.

You know this bowl of spaghetti is in a state of transition. Before it became a bowl of steaming spaghetti you had a collection of unconnected ingredients. But what we see in that bowl is not in its end state. That comes later as the spaghetti serves a higher purpose that can only be achieved through your personal intervention.

Some might look at the bowl of spaghetti and call what they see chaotic. Actually, according to Wheatley and others, chaos is the absence of patterns. Pure chaos, in the case of this metaphorical bowl of spaghetti, would be found in an empty bowl—not one with spaghetti in it. An empty bowl would be pretty much like the empty space in the hole we dug for our new azalea plant that we talked about earlier. But the space in our bowl is filled with sauce-covered spaghetti, and all of that spaghetti is organized into patterns, even though the patterns are so complex and nonlinear that we cannot recognize them. That delectable mess of sauce-covered spaghetti has some order to it, and, therefore, it does not represent true chaos.

School Districts as Bowls of Spaghetti

School districts are like bowls of sauce-covered spaghetti. Even though what's happening inside a school district may seem chaotic, it is not. The behaviors and processes may be complex, nonlinear, and disorderly, but, by the New Sciences definition, they are not chaotic.

Yet, life in school districts is often characterized as chaotic. The complexity and nonlinearity you perceive create an almost impossible managerial situation. There are so many possible relationships and connections between and among people, tasks, roles, priorities, and processes within your school system that no manager can identify all of them, much less manage them! Yet, that same complexity and nonlinearity are rich with possibilities and synergistic energy, just like our bowl of sauce-covered spaghetti.

The insights and viewpoints offered by the bowl-of-spaghetti metaphor are important for making chaos productive. Despite the best work and fondest wishes of education leaders, teachers, parents, and community members, school systems do not act like the ideal organization charts used to depict them. In fact, school systems are more like our metaphorical bowl of cooked spaghetti in a thick, rich sauce. And each school within a district is like each single strand of spaghetti in the bowl.

Where You Stand in a System Shapes Your Perspective

Whether you perceive a work process, problem-solving method, or teaching tool as linear or nonlinear depends on where you stand in a system. In change-leadership terms, where you stand in your system can be identified as being at the strategic level, operational level, or tactical level.

The strategic-level perspective is found at the level of concepts, vision, icons, and ideas. This is the level at which futures are shaped. Strategic thinking envisions what does not exist and counts on using resources that do not yet exist. In this way, strategic thinking relies on intangibles. Relying on intangibles is why strategic planning is so hard to do properly and why so few people are able to do it well.

The operational-level perspective is gained when you examine the relationships between organizational activities. If you look at the relationship between your curriculum and what happens during classroom instruction, for example, you are taking the operational perspective. At the operational level, you create sequences or networks of activities. The focus is not on individual people or tasks, but on organizing those tasks and people into a process or pattern to create a desired outcome, product, or service. At this level, what lies before you can look chaotic, disjointed, and nonlinear.

The tactical-level perspective is at ground level. It is influenced by people dealing with people. It is where time is measured by ticks of the clock. At this level, for any person at a given moment in time, what is before him or her may appear very linear. In fact, most tactical activities are linear. They are step-by-step, first you do this, then you do that, activities.

Zander and Zander (2000) present a very interesting view of the strategic perspective. They discuss the game of chess as a metaphor for strategic thinking and present the insight that strategy does not lie in the pieces, but in the board. In fact, according to Zander and Zander, the idea of chess is to create possibilities by using the board, not the pieces. Most people focus on the pieces because they are tangible. But the pieces are at the operational level. The "intangible" squares are open to strategy, and this is where chess matches are won or lost.

Another analogy might be useful to understand the difference between the preceding three perspectives. Imagine a fleet of ships making an ocean voyage. At the tactical level, we have crewmen and women doing various tasks to make ships work. At the operational level, there are clusters of activities managed by the captain of each ship; for example, keeping each ship in proper relation to other ships, sailing in the proper direction, steering, propulsion, and avoiding dangers. Strategic-level thinking, ideally, occurs before the voyage starts. The fleet admiral decides which ships best meet projected demands for the fleet, decides upon the needed skill sets and weapons for the fleet's mission, decides where the fleet is going, and so on.

Understanding that linearity or nonlinearity is influenced by your perspective (strategic, operational, or tactical) is important. This understanding can help you use chaos effectively because chaos behaves differently at each of the three levels, and so each level requires unique approaches. In much the same way, to create and sustain systemic school improvement you need change-leadership at the strategic, operational, and tactical levels. The level at which your fellow change-leaders function will influence their perceptions of chaos, complexity, linearity, and nonlinearity. You must be aware that what appears to be true for a leader at his or her level may not be true for other leaders at other levels. Your district, like a fleet of ships, must have change-leadership at all three levels to realize the unified power of your district.

Using Chaos for Productive Change Navigation

Moving your district to the edge of chaos (a term coined by Roger Lewin, 1992) can be an exhilarating and frightening journey. We talked about this journey earlier in the chapter. We said that the way you move your district to the edge of chaos is by questioning everything your district does—everything. You don't have to abandon all that you do, but you do need to question everything you do. In this way you and your colleagues are like people dancing on ice as you slip and slide, struggle to maintain balance, start to fall, regain balance, and slip and slide some more until your dance is ended by fully implementing all of the wonderful ideas that are proposed to improve student, teacher, and system learning. It is this questioning, this dancing, and this movement toward the edge of chaos that require so much of your personal courage, passion, and vision.

If managed properly your dance on ice can yield unprecedented opportunities to create a school system that performs at a higher level. A critical part of your role as a superintendent who wants to provide leadership for systemic improvement is that you have to move your district to the edge of chaos. More important, not only do you need to move your district toward chaos, you have to ensure that you and your staff "dance" at the edge of chaos in a productive rather than destructive way.

The Need for Effective Communication

One of the keys to managing life at the edge of chaos is to create and use effective communication strategies. Managing your system's dance at the edge will require you and your colleagues to exercise strategic, operational, and tactical thinking; facilitate productive and appropriate connections between your people and processes; and create the right elements for a "binding frame" that you then use to manage communication during times of great change.

We need to explain the concept of binding frame. To do that, we would like to take you back to the metaphorical bowl of sauce-covered spaghetti. This time think about the sauce. What does the sauce physically do when it's mixed with the spaghetti? Here are some of the ideas we have. It

- binds the strands of spaghetti and facilitates interaction among the strands;
- facilitates interaction and connections among the strands of spaghetti (two strands of spaghetti do not have anything to hold them together—the sauce binds them and creates interaction);
- communicates richness within the bowl of spaghetti;

- provides some stability to the otherwise fluid and relatively disorganized structure of the cooked spaghetti; and
- makes the spaghetti appealing and invites your interaction with the food.

In school systems, district-wide communication processes are like the metaphorical spaghetti sauce because they can "bind" together people, tasks, roles, processes, and so on. Good communication also creates places where faculty, staff, parents, and other external stakeholders can interact in Community Engagement Conferences, District Engagement Conferences, Redesign Workshops, and Organizational Learning Networks (each of which is described in chapter 6), as well as in other forums such as parent meetings, parent-teacher meetings, and training workshops. Collectively, these kinds of communication strategies can be called a "binding frame" because, like the sauce, they bind processes and people together.

Many communication models overlook or only incidentally acknowledge the need to bind together participants in a communication setting. An example of a binding frame is presented in figure 4.5. This

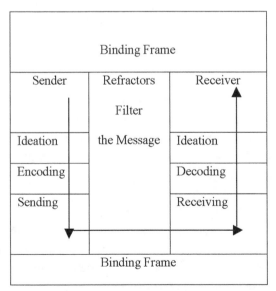

Figure 4.5. The communications process as a binding frame. © 2002 by Edward E. Hampton, Jr. All rights reserved.

figure is an adaptation of a communication model developed by the U.S. Army's Organizational Effectiveness Center and School (circa 1982).

In figure 4.5 you see a model depicting communication between a sender and a receiver. Working through the process, the model shows that the sender first comes up with an idea to communicate. This process is called ideation. Then the sender formulates that idea by encoding his or her message at three levels: verbal, nonverbal, and symbolic. Then the message is sent via one of several channels or multiple channels; for example, voice, telephone, fax, email, television, or letter.

The receiver then receives the message, decodes it at the same three levels as it was encoded, and goes through his or her own ideation process. Hopefully the idea that emerges in the brain of the receiver is the same as the one the sender intended. But, as we all so painfully know, this is not always the case.

One of the reasons messages get distorted is that refractors operate in the space between the sender and the receiver. Refractors are variables that have the potential to distort the meaning of a message during communication. Refractors include personality preferences, emotional states, environmental factors, the quality of interpersonal relationships, and the prior history of your school system's change efforts. Two special sets of refractors—hope and trust and fear and mistrust—play a pivotal role in change navigation. These refractors are discussed later.

New Mental Models for Change-Leadership

Edward Hampton, the coauthor of this part of the chapter, integrated bits and pieces of many concepts from the works of Seyle (1956), Lewin (1947, 1951), Wheatley (1992), Blanchard and Johnson (1983), and others to create what he calls the Chaos-Facilitated Change-Leadership Model and the Stakeholder Management Model, both of which are described here. Both models are complex. Complexity, as noted earlier, does not mean difficult. It means there is a lot to consider and there is a lot to be done when navigating change and when managing stakeholder relationships. Let's examine the key features of both models.

Hans Seyle (1956) first proposed the idea that stressful events will cause a decrease in human and organizational performance. He calls his model the General Adaptation Syndrome. Figure 4.6 illustrates this

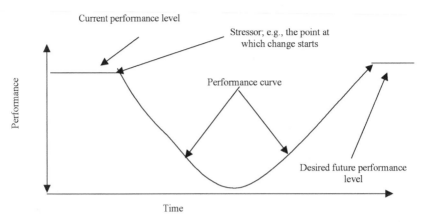

Figure 4.6. Seyle's General Adaptation Syndrome applied to organizational performance. © 2002 by Edward E. Hampton, Jr. All rights reserved.

syndrome. Seyle's concept is a more formal way of describing the "first down, then up" principle that we talked about in part 1 of this chapter.

In figure 4.6, the current performance level of your school district is identified as a horizontal line on the far left of the figure. When a stressor such as systemic change is introduced into your district, your system will experience a drop in performance. Performance drops because people need to expend energy to learn new knowledge and skills. As energy is expended, performance levels deteriorate temporarily. This deterioration process is called entropy in the world of physics.

After a stressor like change is introduced and your system's performance levels begin to decline, the declining performance curve will eventually bottom out near the edge of chaos, and your system will then need to move back up the performance curve toward your district's grand vision. Movement up and out of the declining performance curve is facilitated by replenishing the energy that was used to initiate change. The process of replenishing energy and moving upward toward higher levels of performance is called negative entropy, or negentropy (introduced in chapter 3). Negentropy is not an automatic process. It takes leadership to enact. When negentropy is not generated, instead of moving upward toward higher levels of performance, a system dies or falls over the edge into total chaos.

Interestingly, a study by Ford Motor Company (from a lecture at the U.S. Army's Organizational Effectiveness School) in the early 1970s shows that significant change in that organization caused the same kind of curve as shown in figure 4.6. The Ford study shows that if the change is navigated effectively, it is possible to reduce the depth and duration of a declining performance curve.

The key lesson from Seyle's General Adaptation Syndrome model is that during times of great change, all systems, including individuals and teams, will

- expend energy,
- experience a decline in their overall performance levels, and
- move toward the edge of chaos (not into it, which would result in the complete dissolution of the system).

But, if managed effectively and astutely, systems can

- minimize the depth and duration of the deteriorating performance curve,
- regain energy through negentropy, and
- move upward toward higher levels of performance.

Another lesson from Seyle's theory is that because chaos is the absence of patterns, the goal of systemic school improvement *should not be* to throw a school district into complete chaos by removing all patterns of behavior, processes, and so on. Instead, the goal of whole-system change, as Kevin Kelly (1998) suggests in his book *New Rules for the New Economy*, is to move an organization to the edge of chaos where opportunities for improvement can be identified and seized. This principle takes us back to the hole we dug for our new azalea plant. If you move your district into true chaos, you will totally destroy it. What you do instead is move your district to the edge of chaos by deliberately removing existing and undesirable patterns (e.g., policies, programs, procedures, and the like) to create "holes" (empty places for new policies, programs, procedures, and the like). The empty spaces you create by removing existing and undesirable patterns represent true chaos. By intentionally creating this kind of managed chaos in spots, you make room for new patterns instead of "pancaking" new ones over the old.

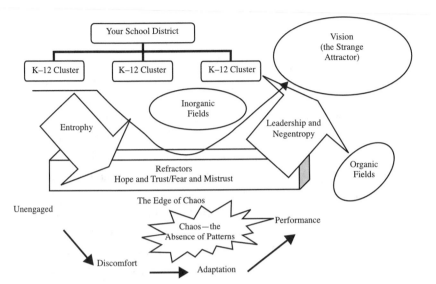

Figure 4.7. The Chaos-Facilitated Change-Leadership Model. © 2002 by Edward E. Hampton, Jr. All rights reserved.

Given everything you've read so far, it is easy to see how challenging it is to navigate change to create and sustain systemic school improvement. A tool you can use to help you navigate systemic school improvement is the Chaos-Facilitated Change-Leadership Model shown in figure 4.7. As a superintendent, you can use the model to navigate systemic school improvement in a positive and advantageous manner. Let's examine the model, one element at a time.

Your School District in the Figure

Starting at the left side of the model, you see what looks like an organizational chart. That chart represents your school district. You also see a thin curved line that represents Seyle's General Adaptation Syndrome and the "first down, then up" principle. Your district's current performance level is represented by the horizontal part of that line to the left and just below the organizational chart representing your district.

Entropy to Initiate Change

Beneath the organization chart representing your district, you see a downward-pointing arrow with the word *entropy* in it. That arrow follows the "first down, then up" performance curve. Entropy is the expenditure of energy. The degree of entropy can be used as a measure of how close you come to the edge of chaos (Wheatley, 1992)—the more entropy you have, the closer you get to chaos. In organizations "energy" is found in human, financial, time, and technological resources. If your school system is not expending increasing amounts of energy, it is not changing.

Your district exists as a set of patterns consisting of behaviors, policies, programs, norms, attitudes, mental models, procedures, relationships, and so on. Organizational patterns are maintained by using personal and system energy. As your system uses energy, it moves toward entropy. To change your district, you must introduce more entropy (i.e., you have to use more resources) into your district because your system must increasingly expend energy to change. The additional energy that you use must dislodge or disrupt unwanted, undesirable patterns to make space for new patterns (just as we used energy to dig a hole for our azalea bush). You will also recall from our earlier discussion that when a system is "stressed" (e.g., undergoing change), the initial movement toward change is downward along the performance curve toward the edge of chaos. This same downward movement is reflected in figure 4.7 in the downward-pointing arrow with the word *entropy* in it.

Megson (circa 1982) identifies eight characteristics of an organization as a system. One of those characteristics is entropy, which was just discussed. Another characteristic is "negative entropy," or as it is sometimes called, negentropy. Negentropy occurs when people put energy back into a system (i.e., replenishing resources) to arrest or reverse the process of entropy. You must introduce negentropy at the appropriate time to prevent your district from spinning into total chaos. Negentropy is a function of change-leadership, and it will replenish your system's energy and help it move up the performance curve toward its desired vision. Leadership to create negentropy and movement toward the future is shown in figure 4.7 as the upward-pointing arrow at the right of the figure.

All of the existing patterns in your school system (e.g., who does what, when, where, and how; your policies, procedures, processes; your relationships; and your district's outcomes) create a comfort zone for you, your teachers, and your stakeholders. This comfort zone, sometimes called the status quo or dynamic equilibrium (this concept was discussed in chapter 3), is a major obstacle to change because people don't want to leave it.

The key to successful whole-system change, therefore, is to reduce or eliminate those comfort zones while simultaneously creating a powerful, attractive vision of future patterns that will attract people and motivate them to move out of their old ways and toward the desired new ones. To create this movement, as we said earlier, you need to introduce entropy (an increased use of energy) into your system to stimulate change.

However, unchecked entropy leads to a deterioration of system performance and eventual system death. Therefore, at the proper time, you will then need to introduce negative entropy to replenish system energy and to move your system toward higher levels of performance. Using entropy and negative entropy effectively is one of the major challenges of navigating systemic change.

Using Entropy and Negentropy Effectively

Effective change navigation requires the purposeful and effective use of entropy and negative entropy. You introduce entropy into your school system by doing the following:

- Engage your teachers, support staff, and stakeholders in creating a new powerful vision for the future of your school system. A vision is a compelling description of some future place or state of being. A properly defined vision begins to create a desire for change. A well-crafted vision acts like what chaos and complexity theorists call a "strange attractor." A strange attractor does two things. First, it creates a space (like the hole we dug for the azalea) within which new patterns can emerge; and, second, it attracts new patterns, people, and ideas to it.
- Boundaries influence behavior in ways that create new patterns. For example, imagine a small pond on a windy day. You can see

the ripples of water moving in many directions simultaneously. At first glance, the perceived disorderliness seems unpatterned—chaotic. But as the waves move within the boundaries that confine the pond (the shoreline), you eventually begin to perceive patterns of wave action. As a change-leader using principles of chaos management, you want to help your colleagues create a boundary within which new patterns of behavior, policies, programs, procedures, relationships, and so on can be recognized, organized, and used to create improved student, teacher, and system learning. A compelling vision for your district is a well-defined boundary that shapes new patterns of behavior, processes, activities, and outcomes.

- Create discomfort with the present. This is an important change-principle that is often overlooked. Discomfort is often assumed. The problem with assuming discomfort is that if it does not exist, then there probably will not be enough energy to cause people to move out of their comfort zones toward the new vision.
- Remove or destabilize existing patterns; for example, suspend rules, set aside constraining policies, or declare an end to something (i.e., "holes").

You use negative entropy by doing the following:

- Create hope that the temporary state of discomfort caused by the disruption in comfortable patterns will not be forever; and assure people that the district's new vision can and will be achieved.
- Develop and reinforce your trust in people and their trust in you. Trust is a binding element that holds people together in times of great change (please take another look at chapter 2 for information about the importance of trust).
- A key change activity is to ensure that those patterns (programs, procedures, policies, roles, and so on) that you want to maintain are protected. You do this by infusing energy into them (i.e., by using human, financial, time, and technical resources to protect them).
- As your district approaches its desired future, stabilize the new patterns you created. You can think of this as a reinforcement and maintenance stage. You provide rewards and incentives to ensure that the new patterns are stabilized. And, as any good

gardener would do, you may need to prune the new patterns as they flourish and grow to keep them at optimal levels of performance.

- Related to the preceding, as you see new desirable patterns emerging, you want to support and protect them just as you would protect new shoots that are delicate and easily harmed on a prized plant.
- You will also need to encourage and support risk taking, while devising creative, positive, and effective ways to manage the inevitable critics and "doom and gloomers" who emerge as you engage in systemic school improvement.

Refractors

The next elements in figure 4.7 that we'd like to call to your attention are called "refractors." There are two sets of refractors in the Chaos-Facilitated Change-Leadership Model: hope and trust and fear and mistrust. Refractors serve as filters through which people's perceptions, attitudes, and beliefs are shaped, and therefore through which their behavior is influenced.

Hope and Trust: Some of your faculty, staff, and stakeholders will resist your efforts to lead systemic school improvement—you can count on it (there is more about resistance in chapter 6). Hope and trust are critical variables within the Chaos-Facilitated Change-Leadership Model that can help reduce levels of resistance and unhelpful criticism.

Hope and trust are also important for helping people take risks. Leaving the comfort zone defined by current patterns of behavior, processes, activities, and outcomes requires risk taking. To take a risk, people must have *hope* that what they do will lead to desired results, and they need to *trust* that they will not be punished for their efforts.

Fear and Mistrust: Two critically important and deeply influential refractors during times of systemic change are fear and mistrust. Fear and mistrust could become perceptual filters through which your faculty and staff will view the changes that you are working so hard to create. Fear and mistrust present two threats to your change-leadership efforts: (1) people may block the use of energy needed to create change because they may fear what lies ahead; or (2) they may not trust your vision of the future, and therefore they may resist going there by trying to stay put. Either of these actions can throw your district off of its change-path.

The Developmental Change Process

The next key element of the Chaos-Facilitated Change-Leadership Model is the developmental change process. This process refers to the predictable stages through which people, including yourself, will move through your systemic change process. The stages are unengaged, discomfort, adaptation, and performance. These phases are shown at the bottom of figure 4.7.

Unengaged and Discomfort: It is important to understand that these two stages emerge on the downward side of the performance curve shown in figure 4.7. At the beginning of a downward movement toward the edge of chaos, there will be a period when your faculty and staff will be unengaged; that is, they will not fully support your efforts to change your district.

People may be unengaged for a number of reasons. They may be in denial (i.e., they believe the changes will not affect them), or they may simply be uninformed about the requirements of the change process. They also may not be sufficiently uncomfortable (remember, a feeling of discomfort with the present is needed to move toward the future). Given this feeling of being unengaged, your people may stay in their comfort zones, and you will perceive this as resistance to change. Again, the key to moving people out of this phase is to increase entropy as described earlier.

Next, once your faculty and staff accept the changes as important or unavoidable, they will enter a phase of emotional discomfort. This feeling of discomfort is needed to motivate people to move toward the future.

As your people work through these first two stages, their actions will tend to destabilize existing patterns of behavior and processes, and this will cause downward movement along the performance curve. At the bottom the declining performance curve shown in figure 4.7, your system will be at the edge of chaos and it will appear to be like the metaphorical bowl of spaghetti that we've been talking about. At this point—at the edge of chaos—you and your people will discover unprecedented opportunities to improve student, teacher, and system learning. You will also face dangerous threats to the well-being of your system. So, you need to seize the opportunities and eliminate or minimize the threats. This takes adaptation and performance.

Adaptation and Performance: It is no trivial thing to note that adaptation to change begins at the lowest point in the declining performance curve—right at the edge of chaos. At this place, people can easily become disoriented by all of the craziness, silliness, hopes, confusion, and fear that often characterize it.

There is also no guarantee that your district's movement along the declining performance curve will bottom out and then move upward toward higher levels of competence and performance. To create upward movement you need to introduce negative entropy (i.e., by replenishing your system's resources). Negentropy creates and reinforces new, desirable patterns of behavior and processes. Replenishing energy will move individuals, teams, schools, clusters, and the whole district up the performance curve toward your district's vision.

It is important to point out that sometimes you may want your school district or a part of the district to linger at the edge of chaos in a high state of malleability and remain open to yet undiscovered opportunities. However, let's assume that you want your school system to achieve its desired vision in the shortest time possible. To do this, you and your colleagues need to introduce negative entropy into your system by feeding increasing amounts of energy (in the form of human, financial, time, and technological resources) back into your district to help everyone to begin moving up the performance curve toward the vision. Moving up the performance curve toward your district's vision is the last stage in the developmental change process.

Effective individual, team, school, cluster, and system performance means that people are working purposefully and constructively through the developmental change process toward your district's grand vision. Movement up the performance curve is stimulated by your and your change-leaders' leadership and influenced by the power of two force fields.

Inorganic and Organic Force Fields

Force fields in organizations are like magnetic fields because their energy influences the emergence of new patterns. Most of us can look back at our high school physics labs and recall using magnets with piles of disorganized iron filings. Do you remember what happened as the magnet approached the iron filings? The magnetic field created patterns by attracting the iron filings to it. In essence, the magnetic field transformed chaos into order. This is what a force field does. In this way, force fields also act something like what physicists call "strange attractors." We talked about strange attractors earlier. For change navigation purposes, there are two primary types of force fields, organic and inorganic.

Inorganic Force Fields: Inorganic force fields are formed by structural things: rules, organizational charts, policies, job descriptions, and so on. These structural elements are also part of a school district's internal social architecture and must be improved if you want to create and sustain high performance. You and your colleagues must create inorganic force fields that compel, facilitate, and otherwise help ensure that new, desirable patterns are developed.

Organic Force Fields: Organic force fields come from people, ideally supportive people. These people are normally internal and external stakeholders. As can be seen in the Stakeholder Management Model shown in figure 4.8, stakeholders can react to your leadership in one of three ways: they can support, block, or ignore your leadership. Of course, you want key internal and external stakeholders to support your leadership for

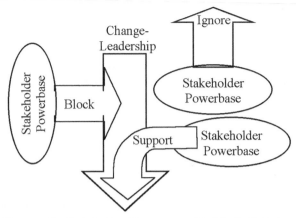

Figure 4.8. Stakeholder Management Model. © 2002 by
Edward E. Hampton, Jr. All rights reserved.

change. You can get their support by working with them to create three
crucial beliefs:

- Belief that they are empowered to help you succeed; that is, that
their contributions will be perceived as adding value rather than as
being frivolous or unimportant.
- Belief that achieving what you are advocating is desirable, not
only for them but for children. Sometimes this means communicating and helping them understand the WIFM ("what's in it for
me") principle.
- Belief that if they take risks they will not be punished.

Earlier, we talked about the powerful influence of strange attractors.
In organizations, behavior is influenced by strange attractors. In
physics, when strange attractors are plotted mathematically, the resulting graph looks like a basin—much like an empty pond of water. Just
as the shape of a pond's basin influences how the surface waves self-
organize, organizational forces acting like strange attractors influence
human behavior in school districts.

Your district's internal social architecture is like a pond basin. In
much the same way that a pond's floor influences the organization and

movement of surface waves, your district's social architecture influences the organization and movement of behavior, tasks, roles, work
outcomes, processes, and so on. So, another key to effective change-
leadership is to redesign your district's internal social architecture so
that it has a positive "strange attractor" kind of influence on the organic
and inorganic force fields that support your district's journey toward
high performance.

The Leadership Arrow

In figure 4.7, you see an upward-pointing arrow that is identified as
"leadership and negentropy." Organic and inorganic force fields are not
enough to move your district up the performance curve toward its desired vision. Leadership to replenish energy (i.e., replenish resources)
in your school district is needed—not just from you, but from many
others in your system, including union heads, principals, supervisors,
senior staff, and senior teachers. You recall from chapter 1 that leadership for change must start with you, but for whole-district improvement
to succeed, that leadership must spread throughout your district so that
many others are empowered to exercise it. Broad and deep leadership
is needed to unfreeze, move, and refreeze (see Lewin, 1951) your
school system.

The terms *leader* and *leadership* are not synonymous. A *leader* is a
person with the ability to exert control, authority, or influence over
other people and situations. *Leadership*, on the other hand, is a process
that often exists in many different parts of your school system and
which is exercised by many different people in many different roles.
Leadership, as a process, must be established throughout your district
to create and sustain effective systemic change. Leadership links the organic and inorganic force fields together and enhances their power to
influence your district's movement up the performance curve toward a
desirable future.

Good leadership deals with four imperatives. These imperatives
were developed by the U.S. Army (1983) to control the dynamics of its
very fluid "Air-Land Battle" doctrine. These imperatives are represented by the acronym SAID:

- *S* stands for synchronization. All the pieces of your system must function in an orchestrated manner. Change activities must be timed and coordinated so they work synergistically.
- *A* stands for agility. Agility is the ability to take advantage of opportunity. Agility is often dependent on resources and skills. A good change-leader will plan a robust set of skills and resources to capture a full range of expected and unexpected options.
- *I* stands for initiative. Initiative is the ability to create opportunities. Like agility, this takes resources and skills.
- *D* stands for depth. Actions must take place in terms of physical depth, time depth, and depth of activity (at the tactical, operational, and strategic levels).

Dissipative Structures: Another New Science concept related to change-leadership is the "dissipative structure." As defined by Prigogine and Stengers (1984), a *dissipative structure* is something that changes states and, in the process, creates energy. Wheatley (1992) comments on dissipative structure in this way:

> To understand the world from this perspective, scientists had to give up their views of decay and dissipation. They had to transform their ideas about the role of disequilibrium. They had to develop a new relationship with disorder. . . . Prigogine's work on the evolution of dynamic systems demonstrated that disequilibrium is the necessary condition for a system's growth. . . . He called these systems dissipative structures because they dissipate energy to recreate themselves into new forms of organization. Faced with amplifying levels of disturbance, these systems possess innate properties to reconfigure themselves. . . . For this reason, they are frequently called self-organizing or self-renewing systems. One of their distinguishing features is system resiliency rather than stability. (p. 88)

Dissipative structures create energy. Leadership is a dissipative structure because energy is created in the give-and-take of leadership and followership. Thus, to tap into the power of leadership as a dissipative structure you must create collaborative relationships among you and your followers that will, in turn, release energy back into the school district. By releasing energy back into your system you are introducing negative entropy (negentropy), which is required to move your system up the performance curve toward its vision.

Models for Creating Agile and Adaptive Organizations

You will recall our earlier metaphor that had us digging a hole to make room for a new azalea plant. We removed existing patterns (grass and dirt) to create an empty hole (the empty space representing chaos). We introduced new patterns (the azalea's root ball and the life forces in it) into the empty hole. Essentially, we reintroduced order to that chaotic environment by putting the root ball in that hole and covering it with freshly enriched soil.

A necessary precursor to our hole-digging experience was not discussed. The elements we removed to create the hole had to be removable or malleable or fluid. Imagine, for example, trying to dig a hole in what our friends from Tennessee call "rocky top"—a thin layer of soil on top of layers of shale-like rock. The rock just below the surface is not malleable and digging a hole is difficult. The point we're making here is that a necessary precursor to systemic change is malleability or fluidity—your system has to be capable of changing. You create fluidity by increasing your system's use of energy (entropy), which in turn creates a pliable organization ready to change.

Fluidity softens rigid organizational hierarchy and creates agility. Agility is the ability to move quickly and effectively. Pinchot (1996) argues that one of the keys to success of an organization is "liberating the spirit of enterprise." In other words, an organization that allows its people to behave entrepreneurially will be more successful on the whole. He argues that entrepreneurial teams, departments, or individuals cannot and should not be linked to an organization's old hierarchical structures. These old structures are arthritic and prevent celerity in either seizing opportunities or responding to threats from the organization's external environment. Rather, these teams, departments, and individuals should be linked together as a human network with others who have the data, information, or knowledge needed to innovate and self-organize.

Given the preceding points, a key leadership decision prior to launching a whole-district change effort is knowing when, where, and how to create fluidity and promote agility within your district. The following advice can help you make these decisions in an artful way.

Boundary Management

Each task, activity, process, role, and unit in a school district has an invisible but real boundary around it. These boundaries can impede or facilitate interaction. Although boundaries are needed to maintain stability, if you want to increase malleability (or fluidity, as it is sometimes called), introduce entropy, and stimulate change, then you must make those boundaries more permeable and malleable.

As you begin your redesign effort, you also need to prevent the premature and unnecessary formation of new boundaries. Remember when you start systemic change, you are creating "empty spaces" (holes) in your school district by removing old, ineffective programs, policies, procedures, and so on (which we collectively call patterns). Empty space begs to be filled, and it is awfully attractive to would-be "empire builders." These people see empty places left by the removal of old patterns and they attempt to carve out new turf for themselves; or, being impatient with the emptiness, they rush to introduce new patterns that may not be appropriate. The problem with the premature reestablishment of boundaries is that it stifles agility and initiative as new rules, guidelines, and the staking out of "available" turf block the free flow of new ideas and activity.

Enable Equifinality

Equifinality is a core concept from the field of organization development. "The idea of equifinality suggests that similar results may be achieved with different initial conditions and in many different ways. This concept suggests that a manager can use varying degrees of inputs into the organization and can transform them in a variety of ways to obtain satisfactory outputs" (Cummings & Worley, 2001, p. 87). Megson (circa 1982) includes equifinality as yet another characteristic of a system. To create fluid situations, you need to empower your faculty and staff to apply the principle of equifinality. Such freedom gives them the opportunity to find the best solution and to handle uncertainty better.

Leaders, like managers, are interested in processes that work. This sometimes means maintaining a certain level of discipline for managing people and processes during times of great change. In other words, you and your fellow change-leaders should not simply take an "anything goes" attitude about equifinality. This might seem like a contradiction when compared to the definition of equifinality. But an important criterion for defining equifinality is that there are many different *acceptable* ways to achieve the same goal. The word *acceptable* implies that there are certain predefined boundaries within which equifinality may be exercised. Not everything is acceptable—only some things. Therefore, when encouraging people to exercise equifinality, leaders define the playing field in ways that make it sufficiently broad to allow many different innovative approaches to achieving school district goals. When equifinality is used within predefined boundaries of acceptability, leaders are better able to tolerate their system's movement to the edge of chaos.

By creating a wider, looser playing field within which people can work and innovate, you increase fluidity and agility. As fluidity and agility increase, and as your system moves to the edge of chaos, opportunities for improving your system explode in a combinatorial fashion.

All of the fluidity and movement you create through your change-leadership have to be monitored carefully. Remember that too much entropy can diminish the overall effectiveness of your school system and, in some cases, it can lead to the death of an organization. You have to watch all the "flux" with a mindful eye focused on your district's desired vision, and you must ensure that your district's vision is kept in synchrony with the requirements and expectations of its ever-changing external environment.

To preserve synchrony, you may have to make adjustments to your vision or you may have to fine-tune how you interact with your external environment; or both. We think that the leadership task of adjusting the vision or fine-tuning your district's interaction with its environment to preserve synchrony marks an important distinction between a leader and a manager. While managers may also want system fluidity to stimulate change, there is the occasional manager who rarely is willing to change the vision or change how his or her system interacts with the outside world. In fact, this kind of manager often forces his or her organization to stay on the misperceived straight-as-an-arrow change-path with the assumption that the system's future is sitting out there waiting for them to arrive.

One final thought on creating malleability to stimulate change. Adizes (1990) argues that once an organization matures, it begins to decline as a bureaucracy, and he says aristocracy takes hold. To counter this decline, Adizes suggests that fluidity (which is another way of describing malleability) cleanses an organization and creates growth through renewal. This same kind of suggestion is also implied by the imperatives for life delineated by Wheatley and Kellner-Rogers in their book *A Simpler Way* (1996, pp. 13–14):

- Everything is in a constant process of discovery and creating.
- Life uses messes to get to well-ordered solutions.
- Life is intent on finding out what works, not what's "right."
- Life creates more possibilities as it engages with opportunities.
- Life is attracted to order.
- Life organizes around identity.
- Everything participates in the creation and evolution of its neighbors.

Random Thoughts, Deeply Felt

We conclude by summarizing a series of random thoughts that represent deep feelings we have about navigating change to create and sustain systemic school improvement.

- Whole-district improvement must create a new social architecture for your school district that has three distinguishing characteristics: (1) it must favor knowledge, skills, and relationships; (2) it must be anchored to a network of teams and their resources; and (3) it must seek to align teams, their knowledge and skills, and their resources with a district's strategic goals and vision.
- The new social architecture you create for your district must focus on developing capacity for trust, commitment, and collaboration that is deep and wide.

- There is a downside to creating more information for people through increased collaboration. Simon (as cited in Kelly, 1998, p. 59) says, "What information consumes is rather obvious: It consumes the attention of its recipients. Hence a wealth of information creates a poverty of attention." So, with the wealth of information that comes with a networked social architecture, you have to figure out creative ways to capture people's attention.

- In a social network, all information and communication demand extensive consensus. Participants in networks also have to speak and understand each other's jargon. In your school district you do this by building an organization-wide mental model (see chapter 3 for more on mental models) that serves as a conceptual frame of reference for understanding your district's values, beliefs, and expectations. You must create a shared defining metaphor (i.e., an organizational mental model) for your district—a metaphor captured and expressed in your district's vision. This mental model helps create consensus and a common language expressed in terms of art (i.e., jargon).

- When people are connected in a networked organization design, each individual becomes a node—a connection point—in that network. The connections among the nodes form a matrix through which flows the professional intellect of a school system. When this matrix is fully functioning, it releases an extraordinary amount of human energy, ideas, commitment, and learning.

- Social networks don't eliminate individuality. Your school district will continue to have teachers and staff, each with his or her individual mental models, individual decision-making styles, and individual ways of doing things. What the network does do, however, is create a powerful district-wide "organizational intellect."

- The individual participants in a web of connected relationships create a collective professional intellect. Each individual contributes what he or she knows, and the resulting organizational knowledge creates an incredibly "smart" school district. There is no way one person can be as smart or as skilled as the "whole."

- The goal of creating this kind of networked social architecture is to create, as much as possible, a school system that is self-regulating and self-optimizing (as opposed to being externally regulated and externally forced to improve). This kind of social architecture produces superior performance in a turbulent environment because it allows individuals and teams to respond to unanticipated events quickly and appropriately (Daft, 2001).

- Biological metaphors most accurately describe how social networks function. The biological metaphor that seems to work best for school districts with a networked internal social architecture is "ecosystem." In an ecosystem, the entire ecosystem does not have to change simultaneously for one species to change. Yet, some proponents of systemic school improvement argue that true whole-system change can only happen if the entire ecosystem changes at once. We disagree. Like an ecosystem, systemic school improvement can start with a cluster of schools and then spread to all remaining clusters until the whole district is redesigned. Wheatley (as cited in Duffy & Dale, 2001) makes this argument, too, when she says, "Start anywhere and follow it everywhere" (p. 15).

- In nature, some ecosystems offer scarce opportunities for life (polar ice caps), while others offer overflowing opportunities (equatorial jungles). If you think of your school system as an ecosystem, it too can offer scarce or abundant opportunities for success. Scarcity or abundance of opportunities in school districts, we think, depends on your district's organizational mental model that guides people's thoughts, feelings, and actions. If most of your people choose to think, feel, and act like your district can never improve, it won't. If most of your people choose to think, feel, and act like you do have the creative potential to move your district toward breathtakingly higher levels of performance, you will make that journey. The power of choice, either individually or collectively, has been repeatedly proven to have an extraordinary effect on human performance. Or, as Jean-Paul Sartre once said, "We are our choices."

- Moving a school system toward the edge of chaos (but not into it) can be a good thing for you and your colleagues as you take steps to create and sustain whole-system change. But this dance to the edge of chaos must be managed carefully. Fluidity, agility, and discomfort with the status quo must be intentionally introduced at the right time, in the right places, and at optimum levels. Most important, your leadership must ensure there is enough energy in your system to redesign the whole district and achieve its grand vision.

- All whole-district redesign methodologies are not "perfect" methodologies and they will not create perfect school districts. Instead, they illuminate the general direction for a school district to take toward high performance, but like a flashlight, the beams only run ahead so far and the darkness beyond the edge of light ahead will not be illuminated until you move farther down the path you're on.
- School district leaders who know how to dance on ice adeptly and with agility will create school systems that are more robust, innovative, and increasingly effective. They also need a change process that will move them upward from the edge of chaos toward their collective vision, reintroduce order to their system, and create sustainable improvements in student, teacher, and system learning.

REFERENCES

Adizes, I. (1990). *Corporate lifecycles: How and why corporations grow and die and what to do about it.* Upper Saddle River, NJ: Prentice Hall.

Blanchard, K., & Johnson, D. (1983). *The one minute manager.* New York: Berkley.

Cummings, T. G., & Worley, C. G. (2001). *Organization development and the management of change* (7th ed.). Cincinnati: South-Western College Publishing.

Daft, R. L. (2001). *Organization theory and design* (7th ed.). Cincinnati: South-Western College Publishing.

Deming, W. E. (1986). *Out of crisis.* Cambridge, MA: MIT Center for Advanced Educational Services.

Duffy, F. M., & Dale, J. D. (2001). *Creating successful school systems: Voices from the university, the field, and the community.* Norwood, MA: Christopher-Gordon.

Kelly, K. (1998). *New rules for the new economy: 10 radical strategies for a connected world.* New York: Penguin.

Keltner, B. R. (1998). Funding comprehensive school reform. Rand Corporation. Available: Rand Corporation Web site, www.rand.org/publications/IP/IP175/

Lewin, K. (1947). Frontiers in group dynamics. *Human Relations, 1,* 5–41.

Lewin, K. (1951). *Field theory in social science.* New York: Harper and Row.

Lewin, R. (1992). *Complexity, life on the edge of chaos.* New York: Macmillan.

Megson, L.V.C. (circa 1982). Open systems—theory and planning. In *U.S. Army Organizational Effectiveness Handbook*. Fort Ord, CA: U.S. Army Organizational Effectiveness Center and School.

Morgan, G. (1988). *Riding the waves of change: Developing managerial competencies for a turbulent world*. San Francisco: Jossey-Bass.

Pinchot, G. (1996). Creating organizations with many leaders. In F. Hesselbin, M. Goldsmith, R. Beckhard, & P. F. Drucker (Eds.), *The leader of the future: New visions, strategies, and practices for the next era* (pp. 25–39). San Francisco: Jossey-Bass.

Preskill, H., & Torres, R. T. (1999). *Evaluative inquiry for learning in organizations*. Thousand Oaks, CA: Sage.

Prigogine, I., & Stengers, I. (1984). *Order out of chaos: Man's new dialogue with nature*. New York: Bantam.

Seyle, H. (1956). *The stress of life*. New York: McGraw-Hill.

U.S. Army. (circa 1982). *U.S. Army organizational effectiveness handbook*. Fort Ord, CA: U.S. Army Organizational Effectiveness Center and School.

U.S. Army. (1983). *Field Manual FM 100-5: Operations*. Washington, DC: U.S. Government Printing Office.

Wheatley, M. J. (1992). *Leadership and the new science*. San Francisco: Berrett-Koehler.

Wheatley, M. J. (2001). Bringing schools back to life: Schools as living systems. In F. M. Duffy & J. D. Dale (Eds.), *Creating successful school systems: Voices from the university, the field, and the community* (pp. 3–19). Norwood, MA: Christopher-Gordon.

Wheatley, M. J., & Kellner-Rogers, M. (1996). *A simpler way*. San Francisco: Berrett-Koehler.

Zander, R. S., & Zander, B. (2000). *The art of possibility: Transforming personal and professional life*. Boston: Harvard Business School Press.

ABOUT EDWARD HAMPTON

Edward Earl Hampton, Jr., is president and managing member of Performance Perspectives LLC, a consulting firm specializing in helping organizations and individuals realize their performance potential. He has been an active organizational effectiveness consultant since 1985. He tailors assessment-based programs for organizations, teams, and individuals to perform optimally. He specializes in strategic planning, team structuring, team coaching, change management, leadership development, assessment-based training, organizational troubleshooting, quality management, and executive coaching. Ed also teaches leadership in the department of industrial engineering and management at the University of Central Florida.

NOTE

This chapter has two parts. Part 1 was written by Francis Duffy, and part 2 was coauthored by Edward Hampton. Combined, both parts provide you with ideas for navigating whole-system change.

1. Stan Herman, a well-known and highly respected organization development consultant, coined this phrase in personal correspondence with me on the topic of systemic change.

Role Models and Inspiration

If you want to understand what a science is, you should look in the first instance not at its theories or its findings, and certainly not at what its apologists say about it; you should look at what the practitioners of it do.

—Clifford Geertz, *The Interpretation of Cultures*

Part 2 has one chapter—chapter 5. This chapter is a collection of essays submitted by invited superintendents who are leading or have tried to lead systemic school improvement. The participating superintendents are Diana Lam of the Providence Public Schools (Rhode Island), Jack Dale of the Frederick County Public Schools (Maryland), and Richard DeLorenzo of the Chugach Public Schools (Alaska).

Additionally, two nonsuperintendents wrote essays describing their views on leadership for creating school improvement. Scott Thompson is the assistant director for the Panasonic Foundation, which partners with school districts engaged in whole-district change. And Louise Sundin, president of the Minneapolis Federation of Teachers and the national vice president for the American Federation of Teachers, is deeply involved in systemic change in her leadership roles.

The chapter leads off with Scott Thompson's essay. Scott provides a broad frame for seeing the potential of whole-district change. He talks about eight "critical success factors" that he believes represent a high-performing school system. He follows his presentation of the critical success factors with a powerful analysis of the kind of leadership needed to transform entire school systems into high-performing learning organizations.

The superintendents' essays follow. The first essay is by Richard De-Lorenzo, who led his school district to one of the two Baldrige Awards ever awarded to a school district in the United States. He talks about his vision and passion for change-leadership.

Diana Lam speaks with passion about issues of race, class, and gender and her perspectives on how dynamics surrounding these issues affect a superintendent's ability to lead systemic school improvement. What makes her essay so powerful is that she speaks to the issues from her personal experience of aspiring to and gaining leadership positions throughout her career.

Jack Dale, Maryland's Superintendent of the Year for 2000, writes next. He has a personal vision of distributing leadership throughout his leadership team and of encouraging leadership for change in others throughout his district. He writes about his passion for seeing this vision become reality.

Finally, Louise Sundin offers her views on the leadership needed to create and sustain systemic school improvement. She speaks to this kind of leadership from the perspective of her role as a nationally recognized leader of a teachers union.

I am so pleased with the messages in these essays. These fine people present powerful and compelling ideas about the kind of leadership needed to move whole districts toward higher levels of performance and create unparalleled opportunities for increasing student, teacher, and system learning.

CHAPTER 5

Essays from the Field

ESSAY 1: A HIGH-PERFORMANCE SCHOOL SYSTEM
Scott Thompson, Assistant Director, Panasonic Foundation

The problems we face in public education are dynamically complex, multifaceted, and ever changing. A school district's organization chart, for example, may be static and well ordered on paper, but it becomes fluid in reality as school and district administrators, board members, teachers, students, parents, and community, business, and union leaders act, react, and interact; as unpredictable events occur; and as the unintended consequences of carefully planned actions unfold.

For all of the fluidity and dynamism of school districts as social systems, the fundamental features of their underlying culture and structure tend to be stubbornly inert. It's a well-known fact that the modern public school and school district are direct descendants of the Industrial Revolution. Public schools were modeled after factories, and factories, we know, are built to last. Factories have traditionally been designed with an eye toward optimizing efficiency through routinized or regimented processes. The blood relative of such regimentation is change aversion.

Given the double-barreled challenge of social flux and bureaucratic intransigence, it's no wonder that those involved in efforts to transform factory-style school districts into adaptive, high-performing systems of education have experienced such tough sledding and spotty progress. At the same time, it's important to note that a number of school systems have made important gains, and their stories contain critical lessons and questions that should be thoughtfully explored as the work of systemic change in public education continues.

This essay offers a fairly detailed vision of a high-performing school district, in which each element of this envisioned system is drawn not from imagination, but from the current policies, practices, and structures of existing school districts. In other words, the vision I am offering comprises school system attributes that are already in practice and are beginning to show positive results.

The Critical Factors of a High-Performing School System

A group of Panasonic Foundation colleagues and I developed a set of "critical success factors" at the classroom, school, and system levels of a school district.[1] These are observable features without which we believe it is unlikely that a school district would be high-performing. I would define a high-performance school district as one where the overwhelming majority of students in all schools are meeting high standards of learning regardless of students' ethnic or socioeconomic background and where the district decisively and effectively intervenes in schools where student performance is declining or flat-lining.[2] For the sake of brevity, I will focus in this essay only on system-level critical success factors of a high-performing district. (The school-level and classroom-level success factors are critically important, but they are implied in the system-level factors that follow.)

Critical Success Factors

1. The system is standards-based:
   - Challenging and clearly understood standards define what all students should know and be able to do at each level.
   - Instructional practice throughout the system is based on standards-referenced continuous assessment for tailoring teaching to individual student needs.
2. The school system takes as its purpose enabling *all* students in *all* schools to meet high standards, and this purpose is evidenced by the district's vision/mission statement, policies, contracts, re-

source allocation (budget priorities), human resource practices, and other practices and structures.

3. From classrooms to district offices to school board meetings, the school system climate is nurturing and supportive; it is characterized by respectful relationships.

4. The system holds itself accountable for the success of all schools:
   - It conducts frequent assessment or monitoring of school performance and uses the results to provide prompt and timely assistance and resources to improve all schools.
   - Low performance of schools is promptly addressed with a clear and intensive strategy of human and material resources.

5. The system ensures intensive, ongoing, high-quality professional development for all employees that is driven by classroom, school, and system performance data.

6. System resources (human, financial, material, time, etc.) are strategically focused on its mission to support powerful instructional practice in all schools, and noninstructional burdens on schools are minimized.

7. The system collects and uses data effectively:
   - Data are collected, analyzed, and disseminated to schools and other departments, and the system provides extensive training, helping schools manage and use their data to improve instructional practice in all classrooms.
   - System-wide data are used as the basis for designing initiatives and ensuring equitable allocation of human, financial, and material resources.

8. The system engages in active, open, substantive, and understandable two-way communication with families, business and community partners, and internal stakeholders.

The Critical Success Factors in Action

To my knowledge, there is not one high-performance school district serving a diverse population in the United States that meets the definition I offered earlier. It is equally important to note that all the critical success factors can be observed in several districts, and they are leading to improved performance in those districts. In every instance, these districts have a long way to go, but the progress they have already realized is noteworthy.

What follows are instantiations of the critical success factors (CSFs), drawing on the experiences, policies, practices, and structures of particular school systems.

CSF 1 (standards-based) and CSF 8 (two-way communication) as illustrated by Aurora Public Schools, Colorado. In 1989, the school district launched a strategic planning effort. Curriculum development was suspended for a year and those monies were applied to researching and formulating a path for fundamentally improving educational practice and outcomes. The district studied demographic trends, began exploring standards-based education, examined changes that might be required in classrooms, and investigated alternatives for assessing academic performance. Over the next couple of years, content and performance standards were developed in seven subject areas, including requirements for graduation.

Then near the end of the 1994 school year, a group of parents attended a board meeting and publicly attacked the new standards-based strategic plan. The superintendent and key cabinet members met with the parent group several times in an effort to better understand their concerns. What emerged was a working group that included a number of the concerned parents as well as school and district staff, students, and other community members. This group revisited and reworked the graduation requirements. Finally, seven years after the work began, the board adopted content standards and performance-based graduation requirements (Panasonic Foundation, 1998a).

A visit to an Aurora elementary school reveals what standards-based education looks like at the classroom level. In a fourth- and fifth-grade class, students write compositions in their workbooks. In these books, which are essentially running records of their learning process, the students follow outlined goals that match the standards and rubrics, such as defining the topic, the audience, and the plan for the composition.

Meanwhile, the teacher is roaming about the room, observing student progress and taking notes in her own monitoring notebook with sections for each child. These records help her determine which skills students can perform and which they need to work on (Panasonic Foundation, 1998a).

CSF 2 ("all means all" evidenced in vision, policies, allocations, etc.) as illustrated by Charlotte-Mecklenburg Schools, North Carolina. In September 1991 the board of education adopted the following vision statement: "The Vision is to ensure that the Charlotte-Mecklenburg School System becomes the premier, urban integrated school system in the nation in which all students acquire the knowledge, skills, and values necessary to live rich and full lives as productive and enlightened members of society" (Charlotte-Mecklenburg Schools, North Carolina, 1999).

To make this vision a reality, the district identified schools requiring intensive services and supports to level the playing field. Four factors were considered: student achievement according to state and district assessments; characteristics of licensed staff; student characteristics (socioeconomic status, mobility, language and learning needs, etc.); and other factors, including school climate, parent involvement, educational materials, quality of facilities, and access to technology (Charlotte-Mecklenburg Schools, 2001). Under this policy framework, a significant number of schools qualify for supports and resources over and above those provided to other schools: lower student pupil ratio; a family advocate; a social worker; a school nurse; a full-time mentor if the school has fifteen or more first- and second-year teachers; extra bonus pay for certified staff; free or radically reduced tuition for a master's degree for teachers in these schools; and additional instructional supplies and materials, media center equipment and materials, and technology. One of the most consequential outcomes of this policy framework is that schools serving a majority of students of color and students in poverty are no longer staffed by the least qualified and lowest-paid teachers and administrators, and significant progress has been made toward closing the achievement gap.

CSF 3 (respectful relationships) as illustrated by the School District of Edmonds, Washington. In 1987 the district was in the grip of a thirty-day teachers' strike. What was explicitly at issue were overcrowded classrooms, but if you were to scratch deeper you would find a pervasive feeling among teachers that they were not trusted or respected by district leadership. The following year two new school board members were elected and a new superintendent was hired. The new superintendent worked with the leadership of the teachers association and with a range of stakeholders at various levels to create a set of guiding principles for shared decision making. What came out of this process was not only a document that guides decision making at all levels of the system—now in its fifth draft after more than a decade of development—but a culture of mutual respect and shared commitment to improving the quality of education for all children.

The leadership of the district and the association also developed a trust agreement that is upheld through continuous bargaining and that promotes an active, positive working relationship between the association, central office, and school board. A bargaining team of twenty, representing the association and school and district administration, meets monthly to address issues, with an eye toward preventing policies from interfering with the work that all parties agree needs to go on (Fink & Thompson, 2001).

CSF 4 (system accountable for school success) as illustrated by Houston Independent School District, Texas. The district closely monitors school performance. In the case of low-performing schools, a team of principals, curriculum specialists, and district-based researchers are assigned to the school and conduct a thorough investigation of school capacities and practices. The team then assists the school in the development of a district-funded improvement plan. Funds are available for up to three years for targeted teacher training, extended day offerings, additional teachers, and educational materials. Schools that do not improve as a result of this intervention are reconstituted (Panasonic Foundation, 2000).

CSF 5 (intensive professional development) from District 2 in New York City and San Diego City Schools. Over ten years, through an effort to shift the district's focus from bureaucratic processes to the quality of teaching and learning, the district has increased its budget for professional development from less than half a percent to 5.5 percent. Now every school in the system has at least one full-time staff developer who observes and coaches teachers and who models best instructional practices. These staff developers themselves receive weekly training from district staff and outside consultants. Principals in each school are now accountable as instructional leaders, spending at least two hours daily coaching teachers in classrooms. And district-level instructional leaders, who visit each school in their region three or four times annually, provide principals with detailed feedback on the quality of their interaction with teachers. Principals also attend all-day conferences each month that are provided by the district to enrich their practice as instructional leaders. As a way to develop and refine instructional strategies, teachers throughout the system have opportunities to visit each other's classrooms and principals have opportunities to visit each other's schools (Panasonic Foundation 1998b; 2001c).

CSF 6 (district resources focused on supporting powerful instructional practice) as illustrated by Plainfield Public Schools in New Jersey. Several years ago the district restructured its Curriculum and Instruction Department, moving from a compliance to a service orientation. The department had been organized around compensatory programs and often allocated professional development resources on the basis of personal relationships. With the restructuring, the department was reorganized into technical assistance teams, with a supervisor and several resource curriculum teachers on each team. The teams focus on supporting teachers in the implementation of these practices: the communication of standards to students; using data to select instructional practices that will improve student learning; instructing all students at or above grade-level curriculum; identifying and employing a range of teaching strategies to address the needs of students who are not meeting standards; helping students use assessment results to improve their own learning (Panasonic Foundation, 2001a).

CSF 7 (data system) as illustrated by Chula Vista Elementary School District in California. The district developed a student information system that includes student demographics; the results of state and various local assessments that can be disaggregated according to race, socioeconomic status, and other factors; the results of surveys on parent, student, and teacher satisfaction on a range of issues; and student attendance and mobility rates. Principals and teachers were trained on how to gather and interpret data for making educational decisions.

Based on data analysis, the district discovered that its preschools were generally housed in schools with empty classrooms and that the locations were difficult for the neediest families in the community to reach. Now preschools can be found in areas where, according to the data, the needs of families are the most pressing (Panasonic Foundation, 2001b).

Implications for Leaders

The districts where the critical success factors identified in this essay can be observed are steadily improving their performance according to assessments of student learning. More research is perhaps needed to better understand the conditions and interrelations between these factors that are most likely to systematically improve performance. What is certain is that the processes of embedding these practices in school systems are far messier than I've been able to convey in a brief essay.

So, it's important to note that the critical success factors cannot simply be plugged into the organization like a set of floppy disks. Without strategic leadership, the development of shared vision and ownership, and thoughtful adaptation of the success factors to contextual particulars, they will either remain as rhetorical declarations that do not translate into results or be force-fitted into the system in ways that create new cultural dysfunctions. In other words, the extent to which these factors can be expected to lead to success is proportional to the quality of leadership that is exercised in their implementation.

Strategic Leadership

More than visionaries, strategic leaders are vision builders—that is, they collaboratively build a strategic vision for the organization that is broadly owned, clearly understood, and powerfully reinforced. A strategic leader's success hinges on his or her ability to mobilize the system in such a way that the distance between current reality and a powerful vision for the future is significantly diminished (Senge, 1990; Heifetz, 1994). This work simply cannot be done without a powerful shared vision—or, for that matter, without a clear, deep, and continually updated understanding of the organization's current reality.

A strategic leader is skilled in balancing pressure and support. As Michael Fullan (1991) points out, "Pressure without support leads to resistance and alienation; support without pressure leads to drift or waste of resources" (p. 91). Together, they can build the momentum that is essential for breaking through stakeholder resistance to change and comfort with the status quo.

This point is well illustrated by San Diego City Schools, where Superintendent Alan Bersin, a former U.S. attorney, has teamed up with Chancellor of Instruction Anthony Alvarado, former superintendent of Community District 2 in New York City, to transform practice throughout the 143,000-student system. The pressure in San Diego, whether you are a student, a teacher, a principal, or a district-level instructional leader, is intense. As in many states, it comes in part from California's testing and accountability system. The pressure has been further intensified by Bersin and Alvarado, who have outlined an ambitious program of reform, an even more ambitious pace for implementation, and an accountability system tied to results. As one district-level instructional leader observed, "It's intense and stress producing. It's the first time in my career that I've faced that much intensity in what I do and how I do it" (Panasonic, 2001c).

In San Diego high pressure is fused with high support (Barber & Phillips, 2000). As described previously, the district is making an enormous investment in the professional development of teachers, peer coaches, principals, and district-level instructional leaders (whose job it is to develop the instructional leadership abilities of principals through job-embedded coaching). For one San Diego elementary school teacher that a colleague and I interviewed for a Panasonic Foundation publication, that combination of pressure and support has translated into renewal of purpose: "Last year my heart wasn't here, and it was a struggle," he told us. "Now I know what I have to do this morning. I have a lot more purpose" (Panasonic, 2001c).

The San Diego story is also illustrative of two key leadership characteristics: passion and courage. When Bersin brought Alvarado to San Diego, he employed an educational leader with a passionate conviction that the key to improving learning is the improvement of instruction and that the system-wide improvement of instructional practice cannot be accomplished without a massive investment in high-quality, continuous professional development for teachers and principals and for professional developers throughout the system. The passionate dissemination of this theory of change has much to do with the district's success to date on the system-wide improvement of instructional practice.

But while one finds widespread evidence of improving practice, what is not widespread in San Diego at this time is genuine ownership on the part of all or even most stakeholders. In addition to high levels of stress, there are pockets of fierce resistance. A war has broken out between the teachers union and the administration. The school board is split 3 to 2 in favor of Bersin and Alvarado. The union argues that the unprecedented number of dollars that are being poured into the change efforts could bankrupt the system. So, you see a powerful reform engine that is hanging by a thread.

My colleagues and I asked Alvarado about the balance between pace and pressure, on the one hand, and support and ownership, on the other. Here's what he said:

> I don't know what's the real answer, but I know there has to be real tension on the issue and you have to engage it with a seriousness that puts the organization in some ways at risk. Only when the organization is at risk do you have the opportunity to make it a real-world situation. People learn to solve problems quickly the way real world people do, which is a foreign concept to us as a profession and an institution. (Panasonic, 2001c)

The courage to put everything on the line in a struggle to improve the educational experience of all students may simply be indispensable if large factory-era districts are to be transformed into high-performance educational systems.

At the same time, I must confess to being troubled by the combative relationship that has emerged between the district and union. As the reforms in San Diego proceed, they may shed light on a critical question: Is it possible to make sustainable systemic progress while engaging in battle with an essential part of the system? "Unless management and the union leaders learn to think of themselves as a system working for the same purpose," Margaret Wheatley has noted, "they are going to stay in their present negotiated settlements, which, in many places, are far inferior to what could be created if they thought of themselves as being connected" (Donohoe Steinberger, 1995, p. 16). So, I find myself wondering what would have been more strategic and more courageous in San Diego, what would better have positioned the system reforms for sustainability: the chosen course or a willingness to engage the union as partners in an interdependent system, which could only have been done at the expense of the pace and momentum that have so far been enjoyed?

Strategic leadership is also a habit of mind that involves continual questioning—asking not only detailed questions around specific programs and interventions, but also the kinds of questions that can only be posed by stepping back to look at the system more holistically. One important aim of this questioning is probing into systemic structures and culture in an effort to identify the points of highest leverage. As Peter Senge (1990, p. 114) has noted, "The bottom line of systems thinking is leverage—seeing where actions and changes can lead to significant, enduring improvements." What is underneath a particular event or symptom? Is it part of a pattern of events? How does our current structure or organizational culture contribute to this pattern of events? What in our thinking and modes of communication contributes to this pattern of events?

Authentic Leadership

Strategic leadership that is focused on the critical success factors of a high-performing school system will only take you part of the way in the absence of what Robert Evans (1996) calls authentic leadership. According to Evans, "Transformation begins with trust" (p. 183). This brings us back to courage, passion, and vision, but also to a nonnegotiable commitment to a set of core values. But what gives leaders trust-engendering authenticity is not simply having or spouting such qualities and values, but making them visible and credible through consistent action. The test of authenticity comes down to a simple question: Are these leaders walking their talk?

Here's an example of what I mean. In Charlotte-Mecklenburg Schools the district is committed to the vision quoted earlier about becoming "the premier, urban integrated school system in the nation." That vision has been translated into a policy framework, also described previously, that is aimed at reversing the decades-long practice of providing the best teachers and educational resources to the most advantaged students and the worst to the least advantaged. The leaders have publicly committed themselves to equity.

What gives that commitment credibility and what exemplifies authenticity is an incident that a colleague and I heard about from more than one source during our recent visit to the district. A district-level team that was analyzing student performance data discovered that thousands of African American students in the middle grades had been placed in regular math classes even though white students with the same scores were placed in advanced classes. Within a week, district leaders assembled all middle school principals, explained the problem, and told them to reschedule their schools. At each of the three grade levels, about 2,700 African American students moved from regular to advanced math classes. Shortly thereafter, the old textbooks were collected and the new ones, which had been delivered by overnight mail, were distributed.

That action changed the educational opportunity and experience of 8,000 kids. But it also powerfully communicated to teachers, principals, students, and parents throughout the community the seriousness of the district's commitment to equity. It did so in a way that no combination or amount of words could match.

Conclusion

Few, if any, organizations could rival public school systems for their degree of dynamic complexity. But there is reason for hope. Through strategic and authentic action, school system leaders can use the critical success factors of a high-performance school system as a guide for moving their system from current reality toward a future that holds immense promise for our children and young people.

About the Author

Scott Thompson is assistant director of the Panasonic Foundation in Secaucus, New Jersey; the editor of *Strategies*, an issues series by the Panasonic Foundation in cooperation with the American Association of School Administrators; and the vice president and a founding trustee of the Glen Rock Public Education Foundation in Glen Rock, New Jersey. Prior to joining the Panasonic Foundation, he was director of Dissemination and Project Development at the Institute for Responsive Education in Boston. He began his career as a high school English teacher in St. Louis County, Missouri. He may be reached at (201) 271-3367 or sthompson@foundation.panasonic.com.

ESSAY 2: ALL MEANS ALL
Richard DeLorenzo, Superintendent of Schools, Chugach School District,
Anchorage, Alaska

Last week, the Chugach superintendent, Richard DeLorenzo, stood
before a ballroom full of high-powered executives, explaining how
little Chugach had won the Malcolm Baldrige National Quality
Award. All three of the first education winners represent remarkably successful collaborations among local communities, educators
and businesses in setting common goals and relentlessly measuring
where they stand in achieving them. But it was the Chugach story
that carries the strongest message to districts that take seriously
President Bush's challenge to "leave no child behind."

—David Broder, *Washington Post*

It is the action, not the fruit of the action, that's important. You have
to do the right thing. It may not be in your power, may not be in
your time, that there'll be any fruit. But that doesn't mean you stop
doing the right thing. You may never know what results come from
your actions. But if you do nothing, there will be no results.

—Mahatma Gandhi

Education has never needed great leadership as much as it does now!
Historically, schools haven't been held accountable to educate all students to any level of excellence. In many ways, public schools were
much like the factories in the United States in the mid-1900s. Students
all followed the same traditional course of study, presented in a similar
manner to all who walked through the doors of the public institution. If
they were not successful, the system failed to see the cause-and-effect
relationship. Our education system was intended to sort and classify
students based on their economic background, social status, ability, and
aptitude. Words like *tradition, status quo,* and *routine* were acceptable
for that time and age. However, today we must educate all students to
some level of excellence regardless of socioeconomic status or ability
level. In other words, *all means all*! Thus, the role of an effective education leader looks dramatically different than the traditional leadership
of the past because today we face the daunting task of mobilizing all
stakeholders to reinvent themselves to serve all students. Facing this

daunting task requires extraordinary courage, passion, and vision in superintendents and their leadership teams.

Whether you agree with this notion or not, the current political battle cry is "accountability." President Bush's "No Child Left Behind" initiative is the blueprint for this new and high-profile level of accountability for the public school systems of America. Accountability seems to be the crisis response of politicians and some educators to an education system that has long failed to serve all students. Parent choice, vouchers, and charter schools give options to those looking to find some solution to accelerate the glacial movement of educational reform or, even still, protect their interests (i.e., their children), from an inferior educational experience. This is why in America we now see the mass exodus of children to private, charter, alternative school, and home schooling choices.

The dilemma is that our beloved education system is in danger of becoming obsolete and replaced, but replaced by what? For many educators, politicians, and parents, the specifics of what needs to change in the current system are vague, yet they all agree that something has to change if public education as we know it is to continue to exist. Even more critical, no one is quite sure of how to transition from our traditional system into something new without any guarantees that the new system will be better. Thus, a "systems approach" that includes all stakeholders and that is driven by a sustained framework of excellence is where we *must* aim. This education system of the future must have the capacity to repeatedly reinvent itself as needed. Stagnation, mindless routine, and mediocrity are all states of being from the past that cannot and should not be carried into the future. A redesigned school system that puts children's needs first and benchmarks internally and externally to illustrate positive trends in achieving higher levels of achievement is the only way for public school systems to truly educate all children.

Another vital component of this envisioned school system is staff empowerment. Faculty and staff must feel empowered to become part of the solution, for it is this empowerment that will garner respect for their role in achieving excellence. This type of school system does not just emerge. It is carefully and strategically created at the hands of effective leaders.

Characteristics of Effective Change-Leaders

We need great leadership to create this new paradigm for school systems—leaders who envision bright and powerful futures for their school systems through the involvement of all stakeholders and who clearly communicate next steps by the continuous refinement of traditional school districts. Incremental reform is no longer adequate; systemic reinvention is imperative if the ultimate goal of public school systems is to ensure every child has the means to reach his or her full potential in a manner that will lead to happiness, personal fulfillment, and a decent livelihood—regardless of his or her current socioeconomic status or geographic limitations. Creating this kind of school district takes vision, courage, and commitment, not only to initiate the process, but also to see it to fruition. It is only through the absolute reinvention of our school systems that we will promote the kind of change vital to the creation of excellence.

There are many characteristics of exemplary leadership. I honestly struggle with maintaining these characteristics in my leadership practice as a superintendent of schools. For my leadership, I believe that if I can inspire others to venture, stretch, or even dream of places that they wouldn't choose to go by themselves, I create in them the passion to take the "path less taken" and not only shift their personal paradigms of what education should look like, but to develop the courage to create it! And if this journey makes their lives and the lives of those around them more fulfilling, then I feel as if I am embodying the ingredients of good leadership.

Inspiration is the key word. The depth of your faculty and staff's commitment to any change in your district is a testimony to how well you, as the leader, have led—not bullied, coerced, or manipulated. Inspiration is in many ways synonymous with passion. Passion is work of the heart. Truly effective leaders create in those around them the ability to envision their passion in action.

Once they are able to envision their passion for change, effective leaders strategically guide their people through a process of creating a road map for a change process. Excellent leaders have the ability to see into the future and not only communicate where we need to go, but, more importantly, help others, in a meaningful way, see how this will improve the quality of their lives and lives of those around them. There are many processes that can do this. There is no one perfect process for getting this kind of involvement, yet effective leaders find the process that is perfect for the select group of stakeholders they gathered together, and they are able to facilitate the stakeholders' self-discovery of a road map that will lead them to their agreed-upon destination.

Overcoming Barriers

In 1979, I arrived in a rural Alaskan school district as a special education teacher with the heart and desire to make a positive difference in the lives of the most economically deprived and mentally challenged students. I seem to have an innate sense of empathy with those less fortunate, probably because of my personal struggle through school with a speech impediment and soft signs of a learning disability.

All through my career I struggled with perceiving myself as a leader. Perhaps this struggle arose from my upbringing within a large family and being lost in the shuffle of surviving day to day, or perhaps it was just my innate sense of insecurity. No matter what the root cause, it was unfathomable for me to visualize myself in a leadership role.

I also strongly hold to the truth that if you believe in yourself to the level that you can love those around you and have a strong vision to create a better existence for others, then that vision is an obtainable goal. This moral purpose can give you the courage to cross that great chasm between the *probable* and the *possible*.

Crossing the chasm between the probable and the possible is what happened in our school district. Just eight years ago, 90 percent of the students in the Chugach School District could not read at grade level, and the district had only one college graduate in twenty years. Yet, as I write this essay, I am returning from Washington, D.C., where I was honored to receive on behalf of our diverse district the first-ever Malcolm Baldrige Award for Excellence in Education. This is the highest award for quality ever given in the field of education, and it was bestowed by the president of the United States. This moment for us gives me a perfect time to reflect on how we have accomplished so much.

Reflecting on our past, I think one of the greatest challenges in changing an entire school system is the fact that the task seems insurmountable. You just can't seem to get your arms around all of the components that make change systemic and sustainable. The diverse array of variables in any system often leads to a feeling of despair and sense of being overwhelmed and often leads to simply "applying a new coat of paint" and failing to get to the core of change.

In trying to help other districts create and sustain whole-district change like we did in our district, we frequently meet with resistance to whole-system change in the form of a full list of reasons why districts can't do what we did. This list of reasons for "why we can't" forms attitudinal and behavioral barriers to achieving the districts' visions. In response to these vision barriers I often hear myself telling folks that they have to believe that they can create whole-system change before they will see the results of that effort. I thought you might be interested in seeing the top ten reasons I hear about why school districts cannot engage in whole-system change.

DeLorenzo's Top Ten Excuses Why We Can't Change

- We tried that before.
- Our district is different.
- We don't have the time or money.
- Our organization is too small (or too big).
- If you only understood our situation.
- Micromanagement is our friend.
- We don't have the authority.
- We don't have the right people.
- It's impossible with our bus schedule.
- If only we didn't have any students, we could change a few things.

What Was So Different About the Chugach School District?

The Chugach School District (CSD) is located in south-central Alaska and includes Anchorage, Whittier, Fairbanks, and Valdez. Chugach's 214 students are scattered throughout 22,000 square miles, mostly in extremely isolated and remote areas where planes are the mode of transportation. With thirty faculty and staff, CSD is the smallest organization ever to win a Baldrige Award.

CSD provides educational services to students from preschool up to age twenty-one in a comprehensive, standards-based community school, home school, and school-to-work or college education program. Here are a few of the specifics for the district in 1994:

- Unemployment rate = 52.3 percent
- Poverty level = 75.7 percent
- 50 percent Alaskan native
- 90 percent of students could not read at grade level
- One college graduate in 20 years
- 50 percent teacher attrition rate

During our first year of change in 1994, a comprehensive restructuring effort was initiated. Using input from our schools, communities, and businesses, CSD realigned its curriculum to create ten performance-based standards for mathematics, science, technology, reading, writing, social sciences, service learning, career development, cultural awareness and expression, and personal/social/health development. Individual Learning Plans (ILP), Student Assessment Binders (SAB), Student Learning Profiles (SLP), and Student Life Skills Portfolios all support and document consistent progress toward agreed-upon levels of proficiency in all standards. CSD developed performance standards continua for all content areas, K–14. These continua of standards are a working document for our students, parents, and teachers. The continua encompass our P–14 curricula, report cards, and standards and serve as road maps of clear expectations toward success for all of our students.

To break away from traditional modes of education, CSD applied for and received a waiver from the Alaska Department of Education and Early Development to forego traditional Carnegie units, or credits, as graduation requirements. These requirements would then be replaced by our newly developed performance standards.

The performance standards created by CSD exceed state standards in every area. Student results are measured formally and informally through a system of multiple, ongoing assessments when students are ready to be assessed, not based upon calendar testing dates designated by the state. The support of our partners, in addition to multiple grant awards, has made all of these opportunities a reality for our students. Table 5.1 provides a snapshot of some of the systemic changes we created.

Table 5.1. Examples of Chugach School District Systemic Improvements

Traditional Chugach School District	21st-Century Chugach School District
Institutionally centered	Student-centered
Credits or "seat time"	Standards-based system
Lecture-style instruction	Presentation based on student learning styles
Unclear expectations	Precise targets, P–14
Disconnected reporting	P–14 report card
Traditional assessments	Skills-based, self-analytical assessments
Text book–based curriculum	Contextual curriculum
Poor School to Life Plan	Comprehensive School to Life Plan
Traditional diploma	Performance-based diploma

Where Did It All Begin?

The question educators have for us is, "How were you able to create the need to change and involve all of the stakeholders in this 'Voyage to Excellence' process?" We all know that change, especially whole-district change, is very difficult. Change of this magnitude also involves a personal journey for each stakeholder, and unless every stakeholder has the opportunity to be involved in some meaningful way, large-scale change has little chance of standing the test of time. Humans often resist the conditions of change because they are facing an unknown or vaguely known future, and change often requires personal risk taking. Effective leaders have to orchestrate whole-district change by creating and maintaining an internal organizational culture that encourages people to test unknown waters and to exercise creative problem solving.

In my opinion, the best precondition for stimulating change is where there is either a great opportunity or an agreed-upon crisis. If both of these conditions exist, the stars are aligned for change to occur. Capable leaders have the ability to be honest about current conditions and the foresight to lead stakeholders down another path. They have to speak positively and from the heart, make the intangible tangible, and listen, listen, listen. The opportunities and needs for our district were compelling. We were not accomplishing our goals. We were not educating all students and we knew it.

An example of our needs and opportunities was captured in a statement made by the Alaskan Federation of Natives. The statement summarizes the "burning platform" for the Alaskan natives and the battle cry that caused Chugach to systemically change what it was doing:

> Improvement in their [Alaskan natives'] economic condition seems unlikely . . . without an educational system that works. . . . Children and young adults who are deprived of self-respect by a culturally alien school system and then sent into a society without marketable skills cannot improve their economic status.

The painful reality of the preceding statement caused us to look very carefully at the moral and ethical obligation we have to all students. Still further evidence supported the need to radically alter how we approached learning and the content we taught. These data include the following:

- The dropout rate for Alaskan native youth in urban schools is often above 70 percent.
- There are more Alaskan natives in our jails than in our universities.
- Between 1992 and 1993, 5,563 students graduated from Alaskan schools while 2,156 students dropped out.
- Just recently, one of the school board members from a large, rural district shared with me that they have often awarded the highest-performing students in their district the valedictorian and salutatorian awards only to have those "high-performing" students be required to take remedial courses in basic skills upon entering the state's university system.

Another challenge our school district faced when trying to create whole-system change was that, unlike other organizations, businesses more specifically, we could not shut down for a year to re-create ourselves. Filing for Chapter 11 is not an option when you are dealing with struggling students needing an education. Since closure to re-create ourselves was not an option, we initiated a number of strategies to remove the traditional barriers that impede excellence in education and that allowed us to create a new school system that empowered our stakeholders. We developed a clear road map for success not only for students, but for teachers as well. The clarity of this road map to all stakeholders was at the core of our success. Each stakeholder group had to "see" it and "own" it.

The Change Processes We Used

Many of the accomplishments mentioned so far were achieved through a comprehensive approach involving all stakeholders, particularly committed staff members who persevered to improve the quality of education in our district.

Our change process began with being honest with each of the stakeholders about the answers to these four questions:

1. According to current research, how are our students doing?
2. What happens to our students once they leave our K–14 system?
3. What will students need to know and be able to do in the twenty-first century?
4. If needed, how do we change our current system to meet the needs of all students?

As in most rural districts, our students were failing academically. They didn't have the prerequisite skills to make good choices, and our system was mired in the quagmire of "doing business as usual." Given these kinds of conditions, effective leaders must have the courage to face their reality with objectivity and have the vision to see where their system needs to go, coupled with the passion to inspire all stakeholders to become risk takers.

In the Chugach School District, we initially thought that our staff, community members, students, and businesses would have different visions and varied priorities, but we were wrong. In fact, every visioning process we used ended with stakeholder groups responding in ways that were closely aligned with our district's vision. It is this close alignment that enhanced our success. The shared priorities among our stakeholder groups are summarized here:

1. Basic skills.
2. Meeting the individual needs of all.
3. Character development.

4. Transition skills.
5. Technology skills.
6. Our business community recommended a stronger accountability system . . . and thus our journey began.

Our leaders provided our stakeholders with a clear vision and strategic plan that included specific strategies of deployment that led to successful attainment of the agreed-upon priorities. The road map illustrated in figure 5.1 was used to improve our system, and it also has been used by other school districts in their pursuit of whole-system change.

Once the visioning process is complete, the next step in creating systemic change is to establish the core curricula that will lead to excellence for all students. This includes relevant standards, multiple assessments, meaningful instruction, and aligned reporting systems that link all the components together.

Overall the entire structure functions as a continuous improvement process that refines the components to reach higher and higher levels of excellence. Effective leaders not only provide a clear vision, but instill in others a process to measure success. Figure 5.2 provides an example of one of the continua we used to measure our success using a whole-system perspective. We developed six of these continua to make a complete assessment tool. Each continuum represents one of the six elements of our school district's design: standards, assessments, evaluation and reporting systems, instructional methods, sustainability, and special education.

Each element in our district's design has its own continuum, which represents a range of possibilities. Moving from left to right on each continuum, as you can see in figure 5.2, there are different levels of conditions related to each element. Conditions to the left of the continuum are moving toward minimum levels. Conditions to the right are moving toward maximum levels. The closer your system is to the maximum levels along each continuum, the closer your system is to becoming "excellent."

To use the self-assessment tool with all six continua, you, your stakeholders, and your staff put a check mark at a place along the continuum that you think represents where your district really is. Then you need to reconcile differences of opinion to develop consensus about where your district falls along each continuum.

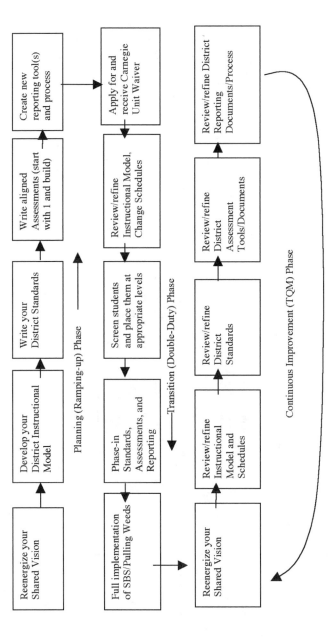

Figure 5.1. Three phases of implementing standards-based education.

Continuum 1: Standards

Some students, staff, and community members have an awareness of district and/or state standards, but do not know how they impact student learning.	Many students, staff, and community members have an understanding of standards and how standards impact student learning.	A majority of students, staff, and community members acknowledges and begins to refer to district and/or state standards in several content areas. A majority of teachers refers to standards when planning, instructing, assessing, or reporting student progress.	Most students, staff, and community members refer to local and/or state standards and routinely consider them when designing learning activities. Local standards are developed and are aligned with state standards.	All students, staff, and community members integrate local and state standards into their daily instruction, assessment, and life activities.	Students, staff, and community members give evidence that local standards are integrated into daily instruction in all curricula and that their standards are edited, revised, and reviewed on a regular basis.

Figure 5.2. Example of an assessment continuum from our Quality Schools Model self-assessment tool. (Note: This is one of the continua we developed; there are five others. If you are interested in seeing all of them, please contact Richard DeLorenzo.)

Quality and Performance Achievements for Our District

Here is a summary of the outcomes of our district's successful Voyage to Excellence.

- Chugach School District (CSD) involved all stakeholders in its strategic planning process—including students, parents, community members, and businesses—to develop a shared vision of organizational performance goals, a five-year time line of activities, and one-year targets. The goals addressed student learning and development in basic skills, individual needs of students, character development, transition skills, and technology. In 2001, stakeholders gave high satisfaction ratings to CSD in these five outcome areas with basic skills at 96 percent, individual needs of students at 89 percent, character development education at 84 percent, transition skills at 89 percent, and technology at 89 percent.
- Results on the California Achievement Tests improved in all content areas from 1995 to 1999. Average national percentile scores increased in reading from 28th to 71st, in language arts from 26th to 72nd, in math from 54th to 78th, and in spelling from 22nd to 65th. In addition, the percent of students in the top quartile in reading increased from 17 to 56, in language arts from 25 to 33, and in math from 42 to 79.
- The state of Alaska began administering the High School Graduation Qualifying Examinations (HSGQE) in third, sixth, eighth, and tenth grades in 2000. In 2001, the percent of CSD students who passed the HSGQE surpassed the Alaska state average in all three subject areas of reading, writing, and math and in all four grades tested. In addition, the percent of CSD's tenth-graders who passed the HSGQE ranked 1st in math, 3rd in reading, and 17th in writing among the state's 54 districts.
- The percentage of CSD students who take college entrance examinations has increased from 0 percent to 70 percent since 1998. Since 1994, 17 CSD students have graduated; 14 currently are attending postsecondary institutions compared to one student who attended, but dropped out, prior to 1994.
- CSD uses a set of developmental levels instead of traditional grade divisions to achieve district and state standards that address ten

content areas that are aligned with CSD's vision and performance goals. The four-step Chugach Instructional Model enables students to progress through the ten content areas by using drill and practice, practical application, interactive simulation, and real-life situations. Embedded in the instructional model are thematic units that cross disciplines so students connect learning in content areas such as reading, math, science, social studies, art, and technology.

- Every CSD student has an Individual Learning Plan (ILP) based on the student's learning style, the ten content area standards, and student and parent preferences. ILPs enable students to learn at their own pace, to move to a higher level in the curriculum only after mastering skills and knowledge at the preceding level, and to achieve high performance levels.

- CSD's Anchorage House, a short-term residential program, prepares students to transition from primarily native Alaskan isolated communities to independent life in higher education or work. The Anchorage House four-phase program is integrated with the district's content standards and specifically addresses personal and social skills, health, career development, and community service. The program provides students with learning opportunities in the district's five student outcome areas, including postsecondary school, full-time employment, service learning, entrepreneurial, and vocational.

- CSD reduced its faculty turnover rate from an average of 55 percent from 1975 to 1994 to an average of 12 percent from 1995 to 2000. The year 2002 will be the first time that CSD will not need to attend a job fair to recruit new faculty. Isolated working conditions contribute to faculty turnover despite high levels of satisfaction that range from 75 to 81 percent on a national satisfaction survey. CSD supplements faculty salaries with pay for performance and provides flexible working conditions, job rotation, job share contracts, and a high degree of empowerment to counter the effects of working in remote, isolated areas.

- CSD provides thirty days of training annually for faculty, twice the number offered by any other school district in the state. Training facilitates strategic alignment among action plans, organizational performance goals, and legal requirements. Training addresses how to assess student needs, instruct and support students, use Individual Learning Plans to monitor learning, analyze results, and determine opportunities to improve student learning.

- CSD uses technology to enhance student learning, improve student technology skills, and improve the efficiency of its academic and administrative operations. Through the aggressive pursuit of grant funding, the district increased the number of computers from 2 per 27 students in 1994 to 21 per 27 students in 2001. In addition, when students reach level IV in all content standards, they receive a personal laptop computer, a vital means of communication for students living in remote sites. Overall student use of the Internet increased from 5 percent in 1998 to 93 percent in 2001.

Next Steps for Chugach

Excellence is a journey, and to the faculty and staff at Chugach it is a challenging journey that continually ignites our passion for doing what is morally and ethically right for *all* students. If in our pursuit of excellence we are able to improve the quality of life for those we teach, it is well worth all of our struggles and failures if we help just one of our nation's greatest assets, a child.

About the Author

Richard DeLorenzo has more than twenty-four years of experience working with high-risk and disabled students of all ages in a wide variety of settings, from urban classrooms with thirty multiage elementary students to rural school settings with at-risk secondary pupils. He is currently the superintendent of the Chugach School District, an award-winning rural school district that made dramatic changes in its approach to education, including a waiver from the Alaska Department of Education to transition from a high school credit system to a performance-based system.

During the past eight years, Richard has been instrumental in the comprehensive, whole-system transformation of his district that yielded phenomenal results in students' academic achievement and transitional skills. The Chugach School District was the only district to receive the New American High School Award and one of the first two school districts to receive the Baldrige National Quality Award. Mr. DeLorenzo may be reached at Chugach School District, 9312 Vanguard Drive, Suite 100, Anchorage, AK 99507 or by calling (907) 522-7400. For more information and additional resources, visit the district's Web site at www.chugachschools.com.

ESSAY 3: THE CONTEXT FOR URBAN SCHOOL REFORM: HOW RACE, CLASS, AND GENDER CHANGE THE LANDSCAPE

Diana Lam, Superintendent, Providence Public Schools, Rhode Island

Introduction

Outside observers might wonder why balancing power, politics, and ethics is a challenge for leaders in public education and what makes this especially challenging for superintendents in urban districts. After all, business leaders juggle power, politics, and ethics, and one could argue that they do so with better results; where their companies show profits, urban school systems for the most part continue to be ranked "low performing" by states and other evaluative entities. I believe that the essential difference between these two contrasting fields is the respective spheres in which the work of each occurs and the context those spheres present.

Business in the United States occurs in a defined sphere, the private sector, which for better or worse is generally more homogeneous than its public counterpart and has a clear accountability structure: one either successfully makes money or goes out of business. The public sector, on the other hand, encompasses broader constituencies and competing interests. Accountability in the public sector is murkier since different groups use different measures to evaluate the success of public institutions. Although educating all our children should be a school district's "bottom line," this primary goal often becomes overshadowed by competing concerns and squelched by cultures in which low expectations of poor and minority children prevail. Given all these realities, superintendents face a host of unique and challenging circumstances.

Personal Observations on the Challenges of Leading Systemic Improvement

Francis Duffy asserts that the ideal superintendent is one who skillfully uses "powerful, political, and ethical behaviors" to lead large-scale systemic improvement efforts. My own experiences as an urban superintendent confirm this assertion. Throughout this essay, I share my observations and reflect on the challenges I have faced as an urban superintendent. I do not purport to represent all urban superintendents, nor do I have the background to comment on the experience of suburban or rural superintendents. I draw on my career as a teacher, a principal, and a superintendent in Chelsea, Massachusetts; Boston, Massachusetts; Dubuque, Iowa; San Antonio, Texas; and Providence, Rhode Island, school districts to illustrate the complexities of balancing power, politics, and ethics.

I begin by sharing the principles that guide my own efforts and discussing how three primary factors—race, class, and gender—have impacted my ability to implement these principles in whole-system reform. I examine my choices, my career, and the success or failure of attempted systemic reform efforts in light of race, class, and gender considerations. Finally, I argue that in order to successfully reform urban school districts, superintendents must acknowledge the centrality of race, class, and gender to their work and must raise the consciousness of the community about these issues carefully and deliberately.

Guiding Principles

I briefly touch on the principles that guide my own work to give you a better understanding of my own vision and approach to education reform; however, I intentionally do not go into great detail about these principles as the purpose of this essay is not to discuss the development of a superintendent's vision. My purpose in this essay is to illuminate the delicate balance of power, politics, and ethics a superintendent must employ to skillfully implement that vision. The building blocks of my own vision, or educational philosophy, can be summed up in the six following basic belief statements:

- Every child can achieve to high levels, and it is the role of public education to believe in and educate every child.
- Reform efforts must focus on promoting high-quality teaching and learning in all schools.
- Leadership at every layer of a school system (central office, school, and classroom) must work toward the ultimate goal of providing every child with a high-quality education.
- Schools should ensure that children learn what they need to know and do by implementing standards-based instruction.
- Students should be provided with clear expectations and should know what they are learning and why they are learning it.
- Schools should acknowledge and address students' social and emotional needs through academic learning and youth development initiatives.

Duffy accurately defines the "passion" needed to lead systemic school improvement as a "burning desire to do what's right for children, teachers, and school systems." This kind of passion is critical to helping superintendents remain true to their own guiding principles, in spite of the many common tests that can make doing so extremely difficult. The following section describes some of the tests that I have experienced over the course of my career.

How Race and Class Shape Our Expectations of Children

When I was superintendent of the San Antonio Independent School District (ISD), 95 percent of our student population comprised children of color, and nearly 90 percent of them qualified for free and reduced lunch programs. A close look at student achievement data revealed significant race gaps in student performance in mathematics. The first time the end-of-course algebra test was given, only three students in San Antonio ISD passed it. With appropriate interventions and strong support for teachers and administrators, the percentage of students passing the test increased incrementally to 3, 4, 9, 18, and reached 34 percent in my last year in that district. Much work still needed to be done, but in a very short time, the district was able to move closer to the state average. It was not that the students got smarter; they were still the same students, coming from the same families, living under the same circumstances. What changed were teachers' and administrators' expectations and practice.

To push for immediate and long-term changes in math instruction, I had to carefully balance the need for urgent action with the importance of having a solid and inclusive process toward our goal. There is an inherent tension between urgency and process in many decisions superintendents make; however, we must live with that tension, pushing for both short-term and long-term change simultaneously.

Acknowledging the racial or class roots of performance gaps or other issues can help to justify the need for urgent action; however, fear of saying the wrong thing and seeming "politically incorrect" often prevents superintendents and other educational leaders from acknowledging these sensitive issues. A superintendent needs courage and faith in her own convictions to make and stand by these kinds of decisions. My career has taught me that pretending these issues do not exist severely impacts our children's futures. If we ignore issues of race, class, and gender, school systems quietly and insidiously track students and lower expectations for low-income and minority students.

A year and a half ago, as superintendent of Providence Schools in Rhode Island, I proposed that we close Feinstein High School and the Alternative Learning Project (ALP) and then reopen those two schools as a single consolidated school with a new philosophy and new leadership. Both schools served a predominantly minority (Feinstein, 83 percent; ALP, 66 percent) and low-income student population. Both were small high schools where student achievement was unacceptably low and where the dropout rate was unacceptably high. Not even 20 percent of either school's students met our reading standard (basic understanding as measured on standardized assessments). Not one student in either school met the standard for problem solving in math.

Even in light of these data, many in the community felt that these schools should not be closed and consolidated. In particular, there was far more opposition to my proposal to close ALP than Feinstein. A number of community members, including some students and their parents, attacked my proposal, arguing that ALP was a good school because it did not demand too much of the students, but rather it helped students who had had a hard time academically to feel good about themselves and kept them out of trouble. They felt it was unrealistic to expect those students to achieve standards that were beyond their reach. One parent, with her daughter sitting next to her, even exclaimed that her daughter would be pregnant if she hadn't gone to ALP.

I was deeply troubled by these remarks, which made apparent many community members' beliefs that our children, by virtue of their race and class, were not capable of doing rigorous work, achieving at high levels, and avoiding negative behaviors. A school district that operates on such a premise is not only undemocratic, it is also tainted by institutionalized racism and classism. Both my personal and professional experience reminded me of the importance of high expectations for poor and minority children. I realized that it was up to me to challenge the expectations of teachers, community members, and the students themselves and to begin the painful cultural shift in our district toward high expectations for every child, regardless of race, gender, or class.

I offered a new vision based on my primary guiding principle that every child can achieve to high levels and that it is our responsibility as public school leaders to provide every child with a high-quality education. I extended an invitation for the community to be part of a new approach to learning, a site-based managed school where performance is the ultimate goal and standards are emphasized above seat time, where students feel challenged and nurtured and benefit from a rigorous curriculum with advanced placement courses. While this created disequilibrium in the community, I felt I had no other choice.

My efforts were a partial success in that Feinstein was closed and reopened; however, community opposition was too strong to close ALP. Instead, that school continued on, but the leadership was changed and the district committed to a major redesign of ALP's instructional program.

Now, just over a year later, Feinstein High School is up and running as a reconstituted school, under new leadership, and with a strong site-based management plan. The principal is building a rich school community where everyone shares in governance and the goal of every effort is to ensure that all students achieve to high levels. With respect to the city's other high schools, including ALP, all are undergoing a district-wide redesign, the community is beginning to be more engaged, and community members are seeing that dropout rates of 30 percent are unacceptable and are the cause for radical change. Students are critiquing their own experience and parents are demanding better for their children, coming to the table with their own ideas, resources, and participation.

This anecdote illustrates one of the most challenging obstacles that superintendents often face as they attempt to implement their vision: namely, low expectations that are based on subconscious or conscious racism and classism. Suggesting that we should have high expectations for all students often counters long-held beliefs of employees of a district and citizens in the community it serves. Furthermore, because racist and classist tendencies are frequently subconscious, many deny their existence. For superintendents, raising issues of race and class is in a sense a double-edged sword. While exposing these can be viewed as an accusation of the community and cost a superintendent her job, it also has the potential to raise consciousness and influence others to work collaboratively toward large-scale systemic reform for all children. In fact, I believe it is the only way to bring high achievement to scale in a district.

How Race, Class, and Gender Impact School Systems

Hiring and Advancement Practices

In addition to affecting our expectations of children, race and class realities affect how urban school districts function in such key areas as human resources. Nationally, there is a movement to diversify the teaching force, especially in urban school districts with large numbers of minority students. Many suggest that race in the classroom matters; however, the research is inconclusive about *how* it matters. While some researchers' studies identify a link between teachers' race and student achievement (Dee, 2001), still other studies suggest that a teacher's race may not be as important as her social class. For example, a Johns Hopkins University study found that teachers who were most successful in raising the achievement of African American students were black teachers from poorer family backgrounds and white teachers from more affluent communities (Viadero, 2000).

While we cannot assume that low-income minority students do better when taught by minority teachers, I still believe it is important for students of all classes and races to be exposed to role models from a variety of backgrounds. Many superintendents across the nation are struggling to recruit and hire highly qualified minority teachers so that their teaching forces can better reflect the diversity of their student populations. And since most administrators are promoted from the teaching pool, it is even more critical to do so. Yet, the research confirms that the *most important factor* affecting student achievement is a teacher's expertise as measured by teacher education, scores on a licensing examination, and experience. Teacher expertise accounts for 40 percent of the variation in student achievement (Ferguson, 1991). It is imperative that superintendents carefully balance diversity concerns with quality, ensuring that qualifications drive the hiring process before any other factor.

In urban school systems, balancing diversity and quality can often be complex in light of community expectations. Most urban school districts are directly impacted by the plight of urban centers (a lack of private-sector employment prospects for local residents and low levels of education among the minority adult population). In such a circumstance, public jobs are precious commodities seen as the path to financial stability and upward mobility, especially for members of minority communities. In such a climate, a large pool of highly qualified minority candidates may not be available, and yet the public may apply great pressure on superintendents to award faculty positions on racial grounds. To hire solely on the basis of race is as detrimental to the candidate as it is to the children she serves because it tokenizes her and sets her up for failure.

Rather than tokenizing them, superintendents can use their power to open doors for women and minorities. In most of the districts I led, I was pressured to hire on the basis of race and gender. In each case, I attempted to elevate quality while being sensitive to race and gender in hiring. In many situations, where I sought but did not find a qualified minority candidate for a leadership position, I hired a white candidate and was criticized by the local community. In other situations, my decisions to hire minorities or women were questioned.

While I was a middle school principal in Boston, there was an opening for an assistant principal. I interviewed many candidates with the help of teachers and parents and selected the best person—an African American woman. The superintendent told me I could not hire her because he could not allow an all-female administrative team, although nine of twenty-three middle schools had all-male administrative teams. The unspoken assumption was that if I did not hire a man, who, then, would handle discipline in the middle school? Younger children, well, that was one matter. Middle school students are older; many are overage for their grade. They're big. I'm physically small. How could a woman handle disciplining the boys?

I left the position of assistant principal vacant rather than hire anyone else. I also filed a sex discrimination complaint with the City of Boston Human Rights Commission; three years later they ruled in my favor. This case spotlighted the need to promote women at the secondary level, whether as department heads or principals. In the years since, significant progress has been made in Boston on this score; today there is not a single all-male administrative team at any middle or high school. Litigation was a tool that opened the doors for other women.

Did I challenge the rules? Yes, because I believed the rules were unfair. Was there a cost for my actions? There is always a cost within an institutional bureaucracy for someone who steps outside the prescribed roles and shouts, "The emperor is wearing no clothes." Like many other women, I remain convinced that I had to be more qualified for equivalent positions held by men. I valued and appreciated my allies— my network of support—but I was honest in my appraisal that my actions had also alienated some in positions of authority who might not have short memories. For example, there were people in the school department who called our middle school "the Amazon school."

This is par for the course. Any issue that touches on race, class, or gender, especially in urban areas, is bound to generate conflict and controversy, often rooted in misunderstanding and mistrust. This is one of the most common tests a superintendent faces in the course of his career, and how he handles it can mean the difference between a well-functioning school district and one that is incapable of meeting the needs of its students.

In every program I designed, I was mindful of diversifying our teacher and leadership ranks. For example, to address the problem of a lack of school administrators in Providence, we created the Aspiring Principals Program, an intensive eighteen-month administrative certification course wherein high-quality teachers are recruited by the district to become school principals. In its first year of implementation, 50 percent or twelve of the aspiring principals were from minority backgrounds. "Grow your own" programs such as this one help tap the potential of minority teachers and promote those qualified candidates within the district organization.

How My Race, Class, and Gender Have Shaped My Personal Expectations

Superintendents bear a heavy burden of political responsibility. My own career has taught me that being a woman from a minority background changes the nature of this burden. Women—for centuries, across continents and cultures—have been socialized to resist accepting this burden. Our responsibilities—survival and traditional motherhood—have left us with few other options. For those of us who have had access to education—and only a tiny portion of females, especially nonwhite females, on the globe have that opportunity even as we speak—the burden of political responsibility weighs even more heavily. Our voices can open doors for those who have been traditionally excluded from leadership roles.

In the field of education, women have barely begun the journey toward full equality. There is no other profession or field in the United States that has an equivalent history of numerical domination by women coupled with a continuing legacy of exclusion of women from key decision-making roles. When I first became superintendent in 1989, only 3 percent of the superintendents were female. That figure has increased to 12 percent (Keller, 1999). Of the superintendencies that are headed by women, most of them are in affluent, suburban districts where the majority of the school board members are women. There are very few female superintendents of urban districts and even fewer who are minority women. Being in a position of power and responsibility, one is constantly faced with the choice of effecting change or maintaining the status quo. The first litmus test for women in authority in public education is whether or not these women who have "made it" promote and mentor other women or whether they adopt more of the "old boys'" values and network than many of the old boys themselves. A token female in power does not address underlying power inequities; but strong representation of women in power can begin to redress the imbalance.

In 1985, when I was a principal of an elementary school in Boston, I attended a meeting with the deputy superintendent. At that time, two of the seventeen high schools were headed by females and one of the twenty-three middle schools had a female principal. I urged the deputy superintendent to consider appointing women to these positions, especially because a middle school principalship had just opened. "Would you be interested?" he asked in a tone of disbelief.

Quite frankly, I had not asked about the position on my own behalf. I had assumed that my next position would be a principalship in a large elementary school, although I had experience working in kindergarten through grade twelve. Like most women in education, I had not thought about becoming a middle school principal and I had been pegged into a limited role. Men are groomed for positions of leadership; women must be assertive and meet higher standards of competency and talent.

The superintendent's question dangled before me. I reached for the brass ring. "Yes," I answered quickly. "I would be."

Remembering the shape my own career took and how, even as a confident and competent woman, I almost did not advance, I try to do the same to help other women now that I am in a position of power. There is plenty of work to be done and we need good leaders to do it. In my view, power is not a limited commodity to be hoarded and guarded; it is elastic and inclusive. Power pivots on relationships and the invisible agendas and cultures of individuals and organizations. Power is derived from the character and integrity of the individual who is exercising influence and who is realizing her vision. When this vision is shared by a group, it becomes a force that can breathe fresh air and hope into urban school bureaucracies that are caught in the vortex of patronage and competing interests of local communities which interfere with providing all students with a high-quality education.

In most school systems, women and minorities have limited power, and yet they are not entirely powerless. As we move into positions of authority, whether as classroom teachers or as commissioners of education, women have a responsibility to hold the magnifying glass up to what we say and what we do. There are no extraneous gestures or comments. A ten-year-old girl may need to hear right now that she not only can become a scientist but that, when looking into the microscope, she already is a scientist. What I have come to realize after many years in public education, working at every level of various school systems, is how much my own voice as a minority female superintendent matters.

Conclusion

I hope this brief discussion of my own experience in public education illustrates how race, gender, and class affect the balance of power, politics, and ethics. I hope it also gives the reader a sense of how challenging addressing these issues can be for a superintendent. In my view, it is only when a superintendent raises consciousness about these notions and faces adversity that her vision, passion, and courage are truly tested. As Frederick Douglass wrote, "If there is no struggle, there is no progress." Every reformist superintendent knows that these personal "tests" have high stakes. If we as leaders compromise on the vision, if we lose our courage, if we yield our passion, another generation of children will be lost.

Many have asked me why I continue to do this work, whether it is worth the sacrifice. I believe that being a superintendent is a calling that is rooted in my deep passion for children that started when I decided to become a teacher. I am a teacher to my bones, but I am a teacher who has change and restlessness and idealism pulsing through her veins. That is why I became a principal, and a district superintendent, and then a superintendent. I cannot stop seeing what I see. I cannot stop knowing what I know, and what I know is the right thing to do.

About the Author

Diana Lam understands what it means to live up to the credo of "success for all children." As superintendent of three very different districts—San Antonio, Texas; Dubuque, Iowa; and Chelsea, Massachusetts—she has helped raise student achievement to new heights. In the communities where she has served as superintendent, she has envisioned the changes required and has put in place structures that facilitated educators and families working together to raise student achievement. Three years ago, she began work in a new community—Providence, Rhode Island—where she has begun to tackle similar challenges. Among her first actions upon taking office in Providence were to establish new, more ambitious achievement goals for all schools—goals that in many cases doubled or tripled the state-mandated minimum adequate rate of improvement. Since the start of reforms, Providence elementary schools have posted marked gains in statewide test results in reading and some improvement in math. Now, with a significant investment from private foundations, Providence public high schools are being redesigned into smaller, more personalized learning communities. Diana may be reached at (401) 456-9211 or Diana.lam@ppsd.org.

ESSAY 4: COURAGE, PASSION, AND VISION
Jack D. Dale, Superintendent, Frederick County Public Schools, Maryland

My passion is to create a leadership team for which there is no need for a single leader. Imagine a leadership team, rather than an individual, that sets direction, sets high performance expectations, and is dynamic rather than static in creating organizational structures to support such capacity.

In the first year of my superintendency, I told the eight members of my cabinet that my goal was to create team leadership of such capacity that, ultimately, the superintendent would not be needed. Many looked askance and internally asked, "Who is this new superintendent?"

Since that day, many in our district have come to understand the importance and power of a shared vision backed by the passion to see the vision attained and the courage to lead all facets of the organization to achieve that vision. My passion to create capacity sometimes leaves me wondering if I ought to be more time line– and outcome-driven. At times I wonder that if I were more driven to attain measurable results as soon as possible, would I be equally successful in my quest to create a "leadersless" leadership team? Sometimes I wonder if society gives educators enough time to build capacity in school leadership teams.

There is no question that much of my time is spent providing leadership to the system; but my simultaneous quest is to create sufficient capacity in others to emerge as members of the leadership team. When I first arrived in the school system, I found most, if not all, staff were quietly awaiting direction from the superintendent. I saw little self-initiated change agent behavior. Much of the leadership team's activities focused on efforts to maintain the status quo in an efficient and effective manner. The school system was growing and new staff were continually being hired and trained to meet ever-increasing demands in the classroom. Leaders of the various divisions and departments spent countless hours aligning their work, but the direction for the alignment was set by the superintendent. I wanted to change the paradigm of leadership from an individual-centered to team-centered leadership. I had a passion for creating a leadership team that had a shared vision, a shared passion, and exhibited the courage to believe in themselves—believe in their abilities, their passion, their core values, and their beliefs.

As I write this essay—five years after I told the cabinet members that my quest was to not be needed—I recently received the following voice mail message from a member of the cabinet who was involved with a fairly pivotal issue in the school system. Over the phone, as she was outlining the issue and her response, she said, "I knew you'd agree. And even if you didn't, it was the right thing and you'd get over it!" I smiled to myself. My vision was becoming a reality!

Many other stories could be told of episodes along our path to creating team leadership. I'll save some of the stories for later. First, let me spend a few moments talking about passion, vision, and courage. While they are intertwined in their workings—not unlike any system—I see a certain sequence to their interconnectedness.

Passion

People can become very passionate about their own core values and beliefs. The most egocentric individual can be very passionate about his or her perspective and will behave very consistently to satisfy that egocentric belief. A hierarchical, or control-focused, leader may likewise be quite passionate about the ability to control all aspects of the organization. Such passion will likewise manifest itself in recognizable ways. Any leader may be quite passionate about his or her particular style of leadership, expectation for performance, or particular beliefs about the people in the organization.

My deeply held value and belief is in team leadership. I have become quite passionate about the importance of team leadership. I believe in the importance of team leadership within our organization, the importance of team leadership to one another in the schools and to those whom leaders supervise. Of course, team leadership requires a certain set of values and beliefs about people. You must firmly believe in and be passionate about the capacity of others to learn and the capacity of others to lead in team leadership settings. One must be passionate about the ultimate good in people and their intrinsic desire to be part of a larger entity and for the entity to be successful. Such is my passion and I seek to work with others who share that passion.

Leadership literature from the effective school movement in the 1980s and the current stewardship leadership literature all recognize the necessity of passion. Each passion may have a different twist or subtlety, but the core passion to realize organizational success is throughout the leadership literature. The passion for organizational success must be in concert with their personal passion for aligning the beliefs and values of an organization. I know of no successful school, school system, or other organization that has no passion. Passion breeds success and success breeds more passion. Without a clear passion, we become static. Passion is necessary for dynamic, focused leadership. Successful schools and school systems are so because of the passion within the system—passion created and led by leadership teams and groups of people with an aligned and shared passion for excellence.

Vision

Vision is multifaceted. A vision for a school system must encompass students, employees, community, the future, and the aspirations for all elements of the system. The vision of our school system, which is shown in figure 5.3, includes not only the success of the school system, but a vision about our students, the adults we employ throughout the school system, the community's relationship with the school system, and the

Education is the foundation of our community. The Frederick County public school system educates its students to become caring, respectful, and responsible citizens and family members.

Students look forward to school each day. They take full advantage of the rigorous academic curricula and strive to develop their talents. They utilize the power of technology to explore a world of new ideas and information. They acquire the knowledge and skills to achieve and the confidence to succeed and are rewarded with a wide choice of offers from higher education and employers.

Outstanding applicants compete to join our system. Employees enjoy the respect of students and the community, opportunities for professional growth, and recognition for their contributions to our system. They value each student and create a learning climate where students can reach for their dreams.

Parents, public officials, businesses, and citizens actively support our commitment to challenge all students to achieve their potential. The Board of Education and school system staff embrace the community's contributions and are responsible stewards of its resources.

Parents choose to send their children to our schools. Businesses and families move to Frederick County because of our schools. Other school systems emulate us.

August 17, 1998

Figure 5.3. Frederick County Public Schools vision statement.

quest for all those who will succeed us as team leaders of the system. More important, it is not my vision. It is the shared vision of all school system leaders—the cabinet and school board. It is a vision that is the result of hours and hours of sweat, angst, persistence, and, at times, frustration. It is a shared vision. It guides us in our decision making, our budget deliberations, and as we develop and revise our strategic plans.

Students, staff, and the community use the vision statement. It has become part of us and is our system.

The vision is us and we are passionate about achieving that vision. Our shared belief in the vision gives us the freedom to act on our beliefs about people. We believe that people want to be successful and want to be part of a successful organization. We spend less and less time "checking" on people and more and more time working to build capacity in others. We are building leadership capacity and we are building learning capacity. Most times it is difficult to see the difference between learning and leading. Each requires the other—learning requires leading others or oneself, and leading requires learning by others or oneself.

We expect our school system to continually learn. We all must continually learn. As another cabinet members tells his division, "If you are doing the same thing in two years that you are doing today, we are not moving forward." Another smile crosses my face. My vision was becoming a reality!

Courage

In the beginning, I questioned myself. This was my first superintendency, so I did not have proven experience "at the helm" of a large school system. Courage was a precious commodity in those early months and first couple of years. I questioned my wisdom for conducting such a large social experiment. Tens of thousands of students' learning was on the line. Thousands of adults were being asked to buy into my vision of empowerment—a level of empowerment that had never been experienced in the system. Sometimes I wondered if one person's courage is another person's stupidity. I knew I was courageous for taking some steps. At times I wondered if I was stupid, but I pressed on.

There was at least one school board member who thought it was stupidity. At the end of my first year, that board member completed his final year on the board. One of his last acts was to conduct a two-hour monologue. It was supposed to be part of my year-end evaluation. From his perspective, it was a monologue and his evaluation of me.

I remember a key part of his evaluative monologue was a reflection about my quest to create greater capacity in one of my cabinet members.

The cabinet member was still learning and didn't meet the board member's level of expectation. The failure to perform at the desired level was appropriately laid at my feet. My quest to build capacity in a cabinet member was not well received, nor was my quest to build capacity in others well received by this board member. We did not share the same values and beliefs about others. He expected a command-control paradigm and I wanted to create team leadership. Courage (or stupidity) allowed me to stay the course. Courage in my convictions about how we wish to treat others allowed me to continue my journey. Courage in my belief in the power of a shared vision allowed me to press onward. In hindsight, my cabinet also lived and learned the importance of modeling that which you believe.

About the time I was receiving my "monologue" evaluation, I spoke with an administrator who was retiring. I remember his words, "You are making the right changes. I would not be comfortable with the change, but it is the right thing to do." We solidify our confidence in many ways; a supportive comment from a respected person is but one venue for courage.

The ironies of my first-year challenges are many. The school board has now been recognized for developing and following a shared vision. Members are frequently quizzed as to how they accomplished such an important task. Ironically, I was selected as Maryland's Superintendent of the Year for 2000; and, after only six years on the job, I am one of the most senior superintendents in the state. Another smile crosses through my mind. My vision is becoming a reality!

As I read and learn more, I am struck by the power of having belief in others. I think believing in others is powerful, bold, and ultimately the most effective leadership strategy. I also know it takes a great deal of time and energy in sharing that belief and the successes of those beliefs. We spend a lot of time sharing our internal belief in people's capacity to learn and grow with external stakeholders.

I find that when we encounter leadership challenges it is because we have not spent the necessary time to build leadership capacity in others. Recently, our district's internal learning curve with a new software system caused external funding agencies to lose trust and confidence in our capacity as a district. What I had failed to do was to adequately teach others. I believe that the funding agencies would also reach the same conclusion if given accurate and timely information.

One of our biggest challenges as leaders is dealing with what many describe as "mean-spirited" individuals. These mean-spirited individuals clearly feel disenfranchised, powerless, and, at times, paranoid. I have found that over time, the community will now automatically believe in the school system instead of believing the mean-spirited people. We have developed credibility and trust that are now difficult, if not impossible, for anyone to damage. We have become our vision, and the community embraces us for doing so.

Our school board was recently given an award for exemplary behavior in the community. It was recognized for modeling the character qualities many members of the community aspire to. The board was living its vision and being recognized for doing so. I am beginning to smile more overtly.

Application

I have studied leadership for decades. We have moved from leadership theories that espoused finding the "great person" as our leader to one that recognizes shared leadership as stewardship. None of us can be all things to everyone. We should stop trying. We must have the courage to believe in a better way, the passion to engage all parts of our organization and communities in that better way, and the shared vision of that better way.

The more I learn, the more I realize how important these three—passion, vision, and courage—are as the cornerstones of learning organizations. All of my personnel selections are now driven by my quest to understand individual job candidates' passion, vision, and courage. I want to know if candidates have passion, and if so what they are passionate about. That passion is at the core of their being. That passion reflects their core values and beliefs. Expecting future leaders in our district to know the values and beliefs of our citizens, stakeholders, customers, and clients is key in our selection process. Many times, candidates are not accustomed to this type of interview. Candidates often focus on what they have done or what they would like to do. It is illuminating when they begin to more fully understand why and how they accomplish tasks. Is it because they were told what to do, or is it because they are passionate about accomplishing a task in a given manner? What is their vision for themselves, the community, and the school system? Do they have the courage and passion to make a shared vision a reality? These are important considerations for us when selecting new leaders in our district.

I spend significant time exploring personal visions and the capacity and desire to create shared visions and shared learning experiences. Many university-based leadership training programs do not train in these areas. A few are beginning to do so, and the candidates are beginning to create and share their visions and the passion behind those visions.

Courage is more than the ability to stick to a value, belief, or vision. Courage includes the ability to recognize when you have made a mistake. It includes the ability to say you don't know and to admit ignorance, but to simultaneously express a desire to learn. At times, some of us have to "swallow our pride." Courage to do so is all part of shared leadership and stewardship.

The more subtle demands for courage arise when we allow others to shape our vision and our passion. Our visions only become shared when they are developed through a sharing process. Courage is present when we give others ownership and credit. Courage is developing the leadership capacity in others so much so that we, as superintendents, are no longer needed as leaders. Courage is smiling when you are no longer needed, knowing you have achieved your vision.

About the Author

Jack Dale was Maryland's Superintendent of the Year for 2000. He has been superintendent of the Frederick County Public Schools in Maryland since 1996. During his tenure, he reorganized the central office curricular and support functions to become services to each of the fifty-six schools in the county (his district is also growing at the rate of one new school per year, so this number changes quickly). Most of Jack's career was practiced in the state of Washington, where he began as a high school math teacher and coach. He received his master's and doctorate degrees from the University of Washington and served in several central office positions responsible for personnel, collective bargaining, curriculum, and school supervision. Prior to moving to Maryland, Jack served as the assistant superintendent in Edmonds, Washington, where one of the first trust agreements between the district

and the teachers' union was implemented—an agreement that later became a model for many other school systems across the nation and for the
National Education Association. He also serves as adjunct faculty for the
graduate program at Mount St. Mary's College in Maryland. He is the author of "The New American School System: A Learning Organization,"
published in the *International Journal of Educational Reform,* and is
co-editor of *Creating Successful School Systems: Voices from the University, the Field, and the Community.* Jack may be reached at (301)
696-6910 or Jack.Dale@fcps.org.

ESSAY 5: THE R FACTOR IN REFORM: RELATIONSHIPS

Louise Sundin, President, Minneapolis Federation of Teachers
and National Vice President of the American Federation of Teachers

Americans want better results from their public schools, and they want
them fast. Polls and surveys consistently show that the public and policymakers want students to develop better reading, writing, and math
skills; become more adept at using computers in their work; work collaboratively with others; and communicate their ideas more effectively.
And they want higher high school graduation rates, much higher.

School districts that are making progress on achieving these improvements have combined the adoption of research-proven educational strategies with the formation of a trusting, respectful working relationship between the district leadership and the local teachers union.
Teachers, who make up more than half of the staff of most school districts, are the ground troops in the war on educational failure and the
district's primary contact with parents and community members. If
teachers don't buy into and enthusiastically pursue reform strategies,
there isn't much hope for success.

Some years ago, a Rand Corporation study of education reform
concluded that "Reform is union made." The researchers found that
teacher unions play an essential role in school reform and in sustaining long-term reform efforts. The teacher union's role may be either as "a reformer or a resister." Real reform only happens when the
union leadership chooses to be an enthusiastic partner, the researchers concluded. Their leadership is particularly important when

the tenure of union leaders extends beyond that of superintendents, which is often the case.

Finding a respectful, trusting, working relationship between an urban superintendent and a big-city teachers union leader is as rare as finding unlimited funding for education. Superintendents and teacher leaders are often pushed into adversarial roles during contract negotiations, and the hard feelings and mistrust that can result can sour their working relationship for years, sometimes permanently.

Superintendents often barge ahead with reform strategies crafted alone or with a small number of administrative insiders. This leaves teacher leaders, even sympathetic ones, caught between a membership offended about being snubbed in the development of the strategy or a membership opposed to some aspects of the strategy for sound educational reasons, but which is left with no recourse except passivity or obstructionism.

In their book, *Boundary Crossers: Community Leadership for a Global Age*, Peirce and Johnson (1997) assert, "There are no magical organizational structures, there are just people and relationships. The table just gets bigger and rounder." Diplomats often negotiate to get countries around a round table. Superintendents and union leaders need to begin at a metaphorical round table, not sitting on opposite sides that often become a gulf between them.

There are many reasons superintendents and teacher leaders often don't work well together, reasons that a savvy superintendent can learn to recognize and avoid. Superintendents who want to succeed can chart a different and more productive path by including teachers in the development of the district's reform strategy, by creating structures that promote and model shared decision making, and by promoting a work culture that stresses continuous learning and continuous improvement. The alternative is to risk dissension and, ultimately, failure.

Rare as they may be, trusting, respectful working relationships between superintendents and teacher leaders are the only partnerships likely to produce remarkable results with students, the kind of remarkable results the public is demanding.

Respectful relationships are necessary for several compelling reasons, not the least of which is that a growing segment of the public is losing faith in our public schools. To a large extent, it is up to superintendents and teacher leaders to restore faith in public education, respect for learning in America, and respect for public educators.

Former American Federation of Teachers president Al Shanker used to admonish, "If the union calls the Superintendent and the Board a bunch of nincompoops who can't administer their way out of a paper bag, and the administrators and Board call the teachers and their union a bunch of incompetents who can't teach, the public believes us both, and goes elsewhere."

Shanker was prophetic, as usual. Look at the evidence. Many families are going elsewhere for schooling for their children. We've seen large increases in home schooling, in charter school applications, in alternative schools, and in the growth of private school enrollment, as well as calls for private school vouchers. At times it seems to those of us who work inside the system that the criticisms of public schools have become deafening. As we move into the first decade of the twenty-first century, school districts all over America are being forced to cut their budgets as states respond to the downturn in the economy following the boom years of the 1990s.

Superintendents' actions will set a tone in their districts that either continues the erosion of faith in our schools or begins to restore the public's confidence that public schools can and will deliver what the society needs and what parents want—students educated to the level necessary to succeed in the Information Age in a world of global economics. The antidote to this educational malaise is a public school system that works—works for all the kids and all the employees; works for the parents and the community's employers and the community as a whole—a school system that focuses its institutional resources, support, and energy on learning, both for its students and its employees; and a school system in which continuous adult learning is as important as progress in student learning. It is a system built on relational competence: healthy, respectful working relationships between teachers, administrators, students, families, colleagues, and community members.

But that kind of work and learning environment doesn't just happen by chance. Meaningful engagement of the various constituents of the school system, including families and the broader community, will only occur in an atmosphere in which the employees feel they are important and valued constituents of the system. Research shows most parents get their school news from their children and their children's teachers, who are more trusted than central office leaders and school board members.

The successful superintendent understands that the primary constituents (or customers, for those who prefer the business term) of the central office are the schools and the employees in those schools. In turn, the primary stakeholders of a school district's teachers, clerks, and bus drivers are the students and their families. Superintendents who don't understand these distinct roles and who don't demonstrate this understanding in their daily practice risk alienating their most important connectors to community.

It's mostly rhetoric to sit in a superintendent's cabinet meeting and ask of a proposed action, "How is this decision going to affect students and their families?" The real question in that meeting should be, "How is this decision going to support the schools and teachers so they better can serve our students and their families?"

Professionalizing Teaching

The key to success in working with teachers lies in focusing on creating a true profession for teaching and in embracing accountability for adults and students to dramatically increase student results. This means creating a collaborative framework for our work and an understanding that adults must model what we expect of students.

It means that employees must be encouraged and even required to work on collaborative work teams; must be supported to innovate; must be provided the resources needed to complete the tasks at hand; must be informed with reliable, timely school district, school-site, and student data; and must receive constant, usable feedback on their work.

District leaders must demonstrate a laser-like focus on student learning through the new Three Rs: Respect, Responsibility, and Results. Under this new belief system, there must be a clear delineation of what Phil Schlechty (1992) calls the new "rules, roles, and responsibilities" through which we all become important partners in the system. The Strategic Direction of the Minneapolis Public Schools states, "As partners, students, families, and all MPS employees (we) accept mutual responsibility and accountability for growth in achievement."

The superintendent must be the primary keeper and promoter of this new vision for a collaborative reform effort. But teachers union leaders must play the role of enthusiastic partners. The union's traditional role has been to limit its focus to pay and working conditions. But union leaders all over the country are recognizing that teachers unions must do more than that. That is why, after first striking out on their own, many like-minded union leaders came together to form the Teacher Union Reform Network (TURN), a group of progressive teachers union leaders from American Federation of Teachers and National Education Association locals.[3]

The TURN mission statement recognizes the larger role unions must play in improving our schools: "Teacher unions also have a responsibility to students, their families and to the broader community to support public education as a vital element of American democracy. What unites these responsibilities is our commitment to help all children learn."

These local unions clearly recognize and accept the role of articulating and focusing their members' attention on improving student learning. They also accept that for student achievement to improve substantially, teachers unions must help by providing teachers access to the knowledge and skills members need to become quality educators; by working to establish and maintain a respectful, collaborative labor-management relationship; and by negotiating a union contract that supports the work of educating kids.

The need for this new role for teachers unions has been reinforced for me in numerous surveys of teachers at all levels of our organization and around the country. When asked what teachers want their union to do to help them, the number one response is always, "Help us do our job better. Help us be more successful with students."

The response of many progressive unions has been to disseminate educational research and to offer professional development and online learning for teachers. Unions are also focusing their efforts on ensuring that teachers and students have a safe, positive, supportive working environment in which to teach and learn.

In New York City, the United Federation of Teachers contract states, "No school is good enough until we would place our own children there." That articulates in a single sentence how union leaders are taking responsibility for improving the skills and knowledge of our colleagues and the viability and effectiveness of schools.

The Vision Thing—Adding Value

Many superintendents come into the job believing and being told that their role is to come up with a vision for reform for everyone else to follow. Superintendents who fall into that trap often meet stiff resistance, even hostility from teachers. Or sometimes the teachers just sit passively and think to themselves, "Okay, Mr. Savior, this is your baby. Let's just see what you've got!"

Superintendents who try to go it alone often interpret that reaction as resistance to their ideas, but many times it's not. It's really resistance to a strategy imposed on educators without their input; and it reflects resentment that the new leader is ignoring the good work, progress, and successful strategies that have been developed in the district.

Educators in many districts, especially the most troubled, have had to endure more than three decades of such grand plans and short-lived superintendents. Minneapolis has had eight superintendents in my eighteen years as union president. Absent a reason to act otherwise, educators' natural instinct in the face of this "big-plan leadership" and frequent turnover is to react to a new superintendent's big new reform plan by saying, "This too shall pass, I'll just keep on doing what I've been doing."

Superintendents who wish to avoid this fate should see their role as "adding value" to successful strategies currently at work in the district by improving their effectiveness and by developing new strategies that build on the successes of the existing ones. Educators are caring, intelligent people who want to do good. The superintendent who can learn how to take their teachers' hard work and focus and steer it has far more chance for success than the one who decides to scrap everything that's come before and start over.

Ron Heifetz, director of the Leadership Project at Harvard's Kennedy School of Government, says today's leaders must have the courage "to interrogate the reality of their organizations" and to engage people in closing the gap between their present reality and the desired future for their organization. He also says, "Leadership is the ability to mobilize people to tackle tough issues" (Heifetz, 1994).

Reform and Professionalizing Teaching

The research is in, and it's abundantly clear: it is impossible to get better student achievement without improving the quality of teaching and the appeal of teaching as a profession. Thus, reform-minded superintendents and teachers union leaders have something in common that, if recognized, can be the foundation for a fruitful and powerful collaboration. By working together to create better professional development programs, more effective curricula, and school governance structures that promote continuous improvement of skills and knowledge, superintendents and teacher leaders can deliver what each of their constituents wants from them.

The Trust Factor

Successful school system reforms have come only where district leadership and teachers union leadership have formed a trusting relationship committed to unity and progress. For that type of trust relationship to form in a system that has been highly adversarial for decades, superintendents need to be willing to trust that union leaders and teacher leaders want the true collaboration necessary for system-wide change to occur. In other words, they have to be willing to work under the assumption that teacher leaders, no matter how much they may disagree on an individual strategy or tactic, will stay the course of collaboration if treated with respect and as equal partners.

One effective strategy for moving from an adversarial relationship to a collaborative one involves creating opportunities for trust relationships to develop and, thus, to set the stage for full collaboration. Minneapolis began creating those opportunities in 1984 when the superintendent and the teachers union president established the Joint Labor Management Committee on Professionalizing Teaching. For the first time in a long time, discussions between administrators and teachers took a constructive turn that both sides gradually embraced. Over time, the committee morphed into an umbrella group overseeing all professional development activities.

The effort led, in 1985, to creation of the Mentor Program, which provides trained, skilled mentors to all new teachers and to tenured teachers who need help.

In 1988, the Five-with-Five Committee of five principals and five teachers was established to discuss ways of cooperating on education improvement strategies. The committee, later known as the Professional Leadership Team, gave administrators and teacher leaders a place and a regular opportunity to interact and exchange ideas outside of the contract negotiation or grievance process. These efforts were followed by many similar initiatives over the next ten years that served to build a lasting, trust-based reform effort in Minneapolis.[4]

In 1992, Standards of District Support for Effective Schools were adopted outlining district support necessary for school success. The standards become the foundation for future discussions around teacher-administrator collaboration.

In 1994, the District Strategic Direction and District Improvement Agenda (DIA) were adopted, once again through extensive collaboration between teachers, administrators, and community representatives. The District Improvement Agenda attempted to align district improvement goals and strategies with school-site improvement plans and with professional development goals.

In 1995, the District Leadership Team was formed and included representatives of major stakeholder groups: students, teachers, principals, parents, business leaders, superintendent's representatives, and various labor leaders. The discussion group worked to surface issues of conflict and potential collaboration and to model shared decision making to schools and district administrators.

In 1995, teachers, principals, and district administrators developed the Accountability Framework, which for the first time required alignment of the Strategic Direction, the District Improvement Agenda, and School Improvement Plans. A feedback process that included teachers and administrators was developed to give schools constructive feedback on their improvement plans. In 2001, the same players completed an intervention process to help schools that weren't succeeding.

From Headquarters to the Trenches

Once a trusting collaboration is created between the district leadership and union leadership, and progress is being made on identifying key strategies for reform, moving that collaboration to the school-site level is the biggest challenge. We're not there yet in most districts, even the ones known for solid collaboration at the district level.

Minneapolis uses school improvement plans, detailed school information reports, feedback processes, school goals, Quality Performance Awards, and more, all under the conceptual umbrella of our Accountability Framework, which lays out the structures and strategies for moving reform into the schools. The framework establishes standards for performance for the district, for schools, for leadership, and for teachers, students, and parents.

Keepers of the Vision

Once a collaboratively devised vision is developed, the superintendent and the union president should be the keepers of the vision—articulating it and promoting it at every opportunity. They should work to ensure that new reform proposals, or suggestions to discontinue existing strategies, are consistent with the stated vision.

They must model the vision, and its emphasis on trust and collaboration, in their daily practices, for they will be watched closely by educators and administrators alike for inconsistent behavior or backtracking. The superintendent must be a cheerleader for change, trusting and believing in the teachers, supporting them, and providing resources for their work.

Superintendents need to model the behaviors they expect in others and challenge building administrators to emulate an inclusive, respectful, supportive professional culture at the school sites. Superintendents who want their work to have lasting impact will also look for ways to embed their reform philosophy in the organization. They'll realize that policy directives are quickly forgotten in the hustle and bustle of educators' lives and that, absent other efforts to embed them in the organization, reform plans can quickly gather dust on shelves.

Rarely do educators at school sites reach for the giant school district policy manual to solve everyday challenges and issues. Living documents and trusting relationships are required for the thousands of daily decisions made at school sites. If we provide the framework, the philosophy, and the flexibility for teachers and administrators at the worksite, they will be empowered to function efficiently, collaboratively, and sensitively. And, if we model the behaviors of trust, they won't be paralyzed into inaction because they fear criticism or retribution if a strategy doesn't produce immediate improvements.

Educators also need the opportunity to learn from each other, from our successes, and from our failures. As an exercise in collective learning, Minneapolis held a one-day reflection conference on four programs that did not succeed and no longer exist. District and teacher leaders felt the need to take the time to learn from the circumstances that led to the programs' demise.

The Union Contract as a Reform Guide

The union contract, if used correctly, can be the most powerful reform document in a school district and an antidote for policy paralysis. The teacher contract can be a blueprint for change, a professional "bible," a resource guide, a "living" manual for reform. It is the document that gives teachers the courage and the confidence to step up and try something new because the contract provides the safety net.

However, such a document can only be created, sustained, and used to educate children in an atmosphere of trust, collaboration, and constant communication. The teacher contract is the one document that teachers trust because it is developed in a process that takes place on a level playing field, where their issues are forcefully advocated and conflicts are jointly resolved, equitable resolution processes are established, and the work of the institution and the institutional relationships are focused.

Superintendents who say to the teachers union, "We will only talk to you about benefits, salary, working conditions, and other traditional bargaining issues" are missing the boat. If school boards and superintendents insist that educational issues are exclusively their purview, then teachers are legitimate in their reluctance to embrace change and to take responsibility for student learning. Why should they, when they have been told that it is not within their purview?

Principles of Quality

A superintendent who leads on the basic principles of quality management will not go wrong. These principles are as essential in the educational setting as they are at the world-famous Saturn auto plant in Springhill, Tennessee, where management and labor set the standard for trust-based, collaborative reform. At Saturn, which regularly ranks at the top of customer satisfaction scales for car owners, all agree that quality equals results. The Minneapolis Schools and the Minneapolis Federation of Teachers have won two Saturn/United Auto Workers Awards for their labor-management partnership and professional development.

The Quality Principles

- Articulate the reform vision clearly, often, and with an easy-to-state and understand focus, vision, and mission.
- Believe in people and the value of workers. Espouse and practice that belief with genuine caring, support, belief, and rewards. It starts with articulation and goes to motivation and inspiration.
- Believe in service as a hallmark of excellence. Establish clarity about clients and customers—school sites are the central office customers; parents and students are the school's customers.
- Believe that we can and will constantly get better at what we do and that we must always be about continuously improving.
- Believe that we must communicate the mission and messages of change and continuous improvement constantly and continually.
- Believe that we are all extraordinarily accountable as a part of an accountability framework focused on results.
- Believe that you can't and won't get better unless and until you measure where you are, and then constantly measure everything to chart progress and improvement.
- Believe that you must celebrate and reward progress toward goals—performance-based pay for teachers and performance-based rewards for schools.

Boomers, Busters, Xers, and Millennials

Educational leaders will also have to focus on a new issue, one that likely wasn't talked about in their education textbooks or leadership manuals—the growing disparities between the generations that produced their employees and their students' parents.

Why worry about such seemingly noneducation matters? There are several reasons, starting with the fact that thanks to longer life spans, more different generations are living today than ever before. The gaps between those generations, in the experiences that formed their work habits and worldviews, in their incomes, in their lifestyles, and in their relationships with the new information technologies, are large and in some cases growing larger.

People from different generations often espouse and strive toward different personal and social values. The potential for conflict in the workplace is great and growing, and internal conflict is the nemesis of effective school reform.

Finally, the aging of the baby boom generation is creating a shortage of workers that will make it imperative that school districts offer working environments that appeal to younger workers. Research suggests that younger workers—the pool from which most new teachers must come—have high expectations. They want to be recognized for their skills and abilities; they expect a safe, environmentally friendly workplace; they expect teaming and collaboration; they expect to be treated as professionals; they expect to work hard, but to balance work time with personal time; and they expect regular, useful feedback on their work.

Young teachers who don't find these traits in their workplace are more likely than previous generations of teachers to say, "I'm outta here!" Clearly, we aren't there yet in meeting those expectations. Turnover in younger teachers is high, much higher than in the past, putting at risk any reform strategy.

Respected leadership researcher and author Tom Peters tells audiences, "If your top leadership hasn't spent at least a half-day in the last month sitting down with a twenty-five-year-old, then they are blowing it."

Leading by Example

Author Joel Barker defines leadership as "taking people further than they would go on their own." To do that, leaders must practice mentoring, modeling, and motivating. Superintendents must model the inclusive, respectful behaviors and belief systems that will help others meet the challenges of change.

A superintendent should also have a mentor or coach to provide him or her with regular performance feedback, just as administrators, teachers, and students need regular monitoring and feedback. The superintendent is the chief motivator through genuine caring for employees and being a cheerleader for change.

It's simple, really. Leaders must model the change they wish for their employees. That means working collaboratively with educators in developing their vision and improvement strategies and evaluating and rewarding progress.

That new place is often a scary one, less predictable than the textbooks would have us believe. The new type of leadership required for systemic reform is more a process than a plan. It's best if leaders go as part of a group that includes the superintendent, the school board chair, and the teachers union leader, the three legs on the stool of successful school district reform. The stool won't stand if any one of the legs tries to act solely on its own.

About the Author

Louise A. Sundin is serving her eighteenth year as president of the Minneapolis Federation of Teachers, Local 59, Minnesota's largest local, representing 6,000 employees. She is also a ten-term national vice president of the American Federation of Teachers. She was recently elected to a three-year term as first vice president of the Minneapolis Central Labor Union Council (CLUC). She is currently in her twelfth term as a regional state vice president of the Minnesota AFL-CIO. Louise taught thirty years as a ninth-grade English teacher. Additionally, she has earned national recognition as a spokesperson for education reform and teacher professionalism. She is known as a progressive labor leader and a powerful advocate for workers. She negotiated a model professional contract that includes accountability and professionalism. She is a founding member of the Teacher Union Reform Network that works to transform unions into agents of change. Louise may be reached at (612) 529-9621 or lsundin@mft59.org.

REFERENCES

Barber, M., & Phillips, V. (2000, September). Big change questions. "Should large-scale assessment be used for accountability?"—The fusion of pressure and support. *Journal of Educational Change*, 1(3), 277–281.

Charlotte-Mecklenburg Schools (2001, March). *Equity Plus II project: A seamless framework for addressing the needs of targeted schools.* Unpublished document.

Charlotte-Mecklenburg Schools, North Carolina (1999, March 18). *Achieving the CMS vision: Equity and student success.* Unpublished document.

Dee, T. S. (2001, August). Teachers, race and student achievement in a randomized experiment. Cambridge, MA: National Bureau of Economic Research. Available: National Bureau of economic Research Web site, www.nber.org/papers/W8432

Donohoe Steinberger, E. (1995). Margaret Wheatley on leadership for change. *School Administrator*, 52(1), 16–20.

Evans, R. (1996). *The human side of school change: Reform, resistance, and the real-life problems of innovation.* San Francisco: Jossey-Bass.

Ferguson, R. (1991, summer). Paying for public education: New evidence on how and why money matters. *Harvard Journal of Legislation*, 28, 465–498.

Fink, S., & Thompson, S. (2001, spring). Standards and whole system change. *Teaching and Change*, 8(3), 244.

Fullan, M. G. (1991). *The new meaning of educational change.* New York: Teachers College Press.

Heifetz, R. A. (1994). *Leadership without easy answers.* Cambridge, MA: Harvard University Press.

Keller, B. (1999, November 10). Women superintendents: Few and far between. *Education Week on the Web.* Available: www.edweek.org/ew/ew_printstory. cfm?slug=11women.h19

Panasonic Foundation (1998a, August). Aurora, CO: A long, bumpy road. *Strategies*, 5(2). Available: American Association of School Administrators Web site, www.aasa.org/publications/strategies/index.htm

Panasonic Foundation (1998b, August). District 2, NYC: Teacher learning comes first. *Strategies*, 5(2). Available: American Association of School Administrators Web site, www.aasa.org/publications/strategies/index.htm

Panasonic Foundation (1998c, August). Standards in action. *Strategies*, 5(2). Available: American Association of School Administrators Web site, www. aasa.org/publications/strategies/index.htm

Panasonic Foundation (2000, May). Houston, TX: Aiming high. *Strategies*, 7(1). Available: American Association of School Administrators Web site, www.aasa.org/publications/strategies/index.htm

Panasonic Foundation (2001a, February). Plainfield, NJ: Moving on many fronts. *Strategies*, 8(1). Available: American Association of School Administrators Web site, www.aasa.org/publications/strategies/index.htm

Panasonic Foundation (2001b, November). Chula Vista, CA: A system of student-centered schools. *Strategies*, 8(2). Available: American Association of school Administrators Web site, www.aasa.org/publications/strategies/index.htm

Panasonic Foundation (2001c, November). San Diego, CA: A high-risk sprint. *Strategies*, 8(2). Available: American Association of School Administrators Web site, www.aasa.org/publications/strategies/index.htm

Peirce, N., & Johnson, C. (1997). *Boundary crossers: Community leadership for a global age.* College Park, MD: Academy of Leadership Press.

Schlechty, P. C. (1992). *Creating schools for the 21st century.* San Francisco: Jossey-Bass.

Senge, P. M. (1990). *The fifth discipline: The art and practice of the learning organization.* New York: Currency Doubleday.

Viadero, D. (2000, March 22). Students in dire need of good teachers often get the least qualified or less experienced. *Education Week on the Web.* Available: www.edweek.org/ew/ew_printstory.cfm?slug=28gapteach.h19

NOTES

1. We used a two-stage process in the development of the critical success factors. A little context is required before summarizing this process. The Panasonic Foundation is a corporate foundation that forms long-term partnerships with public school systems in the United States and provides technical assistance (not grants) aimed at redesigning the educational system so that all students can perform to high standards. A cadre of educational consultants is the technical assistance providers. The foundation's executive director, Sophie Sa, and I met with most of our senior consultants (Dean Damon, Scott Elliff, Larry Feldman, Steve Fink, David Florio, Andrew Gelber, Gail Gerry, Sue Kinzer, Lallie Lloyd, and Deb Winking), and together we created a first draft of the critical success factors at all three levels. About a week later, a subgroup (Damon, Gelber, Gerry, Sa, and I) worked with business consultant Daniel Yaest to hone and sharpen the critical success factors. Panasonic Foundation staff members and consultants drew on their knowledge of literature and from field experience in systemic education reform in developing the factors. The purpose of this effort was to see if we could make our partnership work with school districts more rigorous, but that is a subject for another essay. I should also note that because my name appears on this essay, I felt free to edit the critical success factors according to my inclinations. The literature that identifies similar success factors includes the following: *Dispelling the Myth Revisited* (Washington, DC: The Education Trust, December 2001); *Beating the Odds: A City-by-City Analysis of Student Performance and Achievement Gaps on State Assessments* (Washington, DC: Council of Great City Schools, May

2001); "Doing What Works: Improving Big City School Districts," *AFT Educational Policy Briefs*, no. 12, October 2000.

2. The day after I wrote this sentence, I came across this description of the goal of the Annenberg Institute for School Reform's National Task Force on the Future of Urban School Districts from testimony made by Marla Ucelli before the California Legislative Assembly Select Committee on Low Performing Schools: "Our goal is to help create, support, and sustain urban education systems with two characteristics: all schools in the system meet high academic performance standards and none have significant differences in achievement based on race, ethnicity, primary language, or family income."

3. See the TURN Web site at www.gseis.ucla.edu/hosted/turn/turn/turn2.html.

4. In 1987, the Labor Management Benefits Committee was negotiated to take issues of employee benefits to a problem-solving atmosphere. It was later expanded to include the CEOs of all the district bargaining units.

In 1988, Site Leadership Councils were established for schools as a way of moving the new collaborative working relationship out from the district level into the schools. The councils, composed of principals, teachers, and parents, were charged with developing a basis for shared decision making at the schools.

In 1989, the teachers union contract was expanded to include language on excellence and student performance, system accountability and responsiveness, and a focus on school-based planning and decision making.

In 1989, the Calendar Committee, a joint teacher/administrator/parent group, was established to plan the school calendar for the upcoming year, including release days for staff development, holiday breaks, and so forth.

In 1989, building on the work done in many of the preceding committees and working groups, the Contract Administration Committee was created. This joint teachers union and district labor relations/human resources group meets every two weeks to respond to and hopefully resolve contract-related disputes. One goal is to reduce time-consuming and expensive grievances and arbitration hearings.

In 1989, the first of a series of Memoranda of Agreements between the teachers union and the district was written, focusing on the need for action on various problems, such as teacher dissatisfaction, financial disparities, use of new technologies, and adoption of school effectiveness research. This approach of "agreeing to agree" allowed the two parties to continue working and to make progress on key issues even though they were not yet ready to establish the details for a final agreement.

In 1989, an agreement between the teachers union and the district tied education, professional development, and teacher evaluation under one program that would be designed jointly: the Professional Development Process (PDP). That effort led, two years later, to twelve pilot sites representing 400 teachers trying out a new professional development model, the Professional Development Process, that incorporates peer feedback, annual planning and goal setting, mentoring, and intensive support processes. The PDP replaced the traditional principal-review model of teacher evaluation and professional development with peer review. Soon after, the district made the PDP its official teacher evaluation process.

In order to reward progress in 1995, the district created Quality Performance Awards for schools making progress on their improvement goals, meeting the Principles of Effective Schools, and involving all key constituents in decision making. Winners received cash awards that could be used at the school.

In 1996, in an attempt to establish a higher teacher quality standard, the teacher contract established a salary reward for teachers who achieve National Board Certification. The union negotiated assistance with the application fee, establishment of a candidate support network, and release time for preparing the application.

In 1997, the union negotiated an Achievement of Tenure Process, a rigorous, three-year induction process for teachers that includes mentoring, assessment, peer coaching, action research, and portfolio development. Successful teachers earn tenure and a bonus.

PART 3

A Methodology and a Set of Tools to Create and Sustain Systemic School Improvement

So far, I have shared with you some of the challenges you will face as you try to lead systemic school improvement (in part 1) and several practitioners have shared their views on the courage, passion, and vision they think is needed to lead systemic school improvement (in part 2). In this section, I describe an innovative methodology and set of tools you can use to create and sustain systemic school improvement (chapter 6). And Jason Cascarino, Chris Henson, and I discuss options for financing whole-district improvement (chapter 7).

The Destination of Three Paths and a Methodology to Get There

In a system you can't take away any of the functional structure without providing something to take care of its interdependent relationships, even temporarily. That's why architects and engineers put an external structure—a "scaffold"—around a building so work can go on within it, and doctors provide internal "bypass" mechanisms or processes to ensure that the whole system keeps functioning while they're working on one part.

—Lewis A. Rhodes,
Putting Unions and Management out of a Job

GOOD IS THE ENEMY OF GREAT

There are many good schools in the United States and throughout the world. But at the dawn of the twenty-first century, good is not good enough to bring our children to the knowledge to which they have a right and with which they will bring us and themselves to the future. Not only is good not good enough, but as Collins (2001) says:

Good is the enemy of great. And that is one of the reasons why we have so little that becomes great. We don't have great schools, principally because we have good schools. We don't have great government, principally because we have good government. Few people attain great lives, in large part because it is just so easy to settle for a good life. The vast majority of companies never become great, precisely because the vast majority become quite good—and that is their main problem. (p. 1)

Creating good schools within a school district has been the dominant paradigm for school improvement for many years now. Ever since John Goodlad wrote *A Place Called School* in 1984 and argued that individual schools should be the unit of change to produce school improvement, almost all school improvement efforts in the United States have followed that advice.

Lew Rhodes (1997), the former assistant executive director for the *American Association of School Administrators*, comments on the inadequacies of this approach when he says that educators experience the

> difficulty of perceiving and understanding the role of the school district as the fundamental unit for effective changes that must impact all children. It was a lot easier thirty years ago when John Goodlad popularized the idea of the school building as the fundamental unit of change. . . . But now it is time to question that assumption—not because it is wrong—but because it is insufficient. Otherwise, how can we answer the question: "If the building is the primary unit at which to focus change efforts, why after thirty years has so little really changed?" (p. 19)

School-based improvement is important, necessary, and it must continue. But it is my contention that by itself it is insufficient for improving entire school systems. Not only is the school-based improvement model insufficient, but it also has produced unintentional outcomes. In some districts using this approach, there are excellent schools, average-performing schools, and low-performing schools; or, as they are often called, pockets of excellence, pockets of mediocrity, and pockets of despair.

Please don't misunderstand me. I am not suggesting that school-based improvement is unimportant. What I'm saying is that in my opinion it's not enough. It is wrong and unfair when school improvement is limited to a few buildings in a district while all others are allowed to maintain their status quo. It's unfair to the children in those status quo schools, and it's unfair to the teachers and staff in those schools. Whole districts need to be improved. That's my point.

So, how can you redesign an entire school system to perform at higher levels? And, then, what do you do to sustain those improvements? The answer, I believe, lies at the end of three paths. Each of these paths, if followed alone, will not lead to the kind of transformational change needed to improve entire school systems. All three paths must be followed simultaneously, and by making the journey in this way school districts will, I predict, arrive at a single destination—a place marked by high-quality student, teacher, and system learning that is sustained for the life of a school district.

THE THREE PATHS

Path 1: Improve Your District's Core and Supportive Work Processes

You have to redesign every part of your district, not just your curriculum and not just a single school or level of schooling. The main, or core, work of your school district is teaching and learning. All other work in your district is important, too, but it is secondary in importance to teaching and learning. Nevertheless, even the supportive work processes must be improved if you want to move your district toward world-class standards for educating children.

Path 2: Improve Your District's Internal Social "Architecture"

The social system of an organization is powerful and influential. When your people leave at the end of a day, the curriculum, desks, chairs, books, and so on all become dormant. It is only when people show up the next day that those inanimate things become tools used to do work. This is what brings "life" to your school system—people interacting with each other and with the tools of teaching and learning.

Policies, procedures, methods, techniques, values, beliefs, communication structures, organization culture, and so on support life in a social system. All of these supports are part of what the literature in organization improvement calls social "architecture." These supports need to be redesigned to improve your faculty and staff's job satisfaction, motivation, and effectiveness. Further, the "architecture" needs to be redesigned at the same time you redesign your work processes. Why? Because you want to make sure that the new social architecture and the new work processes complement and support each other. The best way to ensure this complementarity is to make simultaneous improvements to both elements of your school system.

Path 3: Improve Your District's
Relationships with Its External Environment

Your district is an open system. An open system is one that interacts with its environment by exchanging a valued product or service in return for needed resources. To become a high-performing school system you need to have a positive and supportive relationship with stakeholders in your environment. But you can't wait until you improve your work processes and social architecture to start working on those relationships. You need positive and supportive relationships to make the important changes you want to make. So, you also have to improve your district's environmental relationships at the same time you start improving your work processes and social architecture.

The importance of this path is documented in practice. For example, McGee (2002) summarizes several trends in the design of organizations. He identified one of these trends as being "toward reconfigurable organizations . . . ones which continually adjust strategy to meet market conditions and subsequently adapt their organization design to support those strategy changes."

The principle of simultaneous improvement is absolutely essential for effective organization improvement (e.g., see Pasmore, 1988; Emery, 1977; Trist, Higgin, Murray, & Pollack, 1963). In the literature on systems improvement this principle is called *joint optimization* (Cummings & Worley, 2001, p. 353).

THE DESTINATION

Educators throughout the world are on a "School Improvement Quest." The triple societal pressures of standards, assessment, and accountability are motivating them to stay the course. These trekkers carry rucksacks full of contemporary school improvement models, processes, and desirable outcomes. Over and over again, year after year, decade after decade, they all come to a stop at the edge of a broad and deep abyss that goes by the name "The Canyon of Systemic School Improvement." On the far side of the abyss lies "The Land of High Performance." That's where the educators want to be—that's their destination. They stand there frustrated, angry, or depressed, gazing across the wide canyon wondering, once again, how they will ever traverse it.

Standing at the edge of this great abyss, some educators see a threat while others see an opportunity. Some see an impossible crossing, while others see just another puzzle to be solved. Meanwhile, the three great societal pressures for setting standards, assessing student learning, and holding educators accountable for results continue to build and show no sign of dissipating. The pressure drives some of the educators and their school systems over the edge into the depths of the abyss, which is littered with failed efforts to create and sustain systemic school improvement.

Even though the trekkers have walked a lot of ground, and although they have done good things along the way in the name of school improvement, there they stand once more, looking out over the abyss wondering how in the world they will get to the other side. Some of those standing at the edge say, "Impossible, can't be done." Others say, "We've been here before and failed then." Still others stand there and theorize about the complexity of crossing such a canyon. "It's so hard to define the boundaries of the canyon. Just what is a system, what does it mean, is it this or is it that? We need this, this, this, and that or we'll never cross," they suggest, but then they take no action to do what's needed. Still others, looking backward toward their past, say, "What's behind us is the future. What we've done in the past is what we should continue to do."

Crossing the canyon of systemic school improvement is not a new challenge. We have looked out over this canyon many times in the past. People like Seymour Sarason and Michael Fullan have been telling us for years that this crossing must be made. In my opinion, one important reason why the trekkers on the "School Improvement Quest" have not been able to cross the "Canyon of Systemic School Improvement" is that they don't have the right methodology and tools to traverse that canyon. Further, a bridge across the canyon must accommodate three paths that will simultaneously lead educators to "The Land of High Performance."

This book offers a vision of the leadership challenges for crossing the "canyon." In this chapter, I present a methodology and a set of tools (collectively called Step-Up-To-Excellence) that you can use to build a three-path bridge to bring your district across the Canyon of Systemic School Improvement to the Land of High Performance.

THE NEED

Imagine for a moment that you are a parent of school-aged children. Imagine that your sibling, who lives on the other side of town, is sending his or her children to a high-performing school. Then, imagine that your kids, who are *in the same district*, are attending a low- or average-performing school. How would that make you feel? It would make me angry. This is why entire school districts must be improved, not just individual schools within a district.

Focusing school improvement on individual school buildings within a district leaves some teachers and children behind in average- and low-performing schools. Leaving teachers and students behind is a subtle, but powerful, form of discrimination, and America's school-aged children, their families, and their communities deserve better. It is morally unconscionable to allow some schools in your district to excel while others celebrate their mediocrity or languish in their desperation. Your entire school district must improve, not just parts of it. Step-Up-To-Excellence provides the blueprints, methods, and tools to make this happen.

The redesign methodology described in this chapter is a potentially powerful method to improve student, teacher, and system learning by transforming entire school systems into high-performing organizations of learners because it

- develops a school district's capacity to set a strategic direction while simultaneously allowing educators to respond tactically and rapidly to unanticipated events in its environment;
- combines for the first time effective concepts, methods, and tools from several different, but interrelated fields;
- transforms the social "architecture" of a school system from a bureaucratic design to a participative and "networked" design;
- uses innovative methods for analyzing and improving three sets of key school system variables: the system's core and supportive work processes, its social "architecture," and its relationship with its broader environment;
- uses a high-involvement strategy to engage educators in a collaborative effort to improve the quality of education in their systems;
- shifts the focus of school improvement from individual schools to clusters of interconnected schools;
- coordinates school improvement so that the entire school system is redesigned for high performance; and
- is a never-ending process of moving an entire school system toward higher and higher levels of school system performance.

I am firmly convinced that if applied consistently, repeatedly, and with patience, Step-Up-To-Excellence will move your entire school system continuously toward higher levels of performance. The literature on redesigning organizations using similar models confirms this optimism. Further, your school system will never perfectly achieve its new vision because that vision is a moving target; therefore, systemic redesign is a lifelong journey for your district.

THE METHODOLOGY

There are ways to cross the Canyon of Systemic School Improvement; for example, see Kathleen Dannemiller's model in *Real Time Strategic Change* (Jacobs, 1994). One way that was designed specifically for school systems is the Step-Up-To-Excellence methodology described in this chapter. This methodology provides educators at the edge of the abyss with a blueprint for building a three-path bridge across the Canyon of Systemic School Improvement to the Land of High Performance, and once there this new methodology helps you succeed in this new land. This innovative methodology *is not* a particular school improvement reform (i.e., it is not like one of the comprehensive school reform models advocated by the New American Schools, nor is it like a curriculum reform). It is a comprehensive methodology and set of tools designed to help educators navigate change and lead their districts toward *any vision* or to implement *any kind* of whole-district improvement idea.

Prerequisite Conditions for Effective Whole-District Improvement

Successful whole-district improvement is only possible, in my opinion, if certain prerequisite conditions are in place. The conditions for effective redesign are as follows:

- Senior leaders (administrators, union leaders, and informal leaders) acting on the basis of personal courage, passion, and vision, not on the basis of fear or self-survival
- Senior leaders conceiving of their districts as whole systems, not as a collection of disconnected individual schools and programs
- Leaders and followers with a clear view of the opportunities that systemic redesign offers them, not a view of "we can't do this because . . ."
- Leaders and followers possessing the professional intellect, change-minded attitudes, and change navigation skills to move their districts toward higher levels of performance, not people without an inkling about the requirements of navigating systemic change

Criteria for Effective Systemic Change

Rhodes (1999) iterates several criteria he believes are necessary to create and sustain systemic change in school districts. He says effective systemic change

- focuses on needs of children presently in schools;
- does not require resources that draw services away from these students;
- is a part of everyday school operations, not an add-on;
- engages and interacts with present classroom, building, and district operations by providing a safe way to question practices, purposes, and eventually assumptions and beliefs, and from there tries new approaches, learns from what doesn't work well, and tries again;
- enables curriculum design and delivery to be interactive, continuous, and developmental by anchoring it to classroom experiences;
- allows the need for solutions for current problems to serve as the "driver" for training, professional development, and use of new technologies, which provide learning scaffolds to support the continued professional and personal growth of those involved; and
- sustains the district as the unit of change and provides a continual knowledge base that allows those changes to be developmental. (pp. 6–7)

Step-Up-To-Excellence is for school districts that satisfy the preceding prerequisite conditions and that meet Rhodes's criteria. In my opinion, educators in districts that do not satisfy those conditions and do not meet those criteria are not "ready" to adopt a methodology like this.

This new methodology also views educators as knowledge workers and school systems as knowledge-creating organizations. It is also a methodology for navigating rapid, complex, and nonlinear change—a twenty-first-century competency for all organizations (see chapter 4). The methodology assumes that traditional management functions (planning, organizing, staffing, controlling, reporting, and budgeting) will continue to be used. There is an abundance of literature about these functions, so they are not described in this chapter.

Figure 6.1 illustrates the Step-Up-To-Excellence methodology. It is a five-step process that is preceded by a prelaunch preparation phase and followed by a recycle phase.

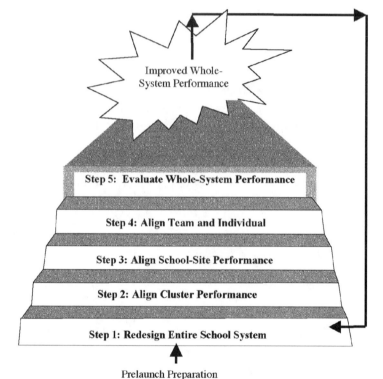

Figure 6.1. Step-Up-To-Excellence: Five steps to whole-district improvement.

PRELAUNCH PREPARATION

Prelaunch Activities

Define the System to Be Improved

One of the first things you do during the prelaunch phase is to define the system you want to improve. Defining the "system" to be improved is critical to the success of your redesign effort. Defining the system properly increases the likelihood of successfully redesigning your school system.

When some people say, "We need to improve the system," they mean they want to improve everything that is connected to education—the federal government, state departments of education, university-based schools of education, communities, the school district—everything. Although theoretically correct, this definition of "the system" is impractical because it is too large a concept to be useful. There is no way people working in a school district are going to create this kind of change.

A reasonable and pragmatic approach to defining the system to be improved is given by Merrelyn Emery, who, along with her husband, Fred Emery, is one of the early pioneers of systems thinking as it applies to organizations. She says (in Emery & Purser, 1996) to define the system to be improved you temporarily draw a circle around those units and people who must work together to deliver a whole product or service. In the case of a school district, the circle goes around all the schools, the central office staff, busing, cafeteria staff, and all others *inside* the district who touch the educational experience of children. Everything *outside* the circle is part of that system's external environment.

The unit of change for Step-Up-To-Excellence is a whole school district. But, to make change navigable, this methodology creates whole-system change by using clusters of interconnected schools that collaborate to educate children. In this chapter, I use a K–12 cluster as an example. A K–12 cluster is a single high school and all the middle and elementary schools that feed into it. Some K–12 school districts have several of these clusters. Some K–12 school districts are so small that the whole district is a single cluster. Some school districts are organized as elementary districts and these will use either K–6 or K–8 clusters. Other districts comprise a single high school (e.g., in California they have high school districts). These kinds of single-school districts will use a single 9–12 cluster. And, there are even some school districts organized as K–14 districts; for example, the Chugach Public Schools in Anchorage, Alaska.

It is clear that some districts are not organized as K–12 systems. Nevertheless, the principle that underlies the use of K–12 clusters to create and sustain whole-district change is useful for these districts, too. The underlying principle is that you must focus your improvement efforts on your district's entire core work process, whatever length it may be. In those districts that are only K–8, the length of the core work process is K–8. In districts that are only K–6, the core work process is

K–6. And in districts that are single high schools, then that single school's core work process is 9–12.

It is also clear that not all districts are designed using the feeder-system strategy. Many of these non-feeder-system districts can still use the cluster principle. What these districts can do is make a map showing which of their schools "tend" to educate the same children, even if one school is physically located on the other side of town. Then, those collaborating schools could be thought of as a cluster for the purposes of creating and sustaining systemic school improvement. Again, each cluster is organized to represent the district's entire core work process, whatever it may be.

The reason clusters are used to create whole-system change instead of single school buildings and classrooms is that a child's education is not what he or she learns in a single classroom, in a single school, or at a particular level of schooling (i.e., elementary, middle, or secondary). His or her education is the cumulative effect of what he or she learns throughout his or her entire educational "career" in a school district.

The entire teaching and learning process in a school district, whether it is K–14, K–12, K–6, K–8, or 9–12, represents its core work process. To make significant and important improvements in schooling, educators must focus their improvement efforts on the entire core work process—not on pieces of it. By focusing on the entire process, change-minded educators can identify where mistakes are being made throughout the teaching and learning process and then take steps either to correct the mistakes or to minimize their impact. This perspective is critical because upstream errors flow downstream (this is a basic principle from the literature on improving organizations as systems).

When upstream errors flow downstream, they enlarge and produce negative consequences later on in the work process. Not long ago, I was describing this principle to a high school principal and his department chairs. He interrupted me and said, "I know exactly what you're talking about. In our district, our middle school curriculum is being 'dumbed-down,' and those kids are coming to our high school unprepared for our more rigorous academic program. And, there's nothing we can do about it." Upstream errors flow downstream!

Build Political Support

One of the main purposes of prelaunch preparation is to build internal and external political support for your redesign effort. You will need explicit and broad support to launch a whole-system redesign effort, so you must spend time doing these prelaunch activities and doing them well. The period of time needed to conduct prelaunch activities will vary from a month or so up to a full year. The amount of time depends on your district's history with school improvement initiatives, the political climate in your community, your relationship with your school board, and your relationship with your teachers union leaders.

An effective tool for building external political support is what I call the Community Engagement Conference. This is a special three-day event organized and conducted using principles of Open Space Technology developed by Owen (1991, 1993). Up to 1,000 people from the community, including school board members and state department of education representatives, can be brought into one room (a large one, of course), and then they are guided through a process in which they self-organize into smaller discussion groups, focusing on topics related to the main theme of the conference, which, for example, could be "How can we improve the overall performance of our school district?" Notes from the discussion groups are entered into laptop computers at the end of each session. At the end of the third day of the conference, you will have a deep and broad database full of wonderfully creative ideas for redesigning your district, a collection of needs and concerns expressed by community members, and an idea of how much political support exists for continuing the redesign process. Most important, you will have demonstrated an authentic interest in the needs, views, and perceptions of a broad sample of your external stakeholders.

Recognize Needs and Opportunities

Before change happens, people must recognize the need to change, especially the people who have a huge stake in the success of your district. Embedded in the need to change are opportunities for significantly improving the quality of schooling you are providing children in your community. Before jumping into a redesign effort you must assess the degree to which internal and external stakeholders recognize the need for redesigning the district and the opportunities this effort presents.

Change-minded educators often focus only on identifying "needs." What doesn't work? What hinders organizational performance? What's missing? Although you need to understand clearly what these needs are, if the motivation to redesign your district is focused solely on the negative, the wrong, the bad, or the insufficient, then these needs become an emotional burden to overcome. An obsessive focus on needs can even make the situation worse if people begin to feel they are failures or incompetent or that there is nothing they can do.

To balance your assessment of the need to redesign your district, you should also determine what opportunities exist for your district. It might be easier to get people to buy in to a redesign effort when they feel good about where they and the district are going and when they know why they're being asked to make that journey. When there is both a statement of need and a description of opportunity, this becomes compelling motivation to improve a district. There is a push from the past conditions (the needs) and a pull toward the future (the opportunities). When being both pushed and pulled, so to speak, people find it easier to disengage from the "old" and move toward the "new."

The Community Engagement Conference described here is a wonderfully powerful tool for collecting data about needs and opportunities and for building commitment. Using the data from that conference you then conduct what strategic planners call a SWOT analysis. SWOT stands for *strengths*, *weaknesses*, *opportunities*, and *threats*. Analyze the data from the Community Engagement Conference and make a list of the SWOTs affecting your school district.

Assess Readiness for Change

Readiness for change occurs when several important conditions exist within your school district. The presence of these conditions, all at the same time, creates a "window" through which your change effort can pass successfully (e.g., Franklin, 1976; Myerseth, 1977). The presence of one or two of these conditions might be sufficient to start a change process, but it may not be powerful enough to sustain the changes. Beer (1980) describes these conditions: key managers must be dissatisfied, the top manager must be committed and lead, slack resources must exist and the resources must match the size and kind of change, and political support must exist.

Another way to assess the level of support for your redesign effort is to conduct a force-field analysis (Lewin, 1951). Force-field analysis is a classic technique that identifies and weighs the forces for and against a proposed change. There are a number of different ways you can depict the results of your analysis. One way to do this analysis is to assume that the "forces" are groups who are for or against the proposed change effort. The second way is to assume that the forces for and against change are "conditions" in your external environment or within your district. Either way, you numerically estimate the strength of each force (e.g., using a scale of 1 to 5, where 1 is very weak and 5 is very strong). What you're seeking is a situation where the forces in support of change outweigh the forces against it.

There are several ways to reduce opposing forces. Many of the techniques are discussed in the literature on dealing with resistance to change (e.g., Evans, 1996). One effective technique is to undertake educational activities whereby your staff, community members, and school board members participate in well-designed activities that help them learn about the need to redesign your district and the opportunities that successful redesign could present. These activities should not be proselytizing sessions or lectures. Instead, they should be designed to present rational *and* emotional reasons why the redesign needs to happen while also promoting group discussion.

Another critical point is that one of the ultimate goals of the prelaunch phase is to generate support through commitment rather than through control (Walton, 1985). Thus, it is imperative to begin modeling this shift in orientation by involving your faculty and staff in the design of the prelaunch activities. As Pasmore, Frank, and Rehm (1992) say:

> In high performance organizations we know that people are expected to be committed to the success of the organization. People move from being employees to being members; from hired hands to volunteers who can engage their heads, hearts, and hands; from simply meeting their

psychological needs for security to meeting social needs through involvement; from a focus on individual jobs to a focus on teamwork; from being uninformed to being informed about relevant business information; from value-less to accepting the values of participation and teamwork; from being powerless to having at least some power to influence local decision making; from no voice in the organization to at least a limited voice; from having a single skill to having multiple skills; from a time orientation of "putting in my eight" to one of concern for the longer term success of the enterprise. (p. 3)

Unlearn and Learn Mental Models

In chapter 3, you read about the significant influence of mental models on human performance. These models can either support or constrain your efforts to create and sustain systemic school improvement. Therefore, it is important to engage your faculty and staff in structured exercises to help them uncover, examine, and change, if necessary, the mental models affecting your district's desire to move forward toward a new future.

As you proceed through all of the preceding prelaunch activities, you will begin to develop a sense of whether your district is ready to engage in systemic improvement. If you sense that your district is ready to begin, then this is when you begin offering structured activities to help people, including yourself, unlearn and learn mental models. A useful tool for doing this was developed by Kegan and Lahey (2001), two developmental psychologists from Harvard University. Their technique, which uses small discussion groups, appears to be a very powerful tool for helping people explore the limitations of their personal mental models. You will also find some ideas for unlearning and learning mental models in chapter 3.

Surfacing, exploring, and unlearning mental models that might block your district's progress along its change-path, I think, is a very important activity to use at this point in the Step-Up-To-Excellence methodology. It is important because you want to have as many people as possible onboard as you get ready to navigate down your district's change-path toward its future. You do not want individuals and teams running off in their own direction toward their personal goals rather than toward the district's goals. Conducting several "unlearning and learning" sessions helps get everyone onboard the same boat.

Make a Launch/Don't Launch Decision

At some point near the end of the prelaunch phase, you and your colleagues will make a "launch/don't launch" decision. Step-Up-To-Excellence moves into step 1 if your decision is to launch the redesign effort.

STEP 1: REDESIGN THE ENTIRE SCHOOL DISTRICT

Redesigning a whole school system is complex work. Complex, however, does not mean impossible. It means there is a lot to do and a lot to consider. This section highlights the key activities and considerations needed to redesign your entire school district. These activities are based on the literature on organization redesign (e.g., Jacobs, 1994; Pasmore, 1988; Emery, 1993; Emery & Trist, 1973).

As you read this section, it will be tempting to feel overwhelmed with everything that has to be done. If you approach the redesign activities systematically (i.e., with an organized, logical plan), you can do this. You will also either appoint or hire someone to navigate systemic improvement on a daily basis. I call this someone a *Knowledge Work Coordinator*. This person will be responsible for the tactical leadership necessary to redesign your whole district. You will also have a network of district improvement teams that will be collaborating with you and the Knowledge Work Coordinator. You are not doing this alone!

The Redesign Activities

Charter and Train a Strategic Leadership Team

After the decision is made to launch systemic redesign, the very first thing you do is charter and train a Strategic Leadership Team (SLT) that will provide broad, strategic oversight for the redesign effort. The SLT is staffed with K–12[1] building administrators and teachers nominated by their colleagues (not appointed by the superintendent), the president of the teachers union, the president of the school board, and the superintendent and a couple of his or her immediate subordinates. A Knowledge Work Coordinator will also be a member of this team, and he or she will serve as a link pin between the SLT and the Cluster Improvement Teams that are set up later in step 1.

Some districts may decide to include students and parents on the SLT, but this is optional, since they will be involved in other ways during your redesign effort. Team size should be limited to a maximum of fifteen members. Beyond that number, group dynamics become unmanageable (refer back to chapter 2 where you saw a mathematical formula for determining the number of possible relationships in a group; a group with 7 members has 966 possible relationships!).

Appoint or Hire a Knowledge Work Coordinator

The literature on organization theory and design (e.g., Daft, 2001) suggests the need for a special "integrator" role during times of organization improvement. Within the context of Step-Up-To-Excellence, this integrator role is called a Knowledge Work Coordinator.

Teaching and learning is knowledge work, and school districts are knowledge-creating organizations. The focus of your district improvement effort is on improving the core work of your district (which is knowledge work), as well as your district's internal social architecture and its relationship with its external environment. The Knowledge Work Coordinator orchestrates this effort on a daily basis.

This role can either be filled by a current employee who has the knowledge, skills, and attitudes to understand the complexities of whole-system change, or you can hire a new person to fill this role. Either way, this person will need to have special competencies related to large-scale organization improvement and the interpersonal skills to bring people together and to keep them together as you collectively move toward your district's desired future. If you have a very large district, you may wish to select and train a cadre of Knowledge Work Coordinators—perhaps one for each cluster.

Conduct a District Engagement Conference

The SLT and the Knowledge Work Coordinator begin planning a special three-day event for teachers and staff in your district. I call this special event a District Engagement Conference. This conference is designed using the principles of a Search Conference articulated by Merrelyn Emery (Emery & Purser, 1996; Emery, 1993).

The purpose of this event is to engage your faculty and staff in collaborative activities to identify a desirable future for your district. Data from the Community Engagement Conference conducted during the prelaunch phase are fed into this conference.

There are four major outcomes of the District Engagement Conference. First, a new grand vision for your district is created. Second, criteria are established to guide the continuing redesign of your district. These criteria provide a framework that defines what will and will not be acceptable redesign ideas. In other words, these criteria put a fence around people's creativity; but the fence is broad enough to allow innovative ideas to emerge and be considered. Third, the vision and the redesign criteria combine to set a strategic direction for the district to navigate. Fourth, the conference will begin to help participants develop and reinforce feelings of trust, commitment, and collaboration.

Organize Clusters

Following the District Engagement Conference, you will have a new grand vision, a set of redesign criteria, and a strategic direction. You now use that information to organize your district into clusters of interconnected schools. If you already have clusters in your district, then you will review their organization to ensure that they are, in fact, representing your district's entire core work process. If your district uses a K–12 work process, then you should have K–12 clusters. If the core work process is K–8, then you should have K–8 clusters. However your district's work process is designed, that's the design you use to create your clusters.

The schools in each cluster should be those that are expected to collaborate to educate children, as in a feeder system. This interconnectedness is important because of the "upstream errors flow downstream" principle. You recall that this principle suggests that mistakes made early in a work process, if not caught, will create larger problems downstream. A cluster organized as a feeder system represents your entire core work process. Educators in those clusters will then be able to examine their entire "work stream" to identify and correct errors.

Even though the unit of change for creating and sustaining systemic school improvement is a cluster of interconnected schools, these clusters will produce whole-district improvement. Thus, the ultimate unit of change in the Step-Up-To-Excellence framework is the whole district.

Charter and Train Cluster Improvement Teams

Once you identify the clusters in your district, then the SLT and the Knowledge Work Coordinator invite each cluster to establish a special team that will lead improvement within each cluster. I call this team a Cluster Improvement Team (CIT).

The Strategic Leadership Team gives each CIT a formal charter. A *charter* is a set of "marching orders" that define performance goals, major tasks, and expected outcomes. Each CIT also receives training on principles of systemic improvement, collaboration, and creative thinking.

Conduct Cluster Engagement Conferences

At the beginning of step 1, you conducted a District Engagement Conference that resulted in a new vision for the future of your district, a set of redesign criteria, and a strategic direction for the district to move along. Now, that information is fed forward to each of the clusters and used by each Cluster Improvement Team and the faculty and staff in those clusters.

Cluster Engagement Conferences are designed and conducted in exactly the same way as the earlier District Engagement Conference. The focus of the Cluster Engagement Conferences, however, is on how each cluster can be redesigned to clearly support the district's grand vision, redesign criteria, and strategic direction. The primary outcome of this special three-day event is a vision statement for each cluster that is unambiguously aligned with the district's vision, redesign criteria, and strategic direction. It is okay if each cluster creates a different vision, as long as it clearly supports the district's grand vision and strategic direction and complies with the district's redesign criteria. A secondary outcome is the continuing development of a climate of trust, commitment, and collaboration.

Charter and Train Site Improvement Teams

Many school districts already have school improvement teams in place. A Site Improvement Team (SIT) is similar in structure and function to a school improvement team. The difference is that in the Step-Up-To-Excellence methodology, these teams are not chartered and trained until after each cluster conducts its Cluster Engagement Conference.

The Cluster Engagement Conference results in a vision statement for each cluster. This vision must support the district's vision and strategic direction and it must fit within the parameters defined by the district's redesign criteria. Each Cluster Improvement Team then charters and trains a Site Improvement Team for each school in its cluster. Each SIT receives training on principles of systemic redesign, communication skills, and creative thinking.

Conduct Redesign Workshops

Up to this point in step 1, you have created a framework for navigating whole-system improvement. This framework provides the foundation for creating innovative ideas to improve your entire school system. Now, people begin collaborating to invent creative ideas to improve your district's (1) core and supportive work processes, (2) internal social "architecture," and (3) relationship to its external environment.

The change navigation framework you created also increases the fluidity of your district's hierarchy and introduces entropy (this was discussed earlier in chapter 4). To increase the entropy and fluidity, you now engage your faculty and staff in what I call Redesign Workshops.

Redesign Workshops are designed using the principles of Participative Design articulated by Emery (Emery & Purser, 1996; Emery,

1993). These are also special three-day events that engage faculty and staff in a structured process of creative thinking to identify improvements in their clusters' core and supportive work processes, internal social architecture, and the clusters' relationships with their external environments (which include relationships with other clusters, with the central administration, and with their neighborhood communities).

Each Cluster Improvement Team organizes and conducts a Redesign Workshop for its respective cluster. The CIT invites teachers and building administrators from each Site Improvement Team in its cluster to participate in the workshop. Each SIT nominates a teacher and a building administrator from its team to attend the cluster's Redesign Workshop.

At the same time that the CITs are conducting their Redesign Workshops, the superintendent of schools is conducting a special Redesign Workshop for the central administration office staff. The purpose of this workshop is to invent ideas to transform the central administration office into a Central Service Center. One of the outcomes of this special Redesign Workshop is a vision statement for the new Central Service Center that views educators in the clusters and schools as customers to be served.

The district's grand vision, redesign criteria, and strategic direction and each cluster's vision statement put a mental "fence" around the Redesign Workshops. This fence creates a boundary within which people can exercise their creativity. In essence, what the fence communicates is that the innovative ideas for improvement that come out of the Redesign Workshops must be unambiguously aligned first with each cluster's vision and then, ultimately, with the district's grand vision and strategic direction. Innovation is encouraged, but it must have a fence around it.

Develop a Redesign Proposal

Each Redesign Workshop lasts three days. Over that period, participants create innovative ideas to redesign their clusters' work processes, internal social architecture, and environmental relationships. The central administration staff do the same thing for their office.

The major outcome of all the Redesign Workshops is a collection of wonderfully creative ideas for improving each cluster's core and supportive work processes, internal social architecture, and environmental relationships, and, thereby, improving schooling throughout your entire district. Each Cluster Improvement Team collects the ideas from their Redesign Workshops. The superintendent does the same thing for the ideas that come out of the special workshop for the central administration office staff. The Knowledge Work Coordinator organizes all of the ideas into a single redesign proposal. The redesign proposal is then submitted to the Strategic Leadership Team for review and approval.

The SLT's review and approval process focuses on making sure that the redesign ideas are (1) aligned with the district's grand vision, redesign criteria, and strategic direction; (2) aligned with any extant state and federal rules and regulations; (3) truly innovative; and (4) fundable.

The SLT may find ideas that do not meet the preceding criteria. If they do find some, they meet with the respective Cluster Improvement Team and Site Improvement Teams to discuss why they think the ideas do not meet the criteria. Unilateral decisions to discard ideas are unacceptable within the context of Step-Up-To-Excellence. In some cases, together, all the involved parties may decide to discard an idea. Or, they may change their minds and re-include it in a redesign proposal.

Find and Distribute Human, Financial, Technical, and Time Resources

After the District Engagement Conference conducted earlier, which resulted in a grand vision for the district, a set of redesign criteria, and a strategic direction, the Strategic Leadership Team starts estimating the kinds and amounts of resources it might need to move its district along the strategic direction toward the district's vision (some ideas about doing this are found in chapter 7). By the time the district's redesign proposal is put in the SLT's hands, team members should have a rough estimate of the resources they will need.

Given the specific redesign proposal and the approved redesign ideas, the SLT now begins the process of finding and allocating the needed resources (see chapter 7 for more advice about this process). A large chunk of the resources will be found by reallocating existing resources and dedicating these to implementing the new, desirable ideas. Another source of funds will need to be "external" monies from the state and federal governments and private foundations. This external money, although needed to jump-start a redesign process, should not be relied upon to sustain systemic improvement. Ultimately, the SLT creates a permanent line item in their district's operating budget to sustain whole-system change and makes the redesign process a part of the core operations of the district.

Once the resources are found and collected, then the SLT distributes the resources to each Cluster Improvement Team, which in turn continues disbursing the resources to the Site Improvement Teams. At this point, the various teams begin implementing their redesign proposals.

Implement the Redesign Proposal

It's one thing to have good intentions and wonderful ideas. It's quite another thing to turn those into reality. Good intentions (as in, "our hearts were in the right place" or "we meant well") are meaningless. If you hold a piece of paper with all your good intentions on it in one hand and a brick in the other, you know what you have—a brick and a piece of paper. You have to do something to turn your ideas and intentions into reality. Doing something requires implementation activities. Everyone has to produce results!

Implementation activities should be planned logically so that the changes you desire roll out in a natural, logical, and flowing sequence. A well-crafted implementation plan is needed. The Strategic Leadership Team, Cluster Improvement Teams, Site Improvement Teams, and the Knowledge Work Coordinator all have important roles to play during implementation.

For implementation purposes, each improvement team should be empowered to seize opportunities at the intersection of anticipatory planning and unexpected events (discussed in chapter 4) as long as these opportunities are in compliance with the district's grand vision, redesign criteria, and strategic direction.

Encourage Formation of Organizational Learning Networks

When you implement your redesign proposals, individual, team, school, cluster, and district performance levels will temporarily decline as everyone moves toward the edge of chaos (see chapter 4). Movement down the performance curve is unavoidable and necessary. At some point, that downward slide will bottom out and everyone will start to move back up the performance curve toward your district's grand vision.

Another tool that is part of the Step-Up-To-Excellence methodology, called Organizational Learning Networks, can be used to facilitate movement of individual and team learning down and up the performance curve. These are small "communities of practice" or study groups for people who share a common interest or common practice. These networks form, explore a topic, learn a new skill together, disband, and re-form with new members to explore different interests. Although these networks are not "ordered" to form, when they do form, they are expected to share their learning with others in their schools and clusters. These networks are absolutely essential for helping your school district create and diffuse organization-wide professional knowledge and skills.

Conduct On-Track Seminars

Another important tool that is part of the Step-Up-To-Excellence approach is the On-Track Seminar. There is an old saying that goes something like this, "There's a lot of slip between the cup and the lip." In other words, even the best implementation plan cannot guarantee perfection—there will be "slip." No matter how well you plan, there will be unexpected consequences, surprising new problems, and stunning unanticipated opportunities.

On-Track Seminars are specially designed discussion groups built on the principles of "evaluative inquiry" (Preskill & Torres, 1999). The purpose of these sessions, which are conducted for the various redesign teams and the Knowledge Work Coordinator, is to conduct what the literature calls "implementation feedback." The results of these periodic seminars are used to make needed course corrections for the redesign effort or to seize unexpected opportunities for improvement that might pop up during the implementation period.

Let's digress for a few minutes to take a look at Preskill and Torres's (1999) model for evaluative inquiry in learning organizations. I'm excited about this model because it complements the Step-Up-To-Excellence

methodology and dovetails nicely with a summative evaluation
methodology that is described later under step 5—Stufflebeam's (2000)
Context, Inputs, Processes, and Products (CIPP) model.

Evaluative Inquiry in Learning Organizations

School districts are learning organizations. Preskill and Torres
(1999) developed their evaluative inquiry model for learning organizations. Their model also reinforces a lot of what I've been talking about
so far regarding Step-Up-To-Excellence; for example, they say:

> Continuous organizational change is resulting in less organizational sta-
> bility and a redefinition of who we are and what we do in the workplace.
> The traditional structures that have given us a feeling of solidity and pre-
> dictability have vanished. This shift has placed a greater emphasis on the
> need for fluid processes that can change as an organization and its mem-
> bers' needs change. Instead of the traditional rational, linear, hierarchical
> approach to managing jobs, which focused on breaking down job tasks
> and isolating job functions, tomorrow's jobs will be built on establishing
> networks of relationships. (p. xvii)

According to Preskill and Torres, their evaluative inquiry model not
only helps you gather information for decision making and action, but
it also helps you question and debate the value of what you do in your
district. The principles of evaluative inquiry undergird the On-Track
Seminars that are used to provide you and your colleagues with implementation feedback.

*Evaluative Inquiry Has Three Phases
and Incorporates Four Key Learning Processes*

Evaluative inquiry moves you through three phases: phase 1—focusing the evaluative inquiry, phase 2—carrying out the inquiry, and
phase 3—applying learning. During each of the phases, people come
together to engage in a learning process that incorporates four key
learning processes: dialogue, reflection, asking questions, and identifying and clarifying values, beliefs, assumptions, and knowledge.

Preskill and Torres's evaluative inquiry model is 100 percent compatible with Step-Up-To-Excellence. It is also compatible with Stufflebeam's CIPP model for summative evaluation that is described later under step 5. This level of compatibility offers a great deal of benefit to your efforts to redesign your district. The linkage of the evaluative inquiry model to the CIPP model provides one powerful evaluation model to assess your district's overall performance. It not only produces evaluation data, but also produces individual, team, and system learning. Now, that's commanding!

How Long Will Step 1 Take?

The amount of time needed to complete all of the redesign activities up to implementation will be relatively short; for example, the various engagement conferences are only three days each. The amount of time needed to implement your redesign proposals, however, will vary depending on the size of your district, the complexity of the redesign ideas, the political environment in your community, and your district's relationship with its teachers union. On average, according to the literature on whole-system improvement, implementation periods may take eighteen to thirty-six months (Pasmore, 1988), with some as long as four years (Odden, 1998), and still others extending to five to seven years (Kotter, 1995).

STEPS 2 TO 4: CREATE STRATEGIC ALIGNMENT

During and following the implementation period, you and your colleagues will need to focus sharply on creating strategic alignment. Alignment activities are conducted during steps 2 through 4 of the Step-Up-To-Excellence framework.

Strategic alignment is a systematic way of linking people, priorities, practices, and processes with your districts' strategic goals and grand vision. More than anything else, strategic alignment is a structured, planned way of ensuring that everyone in your district is committed to making a contribution and adding value to the services you provide to children.

Schwan and Spady (1998, n.p.) talk about the importance of strategic alignment in their comments about why strategic change fails in school districts. They say:

> What's missing in most cases is a concrete, detailed vision statement that describes what the organization will look like when operating at its ideal best to accomplish its declared purpose, as well as a systematic process we call *strategic alignment*. Strategic alignment occurs when the structure, policies, procedures, and practices of the organization totally support the organization's vision.

They continue by observing:

> The alignment of the organizational vision with the actions of those who are part of the organization is a critical step in creating real and lasting change. Such alignment is best fostered and assured through the supervision process. Every supervisor in the district—from the superintendent to the teacher—is a linking pin. Every individual links one part of the organization to another. If the vision is lost by any pin, implementation of the vision becomes an option for anyone supervised by that pin, and in turn for anyone who reports to that pin's supervisees.

Getting All the Horses to Pull the Wagon in the Same Direction

Creating strategic alignment is like getting a team of horses to pull a wagon in the same direction. You can't have each horse trying to pull the wagon in a different direction. In much the same way, change-leaders in school districts cannot have teams, schools, clusters, and individuals all doing their "own thing" with total disregard for their district's strategic goals and grand vision. This is not exactly an effective way to manage a district.

Step 1: Get the Horses out of the Barn

Before you hitch all the horses to a wagon, you have to bring them out of the barn. In the same way, before educators can step up to excellence they have to redesign their district to move toward higher levels of performance. Once a school district is redesigned as described earlier, then educators align the work of individuals with the goals of their teams, the work of teams with the goals of their schools, the work of schools with the goals of their clusters, and the work of clusters with the goals of the district. The alignment process starts at the level of the district and then works inward to the level of teams and individuals. Let me tell you a little bit about each of the steps in the alignment process.

Step 2: Align the Performance of Clusters

Remember, you not only want to align each cluster's work with the grand vision and strategic direction of your district, you also want to make sure that each cluster's newly designed internal social architecture is motivating and satisfying; that each cluster's core work processes (teaching and learning) and supportive work processes (administration, supervision, secretarial, pupil personnel services, cafeteria, busing, and so on) are working as desired; and that each cluster has positive relationships with its external environment. You also want to make sure that policies, procedures, rules, and so forth that may interfere with individual and team performance are removed or changed.

Step 3: Align Performance of Individual Schools

Step-Up-To-Excellence recognizes that school-based management is a necessary element of systemic school improvement; however, by itself, it is insufficient to produce systemic improvement. Instead, the focus of school improvement needs to be "scaled-up" to improve entire school systems. Rhodes (1997) also supports this view when he says, "The scope and nature of the local school system makes it the optimal unit in which can be embedded the needed infrastructures to sustain that process. The process of systemic change cannot end there, but it is the only realistic place that it can start" (p. 33).

Just as each ship in a naval fleet sailing out of port goes under its own power with its captain and its crew, each school in a cluster must do the daily work of schooling. This work is not possible in any other way. It is in the classrooms in these schools that teachers help children learn. But each school should not "sail" alone with total disregard for the goals of its cluster, the work of its sister schools, or for the strategic vision of the entire district. The teaching and learning inside each classroom of each school must be linked clearly and powerfully to the goals of the clusters, and with the district's vision and strategic direction. The fleet must sail together as one.

Step 4: Align Performance of Teams and Individuals

By completing steps 2 and 3, you are applying the "outside-in thinking" technique.[2] This ensures that the conditions for effective team and individual performance are in place and functioning well. Now, you take a look at how teams and individuals are performing in your newly redesigned school district. Please remember that I am not just talking about teachers here—"teams and individuals" include education specialists, administrators, supervisors, cafeteria workers, bus drivers, janitors—everyone in the district.

The logic behind alignment activities (i.e., the reason for moving sequentially from step 2 through step 4) is that if you want your district to achieve higher levels of performance, then you must ensure that conditions to support effective performance are in place and functioning at each level. And if you want to sustain systemic improvement, you want to make sure these conditions stay in place. If the conditions for success are not in place at the district and cluster levels, it is unreasonable to expect improvement in individual and team performance. Further, roadblocks and obstacles to success (e.g., obstructionist policies, faulty procedures, and so on) must also be removed starting at the level of the district and moving inward toward the performance of individuals. Removing obstacles in this manner is called "outside-in" change management (Beckhard, 1983). Here's how it works within the Step-Up-To-Excellence framework:

1. Change-leaders first ensure that the district-level vision and strategic direction are in place as expected.

2. Then, they examine district-level policies, procedures, expectations, and the like to ensure that these things will help people succeed in improving their clusters, schools, and teams.
3. Then, they ensure that each cluster has its conditions for success in place and functioning and that these conditions are aligned with the district's vision and strategic goals.
4. Then, they look at individual schools to determine if they have their required conditions for success in place and whether their performance is aligned with the goals of their clusters.
5. Then, they look at the various teams to make sure that they have their required conditions for success in place and functioning and to see whether their performance is aligned with the goals of their schools.
6. At each point—moving from the outside in, necessary corrective actions are taken to ensure that the desired conditions for success are in place and functioning as expected.
7. Then, *and only then*, the performance of individuals is evaluated and aligned.

The reason for this outside-in alignment sequence is that by doing it this way, you create a work environment within which the performance of teams and individuals is supported by the conditions and resources they need to succeed. Then, if teams and individuals are not performing as expected, they have no excuse for less-than-expected performance levels and they can be held accountable for not performing as expected.

Creating strategic alignment, as described here, accomplishes three things: first, it ensures that everyone is working toward the same district-level broad strategic goals and grand vision. Second, it weaves a web of accountabilities that makes everyone who touches the educational experience of a child accountable for his or her part in shaping that experience. And, third, it removes (by using the outside-in tactic) bureaucratic hassles, dysfunctional policies, and obstructionist procedures that limit individual and team effectiveness. Deming (1986), among others, says that it is these hassles, policies, and procedures that cause at least 80 percent of the performance problems that are usually blamed on individuals and teams.

Using Implementation Feedback to
Create and Sustain Strategic Alignment

Implementation feedback is where you take a good look at how the improvements you are making in clusters, schools, and teams are being implemented. Feedback is also collected about the effectiveness of new policies, procedures, and working relationships. Then, everyone is expected to take the necessary actions either to reinforce what they're doing right or to correct what they're doing wrong. Individuals and teams are then held accountable for taking these actions and producing results (remember, good intentions are not good enough—people have to produce results).

Within the Step-Up-To-Excellence framework, implementation feedback is provided in the On-Track Seminars that are conducted periodically. These seminars produce results that are used to keep your redesign effort on track and to help create strategic alignment.

Cummings and Worley (2001) discuss the importance of implementation feedback for organization development purposes. They say:

> Most OD [organization development] interventions require significant changes in people's behaviors and ways of thinking about organizations. . . . Implementing such changes requires considerable learning and experimentation as employees and managers discover how to translate these general prescriptions [the required changes] into specific behaviors and procedures. This learning process involves much trial and error and needs to be guided by information about whether behaviors and procedures are being changed as intended. (p. 175)

Since Step-Up-To-Excellence is an organization development intervention, and since creating strategic alignment is an important goal for this intervention, implementation feedback becomes a primary tool.

Another important reason for using implementation feedback is related to one of the core principles of sociotechnical systems design; that is, *minimal specificity*. This principle advises change-leaders to define minimally the specifics of desired improvements. In applying this principle, then, individuals and teams have the freedom and authority to add specificity as needed. This freedom to add specificity, however, creates a problem for a school district because as specificity is added, unintentional and intentional deviations from what was expected occur. Thus, to achieve strategic alignment, change-leaders have to bring everything back into alignment. Implementation feedback helps do this.

Weave and Strum a Web of Accountabilities

Another very important outcome of Step-Up-To-Excellence is that when you redesign your district's internal social architecture in accordance with the principles discussed so far, what you are creating is a "web of accountabilities" (Merrifield, 1998). It's ineffective and unfair to hold classroom teachers solely responsible for student success. Instead, you need to adopt the mental model of a web of accountabilities. You weave this web by tying together the various redesign teams that you created with the Organizational Learning Networks that are used to promote organizational learning. The link pin that holds this web together is the Knowledge Work Coordinator. This networked "web" focuses on helping your district achieve its grand vision and strategic direction.

The performance of individual teachers, administrators, and support staff must also be woven into this web. Once woven, the web is strummed so all in it feel the vibration of accountability pulsing through their individual and collective consciousness. Everyone in the web—from school board members to the night-shift janitor—must clearly realize the consequences of nonperformance, and each one must also clearly realize the rewards associated with success and high performance.

Benefits of Creating and Maintaining Strategic Alignment

By creating and maintaining strategic alignment, your school district may experience the following benefits:

1. Greater success as people, priorities, practices, and processes are aligned with a district's strategic goals and vision
2. Improved service to students and their parents because of improved work processes, a more satisfying and motivating work environment for employees, and stronger relationships with external stakeholders

3. Increased effectiveness for individuals and teams because they will be spending less time correcting problems they didn't cause; they will be engaged in effective communication; and they will become an integral strand in a powerful web of accountabilities

4. Greater job satisfaction and motivation because of a redesigned social architecture that increases the level of authentic participation, ownership of improvement plans and goals, shared responsibility for student outcomes, and the use of a retooled reward system

Final Comments About Strategic Alignment

Creating strategic alignment is a primary way to make sure everyone in a school district is moving in the same general direction during times of improvement. School districts should have a vision and a strategic direction, and every blessed soul, program, policy, and procedure must be aligned with that vision and direction. Although each school and classroom is where important improvements happen, educators in all those schools and classrooms cannot each be "doing their own thing." Surely, a teacher in a school may use a special teaching technique that no one else in the district uses. Certainly, a building principal should have the authority to manage his or her school and its resources. But no school, no teacher, no staff person, and no administrator should be permitted to perform in ways that diverge significantly from his or her district's strategic direction. All the horses must pull the wagon in the same direction.

One of the key tasks for sustaining alignment is the ongoing evaluation of processes, procedures, and performance after completing steps 1 to 4, as described previously. After you redesign your school system and align the work of individuals, teams, schools, and clusters with the strategic direction and grand vision of your district, it is time to assess the overall performance of your district to see if everything is going pretty much as desired. Within the Step-Up-To-Excellence framework, this summative evaluation is done during step 5, which is described in the next section.

STEP 5: EVALUATE WHOLE-SYSTEM PERFORMANCE

Up to this point in the Step-Up-To-Excellence approach, you completed step 1 by redesigning your entire school system and took steps 2 to 4 to align the work of individuals with the goals of their teams, the work of teams with the goals of their schools, the work of schools with the goals of their clusters, and the work of clusters with the broad strategic goals and vision of your entire district. Now that you've got everything redesigned, aligned, and performing, in step 5, you're going to evaluate your entire school district's effectiveness in meeting its goals and achieving its vision.

Effectiveness Means Achieving Goals

Goals state where you want to go. They set a direction for a future state of being. Organizational effectiveness is the degree to which your faculty and staff achieve the goals set for your district. Organizational effectiveness is a broad concept that takes into consideration not only the whole organization, but also its component units. Thus, effectiveness measures the degree to which each part of your district is achieving goals.

There are two basic approaches to measuring an organization's effectiveness: contingency approaches and balanced effectiveness approaches (Daft, 2001, p. 64). Let's briefly take a look at each approach.

Contingency Approaches to Measuring Effectiveness

Contingency approaches to evaluation look at various parts of your school district; for example, its clusters, schools, teams, bus transportation, cafeteria services, and athletics. These methods assume that your district functions as an open system. As an open system, your district needs resources (energy) from its environment to do its work. These resources enter your district and are transformed into a valuable service—providing children with an education. Educated children (the product of your work) return to your district's external environment when they graduate.

Contingency approaches to evaluating effectiveness use one of three methods to judge an organization's effectiveness:

* The goal approach (which evaluates organizational outcomes)
* The resource-based approach (which evaluates the quantity and quality of incoming resources)
* The internal process approach (which evaluates how resources are used)

Goal Approach

This approach examines your district, cluster, school, and teams' performance goals and then evaluates how well each unit achieves those goals. The important goals to examine using this approach are called operative goals, rather than official goals. *Operative goals* describe specific measurable outcomes and are often focused on short-term achievement (Daft, 2001, p. 53). Operative goals usually focus on the primary tasks an organization must perform (Stoelwinder & Charns, 1984). *Official goals*, on the other hand, are the formally stated descriptions of what an organization hopes to achieve. These are often referred to as an organization's mission and vision. Official goals tend to be more abstract and difficult to measure. Efforts to measure goal achievement are more productive when you use operative goals rather than official goals (Hall & Clark, 1980). The goal approach is very useful for organizations with performance output goals that can be easily measured; for example, measuring student performance on mandated achievement tests or the number of students graduating and going on to college. However, identifying operative goals and measuring organizational performance against those goals is not always easy because of two thorny problems: multiple goals and subjective indicators of goal achievement.

One of the challenges confronting the goal approach is that most organizations, including school districts, have multiple goals. When an organization has multiple goals, effectiveness cannot be determined on the basis of a single indicator. High achievement on one goal may result in lower achievement on another. Furthermore, each unit in an organization has goals, too. So, the full assessment of your district's effectiveness in achieving goals must take these multiple goals into consideration. To manage the evaluation of multiple goals, many organizations use a balanced approach to measurement (described later); for instance, some businesses set goals for financial performance, customer service and satisfaction, internal processes, and innovation and learning (Fritsch, 1997).

Another issue constraining the effectiveness of the goal approach to evaluation is the unavoidable use of subjective indicators of goal achievement. Someone has to decide which goals are important and which ones to measure. Whenever a person or team makes these kinds of decisions, subjectivity comes into play. In fact, when it comes to evaluation I believe there is no such thing as objectivity. Even so-called neutral third-party evaluators apply some degree of their personal subjectivity to make evaluative decisions. Evaluation is, after all, a process of attaching (*e-*) value (*valuation*) to something or someone. Since there is no such thing as objectivity, the challenge for evaluators then becomes one of managing their subjectivity. Nevertheless, even deeply subjective evaluation data can be useful. For example, if you interview students, teachers, parents, and community stakeholders about their attitudes toward your district, you will not have "hard" numerical data to analyze, but you will sure learn a lot about how your district is perceived by those people.

Internal Process Approach

This second contingency approach to measuring effectiveness examines your district's internal efficiency (not effectiveness). *Efficiency* is a measure of how many of your precious resources you use to achieve your goals. If you use an inordinate number of resources to achieve a few of many goals, your district is inefficient. If you use your resources wisely and with little waste, then your district can be judged efficient.

An efficient organization also has a smoothly functioning internal work process supported by a strong internal social architecture. You will recall that your district's internal social architecture supports people doing their work. Experts such as Chris Argyris (1964), Warren Bennis (1966), Rensis Likert (1967), and Richard Beckhard (1969) (I know these references are old, but they are classics) all emphasize the importance of a healthy and strong internal social architecture. Also, results from a study of almost two hundred high schools showed that both human resources and employee-oriented processes (key elements of a school district's social architecture) were important in explaining the effectiveness of those schools (Ostroff & Schmitt, 1993).

The internal process approach to evaluation also has shortcomings. It doesn't consider how effectively your district achieves its goals and it doesn't evaluate your district's relationship with its environment.

Resource-Based Approach

This third contingency approach to evaluating your district's effectiveness assumes that organizations must be successful in obtaining the resources they need to be effective. From this perspective, organizational effectiveness is defined as "the ability of the organization . . . to obtain scarce and valued resources and successfully integrate and manage them" (Russo & Fouts, 1997).

This approach is useful when other indicators of effectiveness are difficult to determine. In many not-for-profit organizations, including school systems, it is challenging to measure output goals or internal efficiency. Thus, taking a look at how successful these organizations are in obtaining valuable and scarce resources could be a good indicator of their effectiveness. For example, if a school system is succeeding in getting all the money it needs for its operating budget from its local and state governments, and if new teachers are standing in line to work in that district, then this level of "available resources" might indicate the relative success of that district.

This approach has shortcomings, too, one of which is that it barely considers the needs of your district's customers. The ability to secure resources is good, but it is only good if your district is using those resources to provide your customers with what they value.

Balanced Approaches to Measuring Effectiveness

You will recall that Step-Up-To-Excellence helps you redesign your district to create simultaneous improvements in three key areas: your district's core and supportive work processes, its internal social architecture, and its relationship with the outside world. The *goal attainment approach* to evaluating effectiveness is coupled to your work processes; the *internal process method* is linked to internal social architecture; and the *resource approach* is connected to improving environmental relationships. But with Step-Up-To-Excellence you want to evaluate your district's effectiveness in all three areas, not just one. So, what do you do? How do you evaluate all three areas? The answer is found in the literature on organization improvement—it's called a balanced effectiveness method.

Each of the contingency approaches to measure effectiveness described previously has something to offer, but each one gives you only partial answers to your evaluation questions. So, what you need to use is a balanced approach that measures your district's overall effectiveness and one that acknowledges that your district does many things and has multiple outcomes. These balanced approaches combine several indicators of effectiveness into a single evaluation framework. The two main methods that are part of the balanced approach to measuring effectiveness are the stakeholder approach and the competing values approach. Each one is briefly described in the following sections.

The Stakeholder Approach

During the prelaunch phase of Step-Up-To-Excellence, you engage your district's external stakeholders in a large group process called a Community Engagement Conference. The purpose of this conference is to determine the expectations, needs, dreams, and aspirations of your stakeholders in relation to the future of your school district. In step 1, you engage some of your internal stakeholders (your teachers, administrators, support staff) in another large group process called a District Engagement Conference. The purpose of this second conference is to develop collaboratively a new mission, vision, and strategic goals for your entire district.

You can use the stakeholder approach to evaluation during either or both of the preceding large group sessions to assess the level of satisfaction with your district of both external and internal stakeholders. Their measured level of satisfaction is an indicator of organizational effectiveness (Tsui, 1990); that is, the higher the satisfaction level, the greater the perceived effectiveness.

The usefulness of the stakeholder approach is that it views effectiveness broadly and assesses factors in your district's external environment, as well as within your district. This approach is popular because it views effectiveness as a complex, multidimensional concept that has no single measure (Cameron, 1984). Considering the social and political environment that school districts now find themselves within, along with the high-stakes pressure to increase student achievement, this approach seems to be one that could be useful.

The Competing Values Approach

This approach comprises four models for judging organizational effectiveness: the human relations model, the open systems model, the internal process model, and the rational goal model. I talk briefly about each one in a moment, but first let me give you some background information about this approach.

Research on setting performance goals and indicators in organizations indicates that practitioners' views of organizational effectiveness often conflict with researchers' views (Quinn & Rohrbaugh, 1983). To reconcile this conflict, Quinn and Rohrbaugh developed the competing values approach to measure organization effectiveness. Their approach combines the conflicting views of both practitioners and researchers.

To create their approach, Quinn and Rohrbaugh used a panel of experts in organizational effectiveness to identify and classify effectiveness indicators developed by practitioners and another list developed by researchers. Indicators on both lists were rated for similarity, and the final analysis yielded a list of effectiveness indicators representing competing values in organizations (practitioners versus researchers).

Quinn and Rohrbaugh's study indicates that any given manager will have values relating to his or her organization's external environment or values relating to the people who work in his or her organization. This external-internal dimension is called "focus."

A second dimension the researchers identify is "structure." Managers either value stability or they value flexibility. *Stability* refers to a managerial value for efficiency and top-down control. *Flexibility*, on the other hand, represents a managerial value for learning and change.

If you think of the structure dimension (stability-flexibility) as a vertical line that intersects with a horizontal line representing the focus dimension (internal-external), what you get is a grid with four quadrants. Inside each quadrant of the grid is an effectiveness model that complements
the dominant management values for that quadrant. Here's a brief description of the effectiveness model in each quadrant. Combined, these
models are the ones that comprise the competing values approach.

1. *Human relations model of effectiveness* (an internal focus with
   value for flexibility). With this model, managers focus on developing their district's human resources. Employees are given opportunities for autonomy and development. Managers work toward goals of cohesion, morale, and training opportunities.
   Districts adopting this model are more concerned with their employees than with the environment.
2. *Internal process model of effectiveness* (an internal focus with
   value for stability). With this model, managers seek a stable organizational setting that maintains itself in an orderly fashion. Organizations that are comfortably situated in their environments
   with no pressure to change adopt a model like this. Managers using this model work toward goals for efficient communication,
   information management, and decision making.
3. *Open systems model of effectiveness* (an external focus with value
   for flexibility). Using this model, managers' primary goals are for
   growth and resource acquisition. These primary goals are
   achieved through subgoals for flexibility, readiness, and a positive evaluation by external stakeholders. The dominant value in
   this model is for establishing a good relationship with the organization's environment.
4. *Rational goal model* (an external focus with value for stability and
   control). The primary effectiveness goals in this model are for productivity, efficiency, and profit. The focus is on achieving output
   goals in a controlled, rational manner. Subgoals focus on internal
   planning and goal setting, which are rational management tools.

The preceding models represent different perspectives on how to
evaluate the overall effectiveness of your district. All of these models

are examples of summative evaluation—evaluation that sums up how your district and its subparts are achieving their respective goals for effectiveness.

Moving from Formative Evaluation to Summative Evaluation

To create strategic alignment you used a formative evaluation method called implementation feedback (which I talked about earlier). Implementation feedback is provided by using On-Track Seminars. The purpose of the On-Track Seminars is to help you and your colleagues create and sustain strategic alignment. In step 5, however, you need to shift your evaluation strategy from the formative mode to the summative mode. So, let's talk about principles of summative evaluation.

There is a lot of literature on summative evaluation, so I am not going to go into great detail about it. I am also not an evaluation expert and I don't want you to think I am. However, people like Scriven (2001) and Stufflebeam (2000) are evaluation experts, and you can find a lot of helpful guidance about summative evaluation from people like them. In the meantime, let's take a quick look at summative evaluation and how you can use it to evaluate the overall effectiveness of your district, clusters, schools, and teams.

An Approach to Summative Evaluation

The summative evaluation model called Context, Inputs, Processes, Product (CIPP) Evaluation (Stufflebeam, 2000) is one I like because it is based on principles of systems theory, and Step-Up-To-Excellence is based on systems theory. This model also combines principles of formative and summative evaluation, so it complements the On-Track Seminars that are used during steps 2 through 4.

Context, Inputs, Processes, and Products (CIPP) Evaluation

All organizations exist within a *context*. Units within an organization exist within a context, too. All organizations and their units need *inputs* (resources to do their work). They all use *processes* to convert the inputs into meaningful and useful *products* (which is used in the most general sense to include services and other outcomes). So, when you want to evaluate organizational and unit effectiveness you evaluate context, inputs, processes, and products. This is the basic focus of the CIPP model, and it is a systems view of organizational and unit performance.

Stufflebeam's (2000) CIPP evaluation model offers a systematic way to collect, analyze, and report data about the effectiveness of your district, clusters, schools, and teams. The CIPP model is not a new approach to evaluation, but it is still very useful within the Step-Up-To-Excellence framework.

While space constraints do not permit a full explanation of how to use the CIPP model, a brief discussion of how it can provide useful performance data about your district's effectiveness follows.

CIPP is actually composed of four related evaluations: an evaluation of (1) context, (2) inputs, (3) processes, and (4) products. Data from these four evaluations provide you with answers to several basic questions:

1. *What should you do?* Answers to this question will guide your efforts to redesign and improve the performance level of your school district, clusters, schools, and teams. You conduct this sort of evaluation by collecting and analyzing needs and opportunities data to determine goals, priorities, and objectives. Three powerful tools used with Step-Up-To-Excellence are exquisitely suited to answering this question. These tools are the Community Engagement Conference conducted during the prelaunch phase, the District Engagement Conference conducted early in step 1, and the Cluster Engagement Conference conducted later in step 1. These tools will also help you identify the needs and expectations of both your external and internal stakeholders. These needs and expectations comprise the context within which your district must perform. This context will shape your district's new grand vision, redesign criteria, and strategic direction. Context is the *C* in the CIPP model.

2. *How should you do it?* When you get answers to this question you also get operative goals and objectives. In the Step-Up-To-Excellence methodology, the primary tools used to answer this question

are the Cluster Engagement Conference and the Redesign Work-shop, both of which engage your faculty and staff in the creation of innovative improvements in your district's (a) core and supportive work processes, (b) internal social architecture, and (c) relation-ships with its external environment. Seeking answers to this question focuses on identifying *inputs* to your district's improvement efforts. Inputs are the *I* in CIPP.

3. *Are you doing it as planned?* The answers you get to this question will tell you (a) if you are implementing all of the wonderful ideas to improve your district that were created in the Redesign Work-shops, and (b) if everything is aligned with the district's grand vi-sion and strategic direction. Here, you are assessing the processes you used to create improvements. Answers to this question are found by using the On-Track Seminars during steps 2 through 4. Processes are the first *P* in the CIPP model.

4. *Did the improvements work?* By measuring actual outcomes and comparing them to desired outcomes, you will decide if your im-provement efforts were effective. This is the essence of summative evaluation. When you answer this question you are evaluating the products (i.e., the outcomes) of your district's improvement effort. Products are the second *P* in the CIPP model.

SUSTAINING IMPROVEMENTS BY RECYCLING TO STEP 1

You recall that the Step-Up-To-Excellence methodology has five steps and is preceded by a prelaunch preparation phase and followed by a recycle phase. The recycle phase is critically important to your efforts to (1) develop your district's capacity to improve and (2) sus-tain improvements.

Sustaining whole-district improvements requires the enforcement of strategic alignment. It is very easy for people in school systems to re-vert to their past and comfortable ways of doing things. A concerted ef-fort to maintain the alignment of strategy, goals, processes, policies, and rewards is needed to sustain improvements.

Sustaining improvements, however, requires more than maintaining strategic alignment. Your whole-district improvement process must be built into the core operations of your district and funded as a core function (there's more about this in chapter 7). Further, whole-district improvement must be practiced repeatedly for the life of your school system. Please remember that it is the nature of systemic improvement that school districts must move forward from where they stand. They cannot leap to high performance; they must evolve to it, although this evolutionary, first down, then up journey will be punctuated by breathtaking change. It is a school district's lifelong voyage of organization learning and continuous self-renewal that will raise its level of performance. Nothing less will do it!

The Power of Organization Culture

By building your whole-district improvement process into your district's core operations you will be embedding it in your organization's culture. Organizational culture is one of the most powerful organizational forces that will either sustain or destroy all of your wonderful improvements. Organizational culture is a key element of your district's internal social architecture, and you must increase its malleability during step 1 so that it better supports the whole-district redesign process and the subsequent outcomes of that process. Because it is such a powerful force, let's talk about organization culture for a while.

Culture Includes Shared Values, Symbols, Stories, Heroes, Rites, and Rituals

From an anthropological perspective, organization culture creates meaning by ordering relationships, beliefs, and patterns of behavior (Sahlins, 1976). A culture captures and holds shared values, assumptions, beliefs, expectations, and attitudes found within a community or organization. An organization's culture is represented symbolically by "the actions, practices, stories (monologues and dialogues), and artifacts that characterize" the organization (Eisenberg & Goodall, 1997, p. 125).

Each district's culture is unique because it is shaped by the shared goals, values, assumptions, and environmental pressures specific to that district. Eisenberg and Goodall (1997) say, "organizational culture is the result of the cumulative learning of a group of people and that learning manifests itself as culture at a number of levels" (p. 132).

Elements of Organization Culture
Needed to Sustain School District Improvement

Through the Step-Up-To-Excellence approach, three important cultural elements are designed into your school district's internal social architecture. Combined, these elements can help sustain systemic school improvement. They are discussed in the following sections.

Element 1: Trust, Commitment, and Collaboration

Step-Up-To-Excellence creates a highly collaborative and empowered faculty and staff. Everyone in your school system becomes an active participant in the redesign of your district. An essential cultural change that occurs during step 1 is the transformation of decision making from a top-down and bureaucratic approach to a shared decision-making process that allows people to make decisions they are qualified to make and which affect them directly. For school districts engaging in systemic school improvement for the first time, this cultural shift will be more difficult because it requires a significant loosening of the hierarchical and bureaucratic controls, systems, and procedures found in many school districts.

Although leadership and management roles will change in important and exciting ways during the Step-Up-To-Excellence process, these roles *are not* eliminated. Leaders, instead, take on new and exciting roles and responsibilities that liberate them from a need to control events and resources and allow them to focus on becoming cultural leaders whereby they advocate for and facilitate the development of high-performance teaching and learning.

Element 2: A Team Structure

The second cultural element created during the redesign process is a team-based organization design. Teams drive whole-district change. The Strategic Leadership Team initiates and delineates the strategy for the overall improvement process. Cluster Improvement Teams define principles, goals, and directions for making improvements within their respective boundaries and they ensure that the improvements are aligned with the overall mission and vision of the entire school system. Site Improvement Teams do the same thing for their buildings. Organizational Learning Networks take on the critical role of engaging faculty and staff in personal and organizational learning activities.

Element 3: A Belief in Continuous Learning and Improvement

The third cultural element created through Step-Up-To-Excellence is the value for continuous learning and improvement. This value provides a solid foundation for helping your school system become an organization of learners characterized by risk taking, experimentation, question asking, solution finding, data gathering, action research, and the application of continuous improvement techniques. All faculty and staff also need extensive and ongoing training and education to develop new knowledge and skills needed to succeed within a newly redesigned school system. But it is not "anything goes" training and education. What people learn must be clearly and powerfully aligned with your district's grand vision and strategic direction.

RESPONDING TO RESISTANCE TO CHANGE

I would be remiss if I didn't talk about a common and predictable human response to change: resistance. Some people think resistance is in the mind of the people who want to do the changing when they perceive that things are not going their way. They call what they perceive resistance. Others think resistance is a real phenomenon expressed by people who do not want to embrace change for whatever reason. In fact, I think resistance is both of those things. Considering the magnitude of the redesign effort you will undertake when using Step-Up-To-Excellence, you need to anticipate resistance. Here are a few principles to guide your thinking about responding to resistance to change.

Principle 1: Create Feelings of Ownership and Support for Innovation

People often accept or even welcome change if they are involved in designing the course of change (e.g., McGregor, 1960; Emery & Trist, 1973; Weisbord, 1987). When changes are imposed or ordered, resistance and opposition increase, especially when mandated changes focus on the work people do and the way they do it.

The District Engagement Conference, Cluster Engagement Conference, Redesign Workshops, Organizational Learning Networks, and On-Track Seminar tools that are part of Step-Up-To-Excellence provide powerful ways to involve your internal and external stakeholders in your district-improvement process. These tools are used by the people actually doing the work. These tools move your district toward increased trust, commitment, and collaboration and move your school system away from imposed hierarchical decision making.

Principle 2: People Need Both Structure and Freedom

In his landmark studies of group behavior, Bion (1961) describes the tendency of work groups to slip out of "work mode" into predictable and nonproductive work-avoidance behaviors. Slippage occurs when there is not a good balance between structure (rules, expectations, and so on) and professional autonomy. In situations like those described by Bion, groups tend to move into predictably nonproductive behavior. They may look for a leader to "save" them (which is a reflection of psychological dependence), try to pair up and distract the group from the work at hand, get into arguments about who is right or wrong on a given issue, or become distant from one another or from the work at hand. To avoid this kind of slippage and to help your colleagues perform effectively you need to provide people with sufficient structure and with adequate elbow room to exercise their professional judgment. And then you need to hold them accountable for producing desirable results.

Principle 3: Change Happens to
Organizations—Transitions Happen to People

In *Managing Transitions*, Bridges (1991) distinguishes between organization change and human transitions. He says our ability to make dramatic transitions in the way we do our work is much slower than most change-leaders expect. People move through periods of guilt, resentment, resistance, anxiety, self-absorption, hopelessness, apathy, and other emotions when they are required to dramatically change their behavior. These are normal emotions during transitions. These feelings need to be acknowledged and discussed, rather than ignored or criticized. These emotions are greatest for people most affected by change and for those who are least able to participate in making decisions about the changes.

Principle 4: People Need to Hear
About Change Many Times Before Accepting It

Bridges (1991) and Golarz and Golarz (1995) emphasize the number of times people must hear about change before they actually believe it is going to happen and that they have to change. The length of time before accepting the inevitability of change varies depending on, for example, a person's position in the hierarchy or whether a person perceives the proposed change as beneficial or threatening. You must repeat both the need for change and the direction of change many times before everyone gets the message.

Principle 5: Motivation to Move
Forward Must Be Greater Than the Need to Stay Put

Sometimes people and systems don't change quickly. There are different reasons for this "slowness"; for example, inadequate resources, inadequate leadership, or lack of motivation. Principle 5 is about lack of motivation to change.

The lack of motivation to change results in human behavior often referred to as resistance. There are three main reasons for resistance. The first reason is captured in a quote from Merrelyn Emery (1993), "People don't resist change, they resist being changed." The second main reason for resistance is related to human psychology and the need for stability or equilibrium in our lives. The third reason is related to an organization's reluctance to change.

People Resist Being Changed

Most people are open to change. Some of us actively seek it. However, for change to be embraced, the changes have to be on our own terms and must fit our mental models and psychological needs. When imposed change conflicts with our terms, mental models, and personality preferences, we resist changing. This is a normal and expected reaction. When using Step-Up-To-Excellence, you need to apply principles of trust, commitment, and collaboration so people don't feel like change is being imposed on them.

Human Psychology Creates Resistance to Change

Some people assert that people normally embrace change. For example, Clemson and Clemson (1998) comment:

> The idea that human beings naturally resist change is deeply embedded in our thinking about change. Our language . . . , assumptions and mental models about change all seem to imply that there is something in our nature that leads us to resist change. . . . Humans do not normally resist change, but many people do resist the efforts of other people to impose change on them. (p. 1)

I do not fully accept the premise that people normally embrace change. Resistance also comes from our natural tendency as human beings to desire stability in our lives. How would you feel if you had to change your daily routines, patterns of relationships, and work habits frequently? I'm not talking about having these changes imposed on you. I'm talking about you being in a situation that you helped create that required frequent change. Although you might at first be excited by all these changes, you probably would grow resistant to the rate and quantity of change. You would probably begin to resist frequent changes because of your psychological need for stability in your life—some level of predictability, some level of personal control.

Personal anxiety about change, even when you seek it, can also cause resistance, or reluctance to move forward. Cummings and Worley (1997) say:

> At a personal level, change can arouse considerable anxiety about letting go of the known and moving to an uncertain future. Individuals may be unsure whether their existing skills and contributions will be valued in the future. They may have significant questions about whether they can learn to function effectively and to achieve benefits in the new situation. (p. 156)

Organizations Create Resistance

Sometimes an organization can stimulate resistance to change. At the organization level, resistance to change comes from three sources (Tichy, 1993, pp. 114–118). *Technical resistance* comes from the habit of following common procedures and the fact that a lot of resources were invested in developing these procedures, and, therefore, people don't want to give these up. *Political resistance* arises when proposed changes threaten powerful stakeholders such as top executives, senior staff people, or unions. *Cultural resistance* happens when existing norms and assumptions powerfully support the status quo and punish people who try to change.

It is my belief that one of the most powerful ways to respond to all kinds of resistance is through involvement. This is why Step-Up-To-Excellence was designed the way it was, around principles of trust, commitment, and collaboration. Further, this level of involvement is supported in the literature. For example, Cummings and Worley (1997) say, "One of the oldest and most effective strategies for overcoming resistance is to involve organization members directly in planning and implementing change." Vroom and Yetton (1973) describe how participation leads both to designing high-quality changes and to overcoming resistance to implementing them. Cummings and Molloy (1977) observe that because people have strong needs for involvement, the very act of participation can be motivating, thereby leading to greater effort to make the changes work.

Clemson and Clemson (1998) describe other organizational strategies to help people accept change. The first of these is to redesign your school system's reward system. Your reward system is part of your district's internal social architecture, and it must be retooled to ensure that it is aligned with your district's grand vision and strategic direction. Clemson and Clemson say:

> The reward system for the corporation is not a *thing*, but a *relationship* between (1) the needs, desires, and aspirations of the employees and (2) the opportunities provided by the corporation for fulfilling those needs, desires, and aspirations. In most cases the actual reward system is quite different from the formal, ostensible reward system. (p. 4)

This observation implies the need to redesign the reward system to support innovation.

The second way to respond to resistance, according to Clemson and Clemson, is to examine existing school district policies and procedures to determine which ones are obstacles to innovation. These authors state, "System dynamics studies frequently discover that major problems that everyone thought were external are actually the unintended consequences of internal policies" (p. 5).

Principle 6: People's Willingness to Embrace Innovation Varies

Rogers (1995) describes four different roles people play during change. Each role is accompanied by specific behaviors. Each role embraces innovation in different ways and to different degrees. These roles are summarized in the following sections.

Innovators

These people seek out change and innovation. They love it. In fact, they are often described as addicted to it. They are generally on the cutting edge of innovation. Professionally, they tend to hang around with other innovators, rather than their noninnovator colleagues. Often, they will quit their current jobs when their work becomes too routine.

Early Adapters

Early adapters are willing to embrace and support change if they see some solid, practical advantage to doing so. They forecast future trends within a system, and because of this skill they are important to include early in any change process. They often ask challenging questions with the intention of testing the feasibility of an idea, rather than shooting it down. Once they see the feasibility and value of a project, they can become valuable supporters and spokespersons for the innovation.

Middle Adapters

These people will go along with change if they see it is inevitable or if it is to their distinct advantage. They watch the early adapters and take their cues from what they see. These people comprise the largest group of people in any organization, including school districts. If involved early in your redesign effort with real responsibilities for making the redesign successful, they will often become strong supporters of innovation.

Late Adapters

Late adapters will change if they have to, but only then. In school systems, these are the faculty members who say, "Nobody ever told me about this!" weeks after you announced the beginning of the redesign process. They often conspire to resist change by talking against it or by taking covert actions to disrupt the process (e.g., by writing anonymous letters to the school board or to a local newspaper reporter).

These people are best managed by involving them directly in the prelaunch phase or by countervailing their criticism and resistance by amplifying the "voices" of the early and middle adapters. However, it is important not to overreact to their cynicism or criticism. Your overreaction could make them appear as martyrs in the eyes of their colleagues.

Principle 7: Give Voice to People with Courage, Passion, and Vision

Senge (1990) says, "There are two fundamental sources of energy that can motivate organizations: fear and aspirations. Fear underlies negative visions. Aspiration drives positive visions. Fear can produce extraordinary results in short periods, but aspiration endures as a continuing source of learning and growth" (p. 225).

A cornerstone of support for innovation and change is the empowerment of many people who have the courage, passion, and vision to share in leading systemic school improvement in your district. Committed students, parents, and community members are out there, but they are sometimes hard to recognize. The Community Engagement Conference (used during prelaunch phase) is a tool for identifying and giving a voice to external stakeholders who are well informed, influential, and passionate about the work of your district and committed to a positive future for your district.

The District Engagement Conference, Cluster Engagement Conferences, and Redesign Workshops are powerful and exquisite tools for giving "voice" to faculty and staff in your district who have the courage, passion, and vision to participate in leading the transformation of your district.

As you allow people to express their personal courage, passion, and vision, change-leadership in your district will spread outward from you through your entire district. Giving voice to people in this way leads all of you to that future place envisioned in collaboration with internal and external stakeholders.

CONCLUSION

Innovation in a school system is necessarily a shared responsibility among all people—external and internal—who play a part in the education process. People working inside your school system and living outside in your community have a stake in the future of your district.

When attempting to build support for innovation during the prelaunch phase, start with the people who are ready to work with you *now*, while at the same time striving to expand ownership of the redesign process to as many influential people as possible. People working in your school district also have a vested interest in how the school system is structured and what happens to the work they are doing. When communicating with these people during the District Engagement Conference at the beginning of step 1, you need to stress the advantages of innovation for them and point out how the innovations might benefit the work they do.

Innovation in organizations is much more successful if it is neither a top-down nor bottom-up process, but rather an enactment of shared leadership (Beer, 1980). This is why the Strategic Leadership Team, Cluster Improvement Teams, Site Improvement Teams, and Organizational Learning Networks are such powerful tools for creating and sustaining systemic school improvement—these structures are built on principles of distributed leadership.

Whole-district redesign is a complex endeavor. You will recall at the beginning of the chapter I said *complex* does not mean *impossible*, it means there is a lot to do. This is why this has been a long chapter. I needed time to describe for you a methodology. I want you to see its complexity and see its potential. I want you to see its challenges and see its opportunities. But most of all I want you to see that you can, in fact, lead this kind of change in your district. It can be done, and you can do it!

REFERENCES

Argyris, C. (1964). *Integrating the individual and the organization*. New York: Wiley.

Beckhard, R. (1969). *Organization development strategies and models*. Reading, MA: Addison-Wesley.

Beckhard, R. (1983). Strategies for large system change. In W. L. French, C. H. Bell, Jr., & R. A. Zawacki (Eds.), *Organization development: Theory, practice, and research* (pp. 234–242). Plano, TX: Business Publications.

Beer, M. (1980). *Organization change and development: A systems view*. Santa Monica, CA: Goodyear.

Bennis, W. (1966). *Changing organizations*. New York: McGraw-Hill.

Bion, A. (1961). *Experiences in groups and other papers*. London: Tavistock.

Bridges, W. (1991). *Managing transitions: Making the most of change*. Reading, MA: Addison-Wesley.

Cameron, K. S. (1984). The effectiveness of ineffectiveness. In B. M. Staw & L. L. Cummings (Eds.), *Research in organizational behavior*. Greenwich, CT: JAI Press.

Clemson, B., & Clemson, M. (1998). The deep barriers to change and how to overcome them. Available: health.siteseek.com/srch/%7B27079%7D

Collins, J. C. (2001). *Good to great: Why some companies make the leap . . . and others don't.* New York: HarperCollins.

Cummings, T., & Molloy, E. (1977). *Improving productivity and the quality of work life.* New York: Praeger.

Cummings, T. G., & Worley, C. G. (1997). *Organization development and change* (6th ed.). Cincinnati, OH: South-Western College Publishing.

Cummings, T. G., & Worley, C. G. (2001). *Organization development and change* (7th ed.). Cincinnati, OH: South-Western College Publishing.

Daft, R. L. (2001). *Organization theory and design* (7th ed.). Cincinnati, OH: South-Western College Publishing.

Deming, W. E. (1986). *Out of crisis.* Cambridge, MA: MIT Center for Advanced Engineering Study.

Eisenberg, E. M., & Goodall, H. L., Jr. (1997). *Organizational communication: Balancing creativity and constraint* (2d ed.). New York: St. Martin's.

Emery, F. E. (1977). *Two basic organization designs in futures we are in.* Leiden: Martius Nijhoff.

Emery F. E., & Trist E. L. (1973). *Towards a social ecology: Contextual appreciation of the future in the present.* London: Plenum.

Emery, M. (1993). *Participative design for participative democracy.* Canberra: Australian National University.

Emery, M., & Purser, R. E. (1996). *The search conference: A comprehensive guide to theory and practice.* San Francisco: Jossey-Bass.

Evans, R. (1996). *The human side of school change: Reform, resistance, and the real life problem of innovation.* San Francisco: Jossey-Bass.

Franklin, J. L. (1976). Characteristics of successful and unsuccessful organization development. *Journal of Applied Behavioral Science,* 12(4), 471–492.

Fritsch, M. J. (1997, September–October). Balanced scorecard helps Northern States Power's quality academy achieve extraordinary performance. *New Corporate University Review,* 5(5). Available: http://www.traininguniversity.com/tu_pi1997so_10.php22

Golarz, R. J., & Golarz, M. J. (1995). *The power of participation: Improving schools in a democratic society.* Champaign, IL: Research Press.

Goodlad, J. (1984). *A place called school: Prospects for the future.* New York: McGraw-Hill.

Hall, R. H., & Clark, J. P. (1980). An ineffective effectiveness study and some suggestions for future research. *Sociological Quarterly,* 21, 119–134.

Jacobs, R. W. (1994). *Real time strategic change: How to involve an entire organization in fast and far-reaching change.* San Francisco: Jossey-Bass.

Kegan, R., & Lahey, L. L. (2001). *How the way we talk can change the way we work.* San Francisco: Jossey-Bass.

Kotter, J. P. (1995, March/April). Leading change: Why transformation efforts fail. *Harvard Business Review*, 73(2), 59–67.

Lewin, K. (1951). *Field theory in social science.* New York: Harper and Row.

Likert, R. (1967). *The human organization.* New York: McGraw-Hill.

McGee, E. C. (2002, June 13). Designing organizations for sustainability. Message posted to odnet@lists.odnetwork.org. Available: http://www.odnetwork.org/listsinfo/odnet.info.html

McGregor, D. (1960). *The human side of enterprise.* New York: McGraw-Hill.

Merrifield, J. (1998, July). *Contested ground: Performance accountability in adult basic education.* Cambridge, MA: National Center for the Study of Adult Learning and Literacy.

Myerseth, O. (1977). *Intrafirm diffusion of organizational innovations: An exploratory study.* Unpublished doctoral dissertation, Graduate School of Business Administration, Harvard University, Cambridge, MA.

Odden, A. (1998, January). District Issues Brief—How to rethink school budgets to support school transformation. Arlington, VA: New American Schools. Available: New American Schools Web site, www.naschools.org/uploadedfiles/oddenbud.pdf

Ostroff, C., & Schmitt, N. (1993). Configurations of organizational effectiveness and efficiency. *Academy of Management Journal*, 36, 345–361.

Owen, H. (1991). *Riding the tiger: Doing business in a transforming world.* Potomac, MD: Abbott.

Owen, H. (1993). *Open space technology: A user's guide.* Potomac, MD: Abbott.

Pasmore, W., Frank, G., & Rehm, R. (1992). *Preparing people to participate in organizational change: Developing citizenship for the active organization.* Cleveland, OH: Pasmore & Associates.

Pasmore, W. A. (1988). *Designing effective organizations: The socio-technical systems perspective.* New York: Wiley.

Preskill, H., & Torres, R. T. (1999). *Evaluative inquiry for learning in organizations.* Thousand Oaks, CA: Sage.

Quinn, R. E., & Rohrbaugh, J. (1983). A spatial model of effectiveness criteria: Toward a competing values approach to organizational analysis. *Management Science*, 29, 363–377.

Rhodes, L. A. (1997, April). *Connecting leadership and learning: A planning paper developed for the American Association of School Administrators.* Unpublished manuscript.

Rhodes, L. A. (1999). *Putting unions and management out of a job.* Unpublished manuscript.

Rogers, E. M. (1995). *Diffusion of innovation* (4th ed.). New York: Free Press.

Russo, M. V., & Fouts, P. A. (1997, June). A resource-based perspective on corporate environmental performance and profitability. *Academy of Management Journal*, 40(3), 534–559.

Sahlins, M. (1976). *Culture and practical reason*. Chicago: University of Chicago Press.

Schwan, C., & Spady, W. (1998). Why change doesn't happen and how to make sure it does. *Educational Leadership*, 55(7). Available: ASCD Web site, www.ascd.org/otb/benefit.html

Scriven, M. (2001). Hard-won lessons in program evaluation. Available: eval.cgu.edu/lectures/hard-won.htm

Senge, P. M. (1990). *The fifth discipline: The art and practice of the learning organization*. New York: Doubleday.

Stoelwinder, J. U., & Charns, M. P. (1984). The task field model of organizational analysis and design. *Human Relations*, 34, 743–762.

Stufflebeam, D. L. (2000). The CIPP model for evaluation. In D. L. Stufflebeam, G. F. Madaus, & T. Kellaghan (Eds.), *Evaluation models: Viewpoints on educational and human services evaluation* (pp. 279–317). Boston: Kluwer Academic Publishers.

Tichy, N. M. (1993, December 13). Revolutionize your company. *Fortune*, 128(15), 114–118.

Trist, E. L., Higgin, G. W., Murray, H., & Pollack, A. B. (1963). *Organizational choice*. London: Tavistock.

Tsui, A. S. (1990). A multiple-constituency model of effectiveness: An empirical examination at the human resource subunit level. *Administrative Science Quarterly*, 35, 458, 483.

Vroom, V., & Yetton, P. (1973). *Leadership and decision making*. Pittsburgh: University of Pittsburgh Press.

Walton, R. E. (1985, March-April). From control to commitment in the workplace. *Harvard Business Review*, 63(2), 77–84.

Weisbord, M. R. (1987). *Productive workplaces*. San Francisco: Jossey-Bass.

NOTES

1. You will recall that I use K–12 school districts as examples. If your district is designed as a K–8 district, then this team would be staffed with K–8 teachers and administrators. Whatever the design of your core work process—your instructional program—that's the design you use to organize this team.

2. The field of organization development defines four levels of intervention to improve organizations: whole organization, between groups, within groups, and individual. Organization performance is improved starting at the whole-organization level and then by moving inward to the individual level. This outside-in strategy systematically removes obstacles to performance by creating conditions for success at each level.

CHAPTER 7

So, Where Will We Get the Resources to Do This?

Francis M. Duffy, Jason Cascarino, and Chris M. Henson

New dollars will be important for many districts in raising student performance, but not if they are added on top of flawed programs, practices and structures . . . districts and schools must look closely at how existing resources—time, staff and dollars—might better support new comprehensive school designs, improved teaching practice and chosen academic priorities.

—Karen Hawley Miles, *Money Matters*

As we open this chapter, we want to state unambiguously that our ideas for financing whole-district improvement are based on real data about the real costs of school-based improvement; but we did not have any data about the cost of whole-district change. We used school-based costs as a foundation for scaling up our projections about what it would cost to improve an entire school system. We used these real cost data to create a hypothetical case study that illustrates underlying principles of thinking "outside the box" to finance whole-district improvement strategies.

THE CONTEXT FOR FINANCING SYSTEMIC SCHOOL IMPROVEMENT

There is a vicious cycle in improving school systems. *Improve*, after all, is an active verb; you actually have to *do* a whole set of activities that, by definition, is different than what was done before. And because these activities are considered outside the normal practices of the school system, when they are ultimately funded and then implemented, they are almost always seen as add-ons. They are something "extra" that the school system does beyond what it does normally. What the district does normally is funded by existing operating expenses; therefore, anything "extra" must be supported by "extra" money: a federal or state grant, foundation or corporate giving, or new taxes.

The problem is that when extra money goes away, so does the improving activity. Until, of course, some other extra dollars become available that fund some other extra activity. And then that too will come and go with the fleeting funding stream as the cycle continues ad infinitum. The effective result is a culture of education reform in which schools and school systems continue doing basically what they have always done in terms of core functions and at the same time do a lot of different "extra" activities along the way, if the money is available. While the "extras" change from time to time, the core remains the same. Yet, it is this core (the teaching and learning, the internal social "architecture," and relationships with the outside world) that needs to be improved if a school district wants to move toward higher levels of performance.

What this book proposes in its presentation of a whole-district change methodology and the courage, passion, and vision change-leaders need to create and sustain whole-district change is far more core than it is extra. That is why the traditional funding of improvement activities using "extra" money cannot finance whole-system improvement as described in this book. There are two reasons for this. First, there is simply not enough "extra" money out there to fund district-wide change. Second, the only way to institutionalize continuous whole-system improvement, we believe, is to make it the core, the normal practice of the school system, funded initially by reallocating existing operating resources and then funded on an ongoing basis as part of a district's operating budget.

With whole-system improvement, district leaders are not buying a new curriculum or a new program that will be simply "pancaked" on top of their core activities and programs. Systemic school improvement is not about adding on new features. Systemic redesign is about questioning everything your district does at its core, discarding what is not working, keeping and refining what is working, and inventing or selecting new opportunities for student, teacher, and system learning. This kind of systemic redesign requires resources, and plenty of them. This chapter describes some ideas for how to estimate the resources you need to redesign your whole system and then offers you both practical and innovative methods for finding those resources.

FUNDING NORMAL OPERATING COSTS USING ZERO-BASED BUDGETING

Zero-based budgeting is a concept that is neither new nor very complicated. It's a concept driven by a continuous comprehensive needs assessment and supported by individual school improvement plans that are clearly aligned with their district's grand vision and strategic direction. It's a concept that must involve all stakeholders. It's also a concept that can be used to fund whole-district redesign.

Most school district budgets begin with and build on the previous year's budget. A line item is usually carried forward from one year to the next, and an inflationary percentage might be added. Zero-based budgeting begins with a "clean slate" each year. Every line item starts at zero and builds from there as needs are identified and programs are assessed. This process requires much more time and effort, as each line item requires detailed supporting documentation to substantiate requests and to indicate the anticipated results. During this process, it's important to distinguish between actual "needs" and desired "wants" to help keep a district's vision within the bounds of reality and to weigh "personal agendas" against that vision.

Involving Stakeholders in the Budgeting Process

To understand the challenges associated with funding whole-district improvement, it is important to have a clear picture of normal operating costs that must also be funded. What follows is a description of the typical normal costs incurred by a school district.

To appropriately identify needs, the involvement of all stakeholder groups is required. These stakeholders include teachers, school administrators, instructional facilitators, program supervisors, classified staff, parents, and community members. School-based administrators, with the involvement of teachers and parents, can plan for the future by developing improvement plans and performance contracts in collaboration with the superintendent. Likewise, instructional facilitators and program supervisors, through an annual performance review, can envision what they want their particular program or area of responsibility to look like so that it most effectively serves the district's grand vision and strategic direction. Goal statements are established and action plans are developed that include target dates or time lines, estimated resources needed, and measurable means of evaluation.

The kind of involvement described here must also be genuine—not window dressing. There are few things more disheartening and disrespectful than asking a group of people to invest their time and effort to serve on a committee or task force and either not giving serious consideration to their recommendations or making a decision about the course of action that will be taken *before* they even come together to help you.

The appropriate involvement of school board members is also important. Many school board members do not want to consider the details of all budget requests. They expect the superintendent and administration to filter those requests and bring to them a budget proposal for their consideration. Thus, one way to appropriately involve board members is to have nonvoting budget work sessions to share information, discuss programs, and receive input on the many different areas of the budget.

Budgetary information should also not be a mystery or a secret to any of the stakeholders. If it is, skepticism and suspicion could develop. The more people understand what is actually in the budget, the higher the trust level will be. A budget notebook for board members, the press, and administrators can be organized so that all program requests can be viewed in detail.

Data-Based Budgeting

It's been said that information is power. Including statistical data during a budgeting cycle allows both the board members and the public to understand the size of the operation and the current financial status of the district. These data could include the number of employees (certificated and classified), experience and educational level of teaching staff, physical building square footage, number of portable classrooms (if any), the number of students by grade level, and pupil–teacher ratios.

Comparative statistical data from the state department of education can also be very useful. These could include such data as expenditures per student (system, state, national), average teacher salaries (system, state, national), free and reduced percentage of students (at-risk students), ethnic composition of students, accredited schools, student attendance rates, teachers meeting certification standards, and student assessment data by subject area. Some of these data are for informational purposes only, while some of them will showcase positive attributes of the district, and others will highlight areas in need of improvement.

Each area in the instructional program of a school district must be annually evaluated for effectiveness. The curriculum must be properly aligned within the district and with both state and national standards. The district strategic plan, student assessment data (trends), as well as anecdotal evidence, should drive the programs already in place. Staff development must be provided so that teachers and administrators receive the proper training to perform at a high level. Performance data can inform decisions related to these requirements.

Funding Needs for Normal Operating Budgets

Since the mid-1970s, federal legislation has increasingly imposed unfunded mandates on school districts that have required significant increases in resources for special education. Board members and the general public must be made aware of these mandates and the corresponding costs of providing these services. The numbers of students served in these programs, the different types of disabilities, and the amount (percentage) of federal funding (or lack thereof) really can be "eye-opening" information for those who think public education can be funded as it was in the past.

A more recent program that is increasing services and costs is the *English Language Learner Programs* for students whose native language is not English. Again, a list of the numbers of students and the different languages spoken can emphasize the financial challenges associated with this issue.

Costs for textbooks being considered for adoption are greatly influenced by the subject area(s). There is also the potential for consumable texts that will, therefore, have recurring costs on an annual basis.

Instructional and administrative technologies have evolved into a major budgetary component in school districts. It's imperative that the board and the public understand the current status of technology use, as well as plans for the future. If they don't understand the use and benefits of these technologies, they won't support them.

Likewise, each area of a school district's division of finance and administration must be constantly evaluated for cost-effectiveness and efficiencies. The primary function of these programs is to support the schools' and district's instructional program, and ultimately student achievement.

Student attendance reporting is obviously very important because if a student is not at school, the student can't learn. States also base their funding formulas on numbers of students in attendance, so accurate reporting is critical.

School nurses and student health services are becoming a bigger financial cost as local school districts are being held responsible for providing more medical procedures and dispensing more medications than ever before. Data regarding student clinic visits and medications dispensed are very useful.

Fiscal services must follow all accounting and auditing guidelines, pay the bills, pay the employees, administer the fringe benefits package, and follow proper purchasing procedures. The costs of operating and maintaining plant facilities protect a district's investment in buildings. When funds are tight, this area is often neglected, which is a very shortsighted administrative decision. The public expects the investment made in multimillion-dollar facilities to be protected with proper maintenance and care. If a school building is clean and properly maintained, it sends a message to students that education is a priority and should be valued. Most residents in a school district do not have children attending the schools. Their only exposure to the district might be when they drive by the school buildings or when they vote at the schools. To these taxpayers, what they see as they drive by or walk in forms their perceptions of the district, and their perceptions become reality for them.

The cost of energy use in many school districts is significant. Cost savings in energy use can be achieved with computerized energy management systems to control utility costs and by updating older mechanical and lighting systems. These improvements can pay for themselves with the energy savings generated. This not only provides savings, but also provides an environment more conducive to teaching and learning. The dollars saved by creating more efficient energy use can also be reallocated to a permanent budget line for funding whole-district improvement.

Student transportation is a service that, if not provided, would have a significant negative effect on student attendance (and ultimately student achievement). Bus routing should be computerized for maximum efficiency to reduce the number of buses and bus drivers needed. Because transportation costs are significant, all school field trips should be clearly aligned with the district's instructional program.

Human resource staffs not only deal with the many legal issues surrounding employment of personnel, but they obviously play a vital role in the recruitment of quality teachers and staff. This is especially significant as school districts across the country deal with teacher shortages for the foreseeable future. Equally important for school districts is the retention of quality teachers. Providing mentors to new teachers and administrative support through a new-teacher induction program are examples of human resource initiatives that can prove valuable.

The school nutrition program (cafeterias) should be self-sustaining so that local funds are not used to subsidize its operation. This does not mean that the nutrition program is unimportant. To the contrary, it is very important because it may be the only opportunity for some children to receive a healthy meal. Research and common sense tell us that children have a more difficult time learning if they are hungry.

Another self-supporting program should be a district's "before- and after-school care" program. This program is not only offered for the convenience of parents but also for the tutoring and remediation opportunities that can be made available to struggling students.

School staffing is basically driven by numbers of students and student class scheduling. Pupil–teacher ratios are often mandated by state guidelines. To educate the "whole child," special-area teachers may be needed for physical education, art, music, computer, and a variety of additional subjects. The amount of teacher planning time given is a factor in determining the number of special-area teachers needed.

A capital improvement or replacement schedule is essential in planning for the future. Capital improvements and replacements either are usually financed with short-term notes or funds are reserved for a period of years for a designated purpose. These projects typically include roofing, HVAC mechanical systems, school buses, technology, and may include large-scale maintenance items such as carpeting, paving, and painting. Having a replacement schedule shows the board and the public that the district is functioning with a proactive and long-term mind-set.

Some school districts are responsible for issuing bonds and meeting the corresponding debt service requirements. The district's bond rating is very important in reducing the long-term costs of issuing debt. The higher the bond rating, the lower the interest costs. To plan appropriately for meeting debt service requirements, an outstanding debt schedule showing due dates, principal and interest payments by fiscal year, and totals should be shared with the board and the public.

Employee benefits have become a substantial line item in a district's budget as health care costs have risen dramatically. A significant recruiting tool and a considerable ingredient of total employee compensation, benefits are often a part of the negotiated contract with the local teachers union. It's a necessity that employees and the board understand the value of the fringe benefit package that is provided. If employees do not understand the value of the fringe benefit program, then the benefits are not appreciated and utilized fully. An individualized benefits statement furnished to each employee will detail the actual dollar amounts that the district is expending on the employee's behalf as an integral part of his or her total compensation. A flexible benefits plan (e.g., IRS Section 125 cafeteria plan) offers advantages to both employees and employers. This plan allows employees to pay certain insurance premiums and medical and dependent care expenses on a pretax basis. As a result, the district's employer FICA match is reduced. This can be a significant savings depending on the level of employee participation. Insurance rate increases must be anticipated and included in the budget, as well as the costs of any benefit enhancements.

The growing teacher shortage will require school districts to maintain a competitive salary schedule. Considerable research is required to properly analyze salary schedules, as there are numerous variables to consider. The number of contracted days on the schedule may vary from district to district and state to state. The average teacher salary in a district is not the best indicator of the best salary schedule. A district with a very experienced and educated teaching force will have a comparatively higher average teacher salary. However, the same district's starting salary for beginning teachers may not be as enticing. State education associations typically compile and analyze teacher salary schedule data and are usually a good resource for information. Negotiated contracts often dictate the manner in which salary increases are given.

Some school districts are boldly attempting to move away from the traditional method of basing teacher salaries solely on experience and educational attainment and moving toward a more performance-based method, utilizing clearly defined standards and criteria for effectiveness. School districts across the country increasingly are providing monetary incentives and administrative support for obtaining National Board Certification. The corresponding costs of employee salary increases will take a significant portion of any district's *additional* resources available each year.

Finding Revenues to Pay for Operating Costs

After the monumental task of identifying and assessing the needs and wants of the district has been completed, the time comes to prioritize the needs and wants. Identified needs (yearly recurring expenditures) in public education at times appear to be almost infinite, while the resources (revenues) available are always painfully finite. Then, when you add in the cost of making whole-district improvements that are not part of the current operating budget, the challenge of paying for all these costs becomes clear.

One way to find money to pay for whole-district improvement is to look for efficiencies in your current operating budget. It's fiscally responsible to avoid using the term *cut* when referring to *reductions in requested increases*. A true cut is an actual decrease in funding. In most school districts, approximately 80 percent to 90 percent of the operating budget is dedicated to personnel (salaries and benefits) and utility costs. Thus, budget reallocations in the personnel line items are where significant dollars will be found to support whole-district improvement.

In terms of finding money to support whole-district improvement, it's imperative to let good ideas have a decent hearing. Otherwise, good ideas will get stifled, and good employees will become discouraged. However, a good idea may not be considered a "need." Therefore, you should develop strategies to consider and adopt good, "nonneed" ideas. One strategy that works is to stage (phase in) the implementation of good, nonneed ideas; for example, it may be physically impossible to fully implement a new idea (e.g., a new program) in one year. Instead, for example, you could phase the idea in over several years.

Board members and the public should understand the sources of funds available (which are discussed later in this chapter) when discussing revenues to support systemic school improvement. Typically, there are four sources: local, state, federal, and private. If a local property tax is involved, the value of a penny on the tax rate should be shared with stakeholders. This kind of information is usually available through the local assessor of property office. If a local sales tax is a source of revenue, historical trends are also important so you can predict the amount of sales tax that might be available to support whole-system improvement. Understanding the state funding formula also provides a measure of confidence and credibility. Federal funding estimates will round out for your board members the "full picture" of your district's resources.

After prioritized operational needs and fundable "wants" have been brought in line with available resources, the budget can be approved. However, the process is not complete. What has been requested and approved must now be implemented. At this point, because budgeting is a continuous cycle, the comprehensive needs assessment process begins again.

External grants can also be a source of funds to support whole-district reform. Grants supporting the instructional program should be showcased, but they should also be carefully monitored for effectiveness. Grants are commonly thought of as "free money." However, they can take a tremendous amount of school and district personnel time to implement. This time might be better spent doing something more effective.

Another source of resources to support whole-system improvement is discretionary funds allocated by the central administration to each individual school in a district. These allocations are lump-sum amounts, based on a funding formula, that give individual schools the flexibility of determining their areas of greatest need. But their initiatives must be clearly aligned with the district's grand vision and strategic direction.

Final Thoughts about Normal Operating Costs

In closing, the operating budget is a guide that reflects a district's mission, vision, and strategic plan. In presenting budgetary information to stakeholders it is important to highlight the important points in the budget. Board members and the public will not remember all of the details, but the details must be available if someone wants to review them. As educators, we must also remember that the money we get to run our school systems is not our money. We are stewards of the public's money, and we are entrusted with the fiduciary responsibility to spend it wisely.

It's absolutely amazing what a zero-based budgeting process can yield! Budget line items that have been carried forward from one fiscal year to the next over a period of years are suddenly no longer needed. Yes, the money in those line items has been expended, but when the tough questions are asked relating to needs, detailed documentation, and the system's strategic plan, it becomes fairly obvious that funds can be reallocated elsewhere in the budget to further the district's goals. This process is time-consuming and may appear to be insignificant as line items are scrutinized individually, but it can allow significant reallocation of dollars when taken as a whole.

The dollar amounts in each line item, especially the salary and benefits lines, must be carefully calculated to minimize the "fluff" or "cushion." The line items obviously must have enough in them to meet current obligations and identified needs. Many times, however, this is taken to the extreme. Funds that could be available to fund needed changes in a system are often used as "padding" to cover hypothetical catastrophes or to make the reserve fund balance look good at the end of the fiscal year. Don't get us wrong, we're strong proponents of conservative budgeting; but funds should be in place to benefit students during a particular school year, not to serve as "padding" or make an end-of-year reserve-fund balance look good. After all, a child only has one chance to experience first grade or any other grade (hopefully)!

A STARTING POINT FOR ESTIMATING
THE COST OF WHOLE-DISTRICT CHANGE

Most of the available literature on financing school improvement focuses on school-based budgeting and school-based management (e.g., Wohlstetter & Van Kirk, 1995; Goertz & Stiefel, 1998; Odden, Wohlstetter, & Odden, 1995). An example of a key principle undergirding school-based budgeting can be summarized as follows:

> Private-sector research shows that decentralizing four key resources (power, information, knowledge, and rewards) can enhance organizational effectiveness and productivity. In a SBB [school-based budgeting] context, say these researchers, highly involved schools need "real" power over the budget to decide how and where to allocate resources; they need fiscal and performance data for making informed decisions about the budget; their staff needs professional development and training to participate in the budget process; and the school must have control over compensation to reward performance. (Hadderman, 1999, p. 1)

Improving individual schools within a district, however, does not add up to whole-system improvement, which is somewhat like saying, "the sum of the parts doesn't equal the whole." School-based improvement is important and necessary, but we believe it is also insufficient because it has not, does not, and cannot produce sustainable whole-system improvement. This conclusion is implied by the Education Commission of the States (ECS) in its comments on school-based management (SBM). The commission says: "Early research on SBM produced some promising findings, but concluded that school-based management, unless well-designed and well-implemented, had few positive effects. One study noted an 'awesome gap' between the rhetoric and the reality of SBM's contribution to school improvement" (ECS, 2002, n.p.).

To create whole-system improvement, change-leaders need to strike a balance between district-wide budgeting for improvement and school-based budgeting. District-wide improvement needs to be funded through a budgeting process that coordinates and aligns all of the school-based budgets within clusters with the district's grand vision and strategic direction. This requires new outside-the-box solutions for financing whole-district improvement on a sustained basis.

Estimating the Cost of Whole-District Change

Resources Required for Whole-District Improvement

There are basically four kinds of resources: time, money, human, and technology. All of these resources are needed to create and sustain systemic school improvement. The amount of each resource varies from district to district, but more of each is needed.

In this chapter, we focus primarily on financial resources because money can buy the time, extra people, and technology needed to make whole-district improvement a reality. Thus, the success of whole-system improvement depends on careful planning of school and district financial commitments.

Unlike traditional reform efforts, we believe whole-system change cannot be sustained solely through small increases in operating budgets. Because systemic reform touches all aspects of a school district's core operations, it imposes significant resource requirements and demands a rethinking of the way current resources are allocated, as well as some creative thinking about how to use "extra" money that will be needed to jump-start systemic reform.

Financing whole-system change, we believe, also requires the continuation of both school-based budgeting that is coordinated and aligned with centralized budgeting processes. Financing systemic school improvement is not an *"either* centralized *or* school-based" endeavor. It requires a *"both* centralized *and* school-based budgeting"* approach.

Because there seems to be a scarce amount of literature on financing whole-system change, innovative, ground-level tactics, methods, and resource sources are needed. To imagine what the cost of whole-system improvement might be, we first look at the resources needed to support comprehensive reform in individual school buildings within districts. Then, using that information, we scale up the cost estimates to determine a hypothetical ballpark figure for supporting whole-system improvement. We then develop a hypothetical case study to illustrate the cost of whole-system change, followed by some hypothetical thinking about how to pay for all this. You will find the steps we took to arrive at our hypothetical costs in the following sections.

Step 1: Calculate the Cost of
Comprehensive School Reform in Single Schools

The RAND Corporation in its ongoing evaluation of the New American Schools (NAS)[1] comprehensive school reform models provides information on the availability and adequacy of resources to pay for comprehensive reform. This information is provided in a report authored by Brent Keltner (1998). Keltner's findings are from the 1996–1997 academic year, and they were derived from a sample of fifty-eight schools using six of the eight New American Schools designs. Keltner identified resource requirements for comprehensive reform in those fifty-eight schools using four different resource categories: teacher time, personnel, design services, and materials and conferences. A summary of his findings follows. Later in the chapter we scale up the cost data to project the cost of creating whole-district improvement.

Teacher Time

Educators need time to learn new curricula, new teaching practices, and new management techniques, and they need time to collaborate (Purnell & Hill, 1992). The RAND evaluation team collected information at each of the fifty-eight schools in its sample about the amount of teacher time required to implement the various reform models. They counted the total number of hours teachers spent in common planning time, teacher teams, and management teams and the total number of days teachers spent in on- and off-site design training.

Personnel

All of the comprehensive school reform models supported by New American Schools require specialized school personnel to support the designs being implemented. Many comprehensive reform designs use on-site resource experts, such as site facilitators, curriculum coordinators, and technology coordinators. Other comprehensive designs use experts that work directly with students or families and include reading tutors, instructional assistants, and family outreach personnel. The RAND evaluation team collected data on the total number of full-time equivalents (FTEs) dedicated to comprehensive reform for each of these categories of personnel.

Design Services

Other resources needed for comprehensive school reform are design teams that collaborate with school-based educators to implement the selected reform models. Members of these design teams are experts with the reform model being implemented. At each of the fifty-eight schools in the RAND study, information on the costs associated with these design teams was also collected. These costs included consulting fees and travel expenses.

Materials and Conferences

Schools implementing comprehensive school reform models also need materials to support implementation. Most comprehensive designs also require teacher participation in design conferences and visits to other schools outside their district that have successfully implemented the same reform models. To gather data on the costs of materials, the RAND evaluation team collected information on the costs of teacher books, student notebooks, entrance fees, and bus rental fees for students on field trips. Conference costs included the costs of airplane trips, hotel nights, and teacher per diems.

Once the RAND team collected sufficient data to calculate the cost of comprehensive reform, they calculated the total dollar cost for comprehensive reform in each of the fifty-eight schools in their study. They found that the average resource use for comprehensive reform across all fifty-eight schools in their sample was $162,000 per school in the first year of implementation. The average school in their sample had 40 teachers and 740 students. To support design implementation, this average school used 1.8 hours of planning time per teacher per week, 6.5 days of training per teacher per year, 1.7 FTE specialized school personnel, $25,000 for design services, and $12,000 for materials and conferences. As a reminder, these costs were based on 1996–1997 data.

Seventy-six (76) percent of the resources used by the fifty-eight schools in the RAND study was used to pay for a combination of teacher time and for specialized school personnel required by each reform model. The average combined value for these two resources was $125,000 ($66,000 for teacher time and $59,000 for specialized personnel). Design team consulting services averaged $25,000 per school, or about 16 percent of total costs. Materials and conferences averaged $12,000 per school, or the remaining 8 percent of the total cost.

Looking at these costs, it is tempting to jump to several conclusions. The first one is that the total costs are the same as out-of-pocket costs for a school district. Keltner clearly states that the costs of comprehensive school reform in the fifty-eight schools in the RAND study *were not the same* as out-of-pocket costs. The average school in the RAND study *did not actually spend* $162,000 out of pocket to implement its comprehensive reform model. A significant portion of that $162,000 was covered by reallocating funds within each school's operating budget.

Another conclusion that needs to be avoided is thinking that the cost data in the RAND study represent today's dollars. The cost estimates in Keltner's study were calculated using 1996–1997 data. In fact, by 1998, Keltner increased his estimate of the total costs to $180,000 per school.

A third assumption to avoid is that there is no variation in the costs of funding comprehensive school reform. The RAND study clearly shows that there was variation among the fifty-eight schools in the sample. Some schools spent more than others. The main reason for variation in resource requirements is the type of comprehensive reform design a school adopts; for example, two schools in the RAND study had average resource requirements of about $100,000, three had costs within the $150,000 to $170,000 range, and another required approximately $300,000. School size also influences cost variations, but not as much as the particular reform model being used. There will be similar cost variations in whole-system improvement, too.

Step 2: Find Funds to Pay for Comprehensive School Reform

The RAND evaluation team also identified funding sources that schools can draw on to cover the costs of comprehensive reform. They collected data on two types of funding strategies: reallocating resources within current operating budgets and using funds outside existing budgets (or, extra money).

To examine the reallocation of current operating resources, the RAND team included funds from the school district's normal budget allocation to each school for personnel, materials, staff development, and discretionary budgets. One example of the resource reallocation strategy used by the schools in the RAND study was the use of existing in-service days and money for substitute teachers to pay for teacher time to participate in training about the selected reform models. Another example of resource reallocation was when existing positions were retooled to support comprehensive school reform. A third example of resource reallocation was when school-level administrators used their discretionary funds to pay for travel, materials, and conferences to support the selected comprehensive reform model.

To examine the use of outside funds, the RAND team collected data on the use of federal Title I funds, district money beyond a school's normal budget allocation, grants from private foundations, and volunteer contributions (e.g., teachers volunteering their time instead of being paid for it and parents helping with the costs of student field trips). The RAND study tracked Title I funds separately because many of the schools in their sample did not meet the eligibility criteria to receive those dollars.

The sources of funding for the fifty-eight schools in the RAND study were fascinating. About $62,000 (or 38 percent of the $162,000 average cost for comprehensive school reform) was covered through resource reallocation. The other $100,000 came from sources outside a school's normal operating budget—$53,000 from Title I, $30,000 from district budgets, $11,000 from outside grants, and $6,000 from volunteer sources. In other words, each school in the study *was able to find all* the money needed to support comprehensive school reform.

The RAND study also confirmed that for the fifty-eight schools in their sample, district-level leadership for change played an important role in helping schools fund comprehensive reform. Regarding this observation, Keltner (1998) says,

> With many competing resource priorities and fragmented reform efforts, schools may not be able to effectively reallocate their existing resources without district leadership. Indeed, our analysis indicated that reallocation of resources to support comprehensive reform was more likely to occur if district officials clearly signaled that such reform was a key district priority and that reallocation was not only permissible but encouraged. (n.p.)

In summary, the RAND study drew the following conclusions from the assessment of the costs of comprehensive school reform in the fifty-eight schools in the sample.

- Resource reallocation using current operating resources is absolutely essential for funding comprehensive reform. Nearly 40 percent of the funds for comprehensive reform at the schools in the sample came from reallocated resources.
- During the early stages of systemic improvement, and certainly for the first time a district engages in this kind of change, access to "extra" funds should allow most schools to supplement the resources found through the resource reallocation; that is, the analysis showed that before receiving additional sources of extra funds, the "average" school in the study generated $115,000 just by combining its reallocated resources found in current operating budgets ($62,000) with Title I money ($53,000). Remembering that the average total cost of comprehensive school reform in the RAND study was $162,000, the average school in this study would only

need an additional $47,000 from other sources to cover all the costs of comprehensive school reform.

- Access to federal non-Title I funds (e.g., the Obey-Porter funds) is not sufficient for schools without Title I funds. The combination of $50,000 in Obey-Porter funds and $62,000 in internally reallocated resources would still leave most non-Title I schools considerably short of the money needed to implement comprehensive reform. The needed funds, according to Keltner, would then have to come in the form of additional district funding, other outside sources, or both.

- District-level leadership is crucial in funding comprehensive reform. District-level leadership, according to the RAND study, helps prevent school-based practitioners from perceiving comprehensive reform as an add-on.

A HYPOTHETICAL CASE STUDY TO PROJECT COST OF WHOLE-SYSTEM CHANGE

Given the lack of data on the costs of whole-system change, we used the previous real school-based costs as the basis for scaling up our thinking about what whole-district change might cost. To help us do this, we developed a case study in which a hypothetical school district (the Painted Horse School District), with three K–12 clusters of schools and a total of 24 schools, decided to implement three different comprehensive school reform models—one for each of its K–12 clusters. We used real cost data taken from the RAND study and data compiled by Odden (1998) to project the hypothetical costs of whole-district improvement.

Transforming the Painted Horse School District

The superintendent of schools for the Painted Horse School District, the president of the school board, and the president of the local teachers union had met for months over coffee to talk about what might be done to improve the overall performance of their school system. Together, they developed a level of trust that was unprecedented in their district. They viewed each other as partners in this grand vision that was emerging to transform their whole district into a world-class organization of learners that provided unprecedented opportunities for improving student, teacher, and system learning.

Not one of them could remember when it happened, but it did. At some point, over what seemed like their hundredth cup of coffee, the three "change-partners" realized that they had to move forward with the vision they were developing through their conversations. The superintendent agreed that he would begin building political support with stakeholders in the community, with his central office staff, and among building-level principals. The school board president said he would begin sharing the vision with other members of the board and with members of the community. And the union president agreed that she would begin doing the same with her constituents—the teachers and other education specialists in the district.

To deepen and widen political support, the change-partners pulled together a small, unofficial team to plan and conduct an exciting three-day Community Engagement Conference. They invited into one space 500 community members, district leaders, teachers union leaders, and staff to engage in conversations about the future of their district. As a result of this conference, a critical mass of community members and district personnel were in agreement that they needed to take immediate steps to improve their entire school system—not just individual schools within their district. The political support they needed was now there.

Soon after completing the Community Engagement Conference and analyzing the data from that conference, the superintendent, school board president, and union president agreed that there was enough political support to launch the whole-system transformation that they had been envisioning over coffee and sketching on paper napkins.

Their first official action was to issue a joint memorandum calling for the establishment of a change-leadership team of K–12 teachers and building principals nominated by their colleagues to serve on the team, the superintendent and two of his subordinate administrators, the school board president, and the union president. They called the team the "Strategic Leadership Team."

After receiving training on principles of whole-system improvement, the Strategic Leadership Team (SLT) organized another special event.

This event, called a District Engagement Conference, engaged selected district personnel, parents, and students in a three-day event. This conference had four goals: set a new vision for the district's future, define the ground rules and parameters for whole-district redesign, set a strategic direction for the district, and begin developing more trust, commitment, and collaboration among faculty and administrators.

The SLT wanted to move their district toward a vision of whole-system improvement that would create and sustain unprecedented opportunities for improving student, teacher, and system learning. To do this, they believed that the comprehensive school reform models supported by the New American Schools would be helpful. So, a large part of the District Engagement Conference focused on discussions of how the district might use those reform models. At the end of this conference, everyone was in agreement that three of the NAS models were very appropriate for the district and that each of the three K–12 clusters in the district would adopt one of the models.

Given this strategic direction and given the new vision statement collaboratively developed in the District Engagement Conference, the next step the Strategic Leadership Team took was to identify and retrain one of the district's teachers to serve as a change management coordinator. This person was working on a doctorate degree in education administration with a specialty in navigating large-scale change. Because teaching and learning are knowledge work and school districts are knowledge-creating organizations, the title created for this position was "Knowledge Work Coordinator." Together, the Knowledge Work Coordinator and the Strategic Leadership Team planned the next step in their journey toward whole-system improvement: conducting Cluster Engagement Conferences.

The district had three K–12 clusters. So, the next activity for the district's redesign process was to charter and train a Cluster Improvement Team (CIT) for each cluster. The CIT was staffed by K–12 teachers, support staff, and building administrators from within each cluster. The reason they used this kind of staffing pattern was that they knew that a child's education is not what he or she learns in one grade or at one level of schooling; it is the cumulative effect of his or her learning experiences, K–12. So, to improve this learning experience they knew that these improvement teams had to have K–12 representation.

Next, each Cluster Improvement Team conducted a Cluster Engagement Conference for the educators working in their respective cluster. This three-day conference was designed and run the same way as the District Engagement Conference, but with a narrower focus (i.e., on each particular cluster). The purpose of this conference was to engage teachers and administrators in each cluster in discussions about the comprehensive school reform model each chose, and they then developed a vision statement describing the future they desired for each cluster. Participants also continued working on building trust, commitment, and collaboration.

Following the conclusion of the Cluster Engagement Conference, each Cluster Improvement Team set up and trained a Site Improvement Team for each school in its cluster. These building-level teams would be primarily responsible for making the nitty-gritty improvements that would come later in the redesign process.

Once the Site Improvement Teams were chartered and trained, each Cluster Improvement Team then organized a series of Redesign Workshops. The purpose of these three-day workshops was to engage representatives from each Site Improvement Team in a structured process for figuring out how to implement the reform model the cluster selected (thus improving the core work of the cluster), creating innovative ideas for improving the quality of work life in the cluster and schools (thus improving the cluster's internal social architecture), and strategizing about how to relate better to the neighborhoods served by the cluster and the schools, as well as figuring out how to improve the cluster's relationship with the other clusters and with the central administration (thereby improving each cluster's relationship with its external environment).

The outcomes of these three-day workshops were innovative ideas to redesign each cluster and its schools. Each cluster had different ideas about how to improve, and, of course, they each had a different reform model to implement. Although each cluster was doing its own thing, so to speak, what each was doing was clearly and powerfully aligned with the district's grand vision and strategic direction.

The Knowledge Work Coordinator collected all of the redesign ideas and organized them into a single, comprehensive redesign proposal. Each cluster had its own section in the redesign proposal. The redesign proposals were then submitted to the Strategic Leadership Team, which reviewed the proposal to ensure that the innovative ideas for change were aligned with the district's vision and strategic direction.

As a result of the strategic review, some of the ideas in the re-design proposal were marked as infeasible or unsupportive of the district's vision. Others were identified as something that would be nice to do later. Most were acceptable as improvements that could be made starting right now and continuing over the next four years. The ideas in the proposal marked for rejection or "set aside for later" were sent back to the affected Cluster Improvement Teams and Site Improvement Teams and discussed with those people to ensure that they understood the rationale for the changes. In some cases, some of the items marked as infeasible were changed back to feasible and reincluded in the redesign proposal.

At the same time that the three Cluster Improvement Teams were conducting their respective Redesign Workshops to plan the redesign of their clusters, the superintendent engaged his central office staff in a similar conference to create innovative ideas to transform the central office into a central service center. The vision for the new central service center was that it and the staff would view teachers and other education specialists as their primary "customers" and work in service of those customers. The outcome of this special conference was a redesign proposal full of wonderfully innovative ideas.

Given the redesign proposal for the clusters and the redesign proposal for the central office staff, the Strategic Leadership Team began the hard work of finding resources to implement the redesign proposals. The district, as noted earlier, wanted to implement three of the comprehensive reform models supported by the New American Schools — one in each of the three K–12 clusters. The models they selected were the ATLAS Communities, the Modern Red Schoolhouse Institute, and Roots and Wings.[2] Using a different design for each cluster is not a problem, as long as each design supports a district's grand vision and strategic direction. In the literature on organization development, encouraging different approaches to the same goal is referred to as the principle of equifinality.

To estimate the cost of implementing all three designs to improve their whole district, the Strategic Leadership Team relied on cost data developed by a study conducted by the RAND Corporation and by cost projections developed by Odden (1998). Odden's projections, in particular, were central to the team's calculations because they were specifically linked to each of the chosen reform models.

Odden (1998) specifies the expected costs of implementing comprehensive school improvement designs supported by the New American Schools. These costs are calculated at the school-building level. Therefore, to estimate the cost of whole-system change the Strategic Leadership Team needed to scale up those numbers to project the cost of whole-district change. So, the next thing they did was use Odden's numbers to determine the cost of implementing the chosen design in individual buildings.

According to Odden, the three reform models selected had the following first-year costs associated with them. For planning purposes, the Strategic Leadership Team assumed that each design would cost out at the maximum level.

- *ATLAS Communities* require an additional $150,000 to $250,000 per building to implement, plus $32,000 for design team consulting services. Each school would need an additional 3.6 to 5.6 staff slots, but these could be filled using existing district personnel. The maximum total cost per building to implement this design was $282,000.
- The *Modern Red Schoolhouse Institute* required an additional $279,000 per building to implement, plus an additional $75,000 of design team consulting services. Each school would need an additional 7 staff slots, which would be filled using existing personnel. The maximum total cost per building for this model was $354,000.
- The *Roots and Wings* design required an additional $180,000 to $305,000 per building to implement, plus $44,000 to pay for design team consulting services. An additional 4.5 to 7.0 staff slots would be needed per building, which would be filled by shifting currently existing positions. The maximum total cost per building equaled $349,000.

The Strategic Leadership Team now had the first-year per-building cost of implementing each of the chosen reform models. Now, they had to scale up those costs to see what they would be for each of their three K–12 clusters.

Cluster 1 wanted to use the ATLAS Communities design in all of its schools. This cluster has one high school, three middle schools, and six elementary schools, for a total of ten school buildings. Ten buildings at the cost of $282,000 per building equals a total first-year cost of $2,820,000 to redesign that cluster using the ATLAS Communities design.

Cluster 2 wanted to use the Modern Red Schoolhouse Institute design. That cluster had one high school, two middle schools, and five elementary schools, for a total of eight schools. At $354,000 per building, it would take $2,832,000 to redesign that cluster using that chosen design.

Cluster 3 wanted to use the Roots and Wings design. This cluster had one high school, two middle schools, and three elementary schools, for a total of six school buildings. At the cost of $349,000 per building, it would cost $2,094,000 to redesign this cluster using the chosen design.

Finally, their whole-system redesign required the transformation of the school district's central administration office into a central service center. The first-year cost of this kind of transformation was predicted to be $250,000.

So, the total first-year cost for redesigning the entire school district was estimated as $7,996,000. The team rounded that number up to $8 million to give themselves a bit of a financial cushion for planning purposes. That $8 million was needed to redesign the entire school system—three K–12 clusters with a total of twenty-four schools.

Odden and others suggest, however, that it can take up to four years to fully implement the NAS designs. So, the Strategic Leadership Team simply multiplied their first-year estimate of $8 million by four to arrive at a four-year projected cost of $32 million, knowing that the predicted first-year costs would decline over the four-year implementation period.

The team also knew that the cost data they based their projections on were from 1996–1997, so they had to make an upward adjustment in their projection. They also wanted to have money available to cover unexpected "surprises" that might pop up during the four-year redesign period. In addition, they wanted to have some money in reserve to seize unexpected opportunities for improvement that might pop up during the implementation period. So, given these needs, they added a financial cushion of 25 percent to their projected bottom line, giving them a new four-year grand total of $40 million to pay for the total redesign of their entire school system. They were stunned by the size of that number. They wondered, "Where will we get this kind of extra money?"

Finding $40 Million for Four Years of Transformation

If the educators in this fictional school system asked Duffy, Henson, or Cascarino where to find the $40 million, the following is what they would be told. Absent more concrete financial data, we had to make some calculations and extrapolations to make sound estimates. These estimates, along with the underlying principles for finding resources, should provide school system leaders with a good starting point in financing large-scale transformation.

Counting the "Extra" Money

Getting a handle on education funding is extraordinarily challenging, largely because school revenue comes from a complex of local, state, federal, and private resources. The combination of these myriad funding streams differs, often widely, state by state and community by community. For example, in FY2000 the state share for education funding in Nevada was about 30 percent compared to over 71 percent in New Mexico. The share of federal dollars in the same year varied from over 20 percent in the District of Columbia to less than 4 percent in New Jersey (National Center for Education Statistics, 2000). To complicate matters, education spending as a whole has not often been effectively tracked, a circumstance that "discourages accountability . . . since no one person holds responsibility for total spending on teachers or on math" (Rothstein & Miles, 1995), for example. Thus, we have to make some broad assumptions and calculations about funding system-wide improvement absent comprehensive cost data.

The Strategic Leadership Team in the preceding scenario estimated that their school system would need $40 million over four years to implement systemic improvement. We would point out that this estimate is probably on the high side for several reasons:

- First, they repeatedly rounded up their numbers when doing their calculations.
- Second, they used a 25 percent cushion to raise their projected costs.
- Third, our projected per-year per-building cost is significantly higher than any of the maximum costs for implementing the chosen NAS designs.
- Fourth, first-year costs are always the highest in any school reform effort. In subsequent years, the first-year costs would probably decrease on a yearly basis. This reduction in costs was not built into their calculations.

But, to be safe, we would advise them to assume that $40 million is what they needed.

In the case study, the default mental model for financing whole-system change was that they needed 40 million *extra* dollars to do this *extra* set of improvement activities. As long as "extra" remains their prevailing mental model, improving that school system would be unsustainable (we also believe that this mental model would also create unsustainable change in real school districts). The reason for this conclusion is simple: there will never be enough extra money to pay for this kind of whole-system transformation.

The Painted Horse School District is a school system with 24 school buildings organized into three K–12 clusters. In reality, out of the 16,850 public school districts in the United States, only 416 of them have 24 or more schools. The National Center for Education Statistics tracks various data on the top 500 school districts (in terms of student enrollment) in the country, of which the 416 identified previously are a part. While the data are incomplete, revenue and expenditures of 400 of those 416 school districts are available, and we used those figures to make the following calculations.

The 400 largest school districts in our sample are home to 25,817 school buildings that educate more than 18.7 million students. The average per-year per-building expenditure for each of the schools in those

400 districts is $4,146,665. We assumed that the Painted Horse School District would also be part of this group of districts. So, to project where we would find money to pay for whole-district reform in our hypothetical school district we used the yearly per-building expenditure amount of $4,146,665 as a point of reference.

The hypothetical scenario suggests that this district of three clusters and twenty-four schools needs about $40 million over four years to implement the systemic improvement process illustrated in the case study. This creates a rough average of $416,666 per school per year ($40,000,000 divided by 24 schools divided by 4 years).[3]

We think it would be a mistake to look at this $416,666 figure, which in the real world only constitutes about a 10 percent increase in average building-level operating budgets in a district, and think of it as an extra cost. Were this the case, district leadership would be hard-pressed to find those extra dollars even by tapping into the existing universe of federal, state, local, and private resources. But, for the first year of implementation, they would most likely need some extra money to help meet the $416,666 figure. So, let's take a closer look at several of these "outside the district" funding sources.

Federal Education Spending

In 2000, the 400 school districts in our sample with a total of 25,817 schools had combined annual revenues of $107 billion, an average of 9.1 percent of which was federal subsidy (National Center for Education Statistics, 2001), totaling $9.74 billion. In fact, their federal allocation represented roughly 50 percent of all federal monies earmarked for elementary and secondary education in 2000. The figure $9.74 billion divided among 25,817 schools comes to $377,271 per school per year, which very quickly approaches the $416,666 target needed by the Painted Horse School District. Remember, however, that most of the $9.74 billion has already been spent. In the U.S. Department of Education's 2000 budget, 72 percent of monies allocated to public school systems were in the form of *targeted* assistance, or formula programs that are tied to students with certain circumstances, such as poverty, English language learning, migrant status, special needs and disabilities, and so on. Nearly all of this federal money, in fact, is directed toward salaries of additional teachers, often special resource teachers outside the general classroom. Only 28 percent of funding came in the form of competitive grants that typically fund "extra" or new programs, for reading, comprehensive school reform, dropout and violence prevention, and so on.[4] This means that in all likelihood, only $2.73 billion divided among 25,817 schools, or $105,744 per school per year, could be awarded to these school systems to do something "extra." So, let's assume that the school district in the case study qualified for and received the $105,744. This would leave them $310,922 per school per year short of their projected costs ($416,666 minus $105,744).

Local Education Spending

Federal dollars represent approximately 10 percent of all education spending. The remaining 90 percent flows from state, local, and private resources.[5] Local resources generally come from property and other local taxes. Finding extra dollars here means raising taxes, the feasibility of which varies from community to community. There are also Local Education Funds (LEFs), which are private community organizations designed to pool resources together at the local level to distribute to schools. According to the Public Education Network, in the national association of LEFs, there are 70 LEFs in the country that have for over twenty years contributed $1.5 billion to public education.[6] While certainly not insignificant, we think that LEF funding is not large enough on a yearly basis to warrant factoring in to the Painted Horse School District's search for funds.

Private-Sector Education Spending

More broadly, the private sector participates considerably in education. In 1999, the largest 1,000 private and corporate foundations in the United States contributed $751.6 million to elementary and secondary education (Foundation Center, 2001). These foundations represent roughly half of all foundation giving among the more than 14,000 private foundations in the United States. That being the case, private foundation contributions to elementary and secondary education could conceivably be double that figure, or $1.5 billion. Not all of this is applicable, of course. Some of it goes to fund private schools, for example; some of it finances land acquisition, building maintenance and renovation, scholarships, and so on. But even if we assumed that all of this money was made available for financing school system improvement, that would add $751.6 million to our hypothetical kitty, or $29,112 per school per year ($751.6 million divided by 25,817 schools). If the Painted Horse School District received $27,092, that would bring their grand total of improvement funds up to $134,856 ($105,744 plus $29,112), which still leaves them $281,810 per school per year shy of their target.

State Education Spending

Can the Painted Horse School District's state bear the burden of "ponying up" the extra money needed to support whole-district change? Probably not. State funding for school districts, as was mentioned, varies greatly from state to state. Despite lacking a systematic accounting of state spending, it is assumed that nearly all state-level resources are placed toward existing operations.

States do award competitive grants for new programs. For example, Massachusetts has a Bay State Readers program, which allots $2.9 million per year for schools to hire a literacy coordinator and purchase professional development and other technical services in language arts.[7] California has the Immediate Intervention Underperforming Schools Program (II/USP) that grants $200 per pupil to schools needing improvement. A total of $149 million was awarded in FY2001.[8] These awards last a finite number of years, typically two or three. Presumably, new grant programs take their place thereafter.

Most states have similar amounts of dollars set aside for new programs. In general, however, the amount of "extra" funding available to school districts is minimal. A survey of ten states revealed that competitive state grants represented an average of 1.5 percent of total state allocations.[9] In 2000, total state allocations for elementary and secondary public education added up to $180.5 billion,[10] 1.5 percent of which is $2.7 billion. Presuming, again, that the 400 largest school districts in our sample, of which the Painted Horse School District is a part, received a portion of that funding comparable to the percentage of federal monies received, that is, 50 percent (which is a presumption of some magnitude in this instance), they would be awarded $1.35 billion (which is 50 percent of $2.7 billion) in extra state funding, or roughly $52,291 per school per year ($1.35 billion divided by 25,817 schools). Add this to our running total of $134,856 that the Painted Horse School District found so far in federal and private resources, and its grand total of improvement funds now comes to $187,147. That leaves them, in the best of all scenarios, $229,519 short of the $416,666 per school per year necessary to improve their entire school system.

The eye-opening and disappointing conclusion from this analysis is that it seems that finding and getting "extra" money is an inadequate strategy for financing whole-system improvement. What else can our hypothetical school system do to come up with the dollars it needs to transform the entire school system into a high-performing organization of learners?

Using Dollars That Are Already There

Our figures are admittedly rather raw and warrant more systematic study by school finance experts. But beyond the fact that they at least suggest that improving school systems cannot be permanently funded by "extra" resources, there are more critical reasons why it *ought not be*.

We believe that school districts will need to find as many extra dollars as possible to launch their whole-district redesign efforts because their current operating budgets do not have a budget line for supporting whole-system change. But to embed a whole-system improvement process into the core operations of a school district, permanent dollars must eventually become a permanent part of a district's budget.

Even though extra dollars will be needed for the first cycle of whole-district improvement, school districts should not depend on those extra dollars to sustain whole-system improvement. Extra dollars, by their very nature, are unreliable. Schools and school systems have to apply for them, and they may or may not be successful year after year, leaving a shortfall in funding in a given year when the application is not accepted. Extra dollars are also tied to the various "waves" of education initiatives. The "new thing" in teaching and learning will get funded until the next "new thing" comes along. Instead of continuously improving by building on what works, school systems chasing extra dollars will toss out what works for whatever is new and attached to new funding.

Fundamentally, so long as an improvement process remains an add-on activity funded by extra dollars, it will never become a core operational function of a district, part of the common practice, or part of a district's internal social architecture. High-performing school districts are ones that not only improve once, they improve continuously. Improving is normal. It is part of the core, not extra. And it needs to be funded as part of the core, not extra. While extra dollars represent a great way to leverage resources to "jump-start" a systemic improvement process, the school system needs to think seriously and strategically about how it can spend its own money better in order to sustain continuous improvement over a long period of time (Miles, 2000).

There has been a great deal of scholarly and practical work on resource reallocation in public education. Karen Hawley Miles and Allan Odden, among others, have extensively documented their work with schools and districts in reallocating resources to support large-scale improvement efforts. Miles, Odden, and others have outlined strategies that have helped numerous school systems redirect millions of dollars toward improvement. There are probably as many ways to *reallocate* resources as there are ways they are presently allocated in the thousands of school systems throughout the country.

An important fact related to the resource reallocation strategy advocated by Miles, Odden, and others was found in the RAND study cited earlier. In the fifty-eight sample schools that were part of that study, a full 38 percent of the resources used to pay for comprehensive school reform came from reallocating existing resources. This is not an insignificant fact for the educators in the Painted Horse School District. If they could come up with some part of this 38 percent out of their own budget they would probably hit their financial goal.

You will recall that we used the average per-school per-year expenditure rate of $4,146,665 as a baseline point of reference (this is a real number taken from statistics collected by the National Center for Education Statistics, 2001). But not many school districts can reallocate a full 38 percent of that kind of money without causing pain in their districts. The Painted Horse School District couldn't do this either. But it felt comfortable with reallocating about 7 percent of $4,146,665. Seven percent of that figure would be $290,266. This amount put them over their goal by $60,747. They hit their financial goal, and then some.

To reallocate 7 percent of their budget and assign it to whole-system redesign, the Strategic Leadership Team came up with the following strategies.

Rethinking Staff

First, district leadership should think comprehensively and creatively about all resources, including staff, time, and dollars. The largest single resource allocation in any organization, school systems included, is staffing. In Miles's 1993 study of spending in Boston Public Schools, she uncovered that while 70 percent of students in the school system required "regular" education, only 50 percent of the teaching staff served these students. The other half was dedicated to special education, Title I, gifted and talented, bilingual, and so forth (Miles, 1993). A critical part of a whole-district improvement process is to make sound judgments as to what the best staffing allocations are throughout the school system not only to maximize classroom instruction but also to create greater efficiencies in educating the total population of students.

In a study of four schools in different districts, Odden (1997) found significant resources currently allocated for staffing positions beyond "slots" for regular classrooms—categorical specialists for special education, Title I, instructional aides, and so on. Ideas such as contracting out physical education, incorporating art and music in classroom instruction, and redefining the librarian role as a language arts instructor have enabled schools to redirect traditionally noninstructional positions toward regular classroom teaching and learning.

Also, by building capacity among regular classroom teachers to accommodate a greater diversity of students in terms of special needs, numerous resources can be reallocated. Boston Public Schools in 1998 attributed nearly 70 percent of special education referrals to a student's lack of reading progress or inappropriate behavior, sometimes resulting in placing students with challenging behavior in costly, out-of-district private schools. Boston subsequently realigned its special education services to better integrate them with regular classroom instruction, resulting in a 50 percent reduction in out-of-district placements by 2000, freeing resources that were then redistributed to provide greater support to reading and math instruction (Payzant & Durkin, n.d.).

Money Saved through Retirement of Faculty and Staff

Another way to recoup resources from staff positions is through the natural retirement process. As high-paying, senior-level people retire and as those positions are filled with younger professionals at entry-level salaries, the differences in salaries can be redirected to support systemic improvement.

Rethinking Dollars

Reallocating staffing in this way is not easy by any means. In many cases, nonregular classroom staffs are funded through federal and state categorical, formula-based programs like Title I. This is money that traditionally and legally must be spent on specific activities; typically, additional staff support for economically disadvantaged students or students with special needs. However, in recent years, the government has granted a great deal of flexibility in how schools and school systems can use this funding, sanctioning the commingling of funds for financing more holistic approaches. Schools with at least 50 percent of students designated in poverty can combine their Title I allocation for each of those students into a single pool of resources to support improvements for the whole school. These so-called school-wide programs can further be combined with a number of other funding streams so long as they are used to implement a comprehensive improvement plan, a plan that fulfills the overall "intents and purposes" of each of the funding programs (Cascarino, 2000).

Studies have also shown that school systems tend to dramatically underestimate the amount of dollars spent on professional development. This is in part due to poor accounting, because professional development activities are funded by various means (via local, federal, state, and private initiatives) and because districts do not account for teacher time in calculating professional development costs (Miles & Hornbeck, n.d., p. 6). It is also important to examine what school systems are getting for the money they invest in professional development. "Districts that offer 30 or more professional development topics actually may impact teaching and learning less than districts focused on key areas such as literacy" (Miles & Hornbeck, n.d., p. 5). Indeed, it makes little sense to send teachers to seminars for professional development on a wide range of teaching strategies if a school is already purchasing on-site professional development, technical assistance, and coaching from a consulting firm for a single teaching strategy. Reorganizing and realigning the often disjointed professional development activities for teachers could better focus resources on classroom instruction and best practices in teaching and learning.

Creative Strategies

The Strategic Leadership Team of the Painted Horse School District knew they could also use some nontraditional strategies to reallocate money. One of the team members had a colleague who worked in the Frederick County Public Schools in Maryland, which was led by Dr. Jack Dale. The team member recalled how that district was able to save $500,000 by converting two parent conference half days into one full day (this is a real fact taken from the district's online newsletter at www.fcps.org). The team knew they could do the same thing in their district. If this amount of savings was divided by the twenty-four schools in their district, they could reallocate $20,833 per school to support whole-system redesign.

FUNDAMENTAL PRINCIPLES FOR FUNDING SYSTEMIC SCHOOL IMPROVEMENT

We realize that the estimated costs for creating and sustaining whole-system change discussed previously were hypothetical. But we did use real cost figures to make our estimates and extrapolations to illustrate some important underlying principles that we think are important for financing whole-system change. Many of these principles are advocated by "real" school finance experts. The fundamental principles that we would like to uncover are as follows:

- Think creatively about securing resources. Instead of saying "We can't do this, because . . . ," say, "We can do this. Let's be creative in figuring out how."
- Develop a new mental model for financing school system improvement that helps you think outside the box for creating innovative solutions to your resource allocation challenges.
- Reallocate current operating money (according to the RAND study cited earlier, 38 percent of each school's current operating budget can be reallocated to support change. It seems reasonable to suggest that some portion of this figure could be used to create and sustain whole-system change, too).
- Make systemic improvement part of the core work of your school system. Build the improvement process into the social architecture of your district.
- Fund systemic improvement as you would fund a core program or activity—with real dollars that are a relatively permanent part of the budget.
- Over time, reduce "extra" resources for whole-district improvement to near zero while increasing internal resources to support systemic improvement and by creating a permanent line on your yearly operating budget.
- As needed, combine federal funds in innovative ways to directly support district-wide improvements in teaching and learning (see Cascarino, 2000, p. 1).
- Focus your thinking on financing for adequacy rather than on financing for equity (see Clune, 1994a, 1994b).
- When seeking outside (extra) money, make sure that the requirements and goals of the funding agency do not conflict with or constrain the vision and strategic direction of your redesign effort.
- Employ superior communication skills so all stakeholders recognize the true purpose of your budget reallocation strategy, how it will work, and what the benefits will be.

ONWARD TOWARD WHOLE-SYSTEM IMPROVEMENT

This chapter highlights the normal operating costs that school administrators have to pay for through their budgeting process and presents tip-of-the-iceberg options for financing systemic school improvement. The normal operating costs that were highlighted are common and covered through a district's operating budget. Despite increased flexibility in using federal and state funds and the wealth of research on best practices in resource reallocation strategies, the options for funding systemic school improvement that were discussed are far from being common practice in education.

We do not suggest that no less needs to be invested in education. What we are arguing for is to see school districts learning to use their current resources more effectively to better support continuous improvement. We are arguing in support of the position that educators should think more creatively and comprehensively about how to fund systemic school improvement in the short term to jump-start the process and for the long term by making these improvement funds a permanent part of a district's core operations. Finding the "extra" money out there will surely help get a systemic improvement process moving, but it will never be enough to fund the effort completely, nor sustain it over time. Continuous whole-system improvement, we believe, ought to be a core function of the school system, funded by core resources that are already there and that can be spent more wisely.

ABOUT JASON CASCARINO

Jason has been affiliated with the New American Schools (NAS) since January 1998. He is a graduate of the University of Scranton, Pennsylvania, and holds a graduate degree in international relations from Victoria University of Wellington, New Zealand. He spent a year teaching American history and researching issues of international culture and public policy in New Zealand on a J. William Fulbright Fellowship. Currently, Jason works with NAS as a consultant and writer, helping NAS institute strategies and mechanisms to encourage private-sector investment in public schools and to help develop tools for district-level managers to work through comprehensive reform. In addition to his consulting and writing projects with NAS, Jason is an analyst for the U.S. government.

ABOUT CHRIS M. HENSON

Chris Henson is the Assistant Superintendent for Business and Facility Services, Metro Nashville Public Schools, Nashville, Tennessee. He is the former Assistant Director for Finance and Administration for the Franklin Special School District, Franklin, Tennessee.

REFERENCES

Cascarino, J. (2000). Many programs, one investment: Combining federal funds to support comprehensive school reform. Arlington, VA: New American Schools.

Clune, W. (1994a). The shift from equity to adequacy in school finance. *Educational Policy* 8(4), 376–394.

Clune, W. (1994b). The cost and management of program adequacy: An emerging issue in education policy and finance. *Educational Policy*, 8(4), 365–375.

Education Commission of the States (ECS). (2002). Site-based management. Available: ECS Web site, www.ecs.org/ecsmain.asp?page=/html/issues.asp

Foundation Center (2001). *Grant money for elementary and secondary education 2000/2001*. Washington, DC: Author.

Goertz, M. E., & Stiefel, L. (1998, spring). School-level resource allocation in urban public schools. *Journal of Education Finance*, 23(4), 435–446.

Hadderman, M. (1999, October). School-based budgeting, ERIC Digest Number 131. Available: ERIC Clearinghouse on Educational Management, www.ed.gov/databases/ERICDigests/ed434401.html

Keltner, B. R. (1998). Funding comprehensive school reform. Rand Corporation. Available: Rand Corporation Web site, www.rand.org/publications/IP/IP175/

Miles, K. H. (1993, June). *Rethinking school spending: A case study of Boston Public Schools*. Cambridge, MA: National Center for Education Leadership, Occasional Paper No. 22, 13–14.

Miles, K. H. (2000, November). *District Issues Brief—Money matters: Rethinking school and district spending to support comprehensive school reform*. Arlington, VA: New American Schools.

Miles, K. H., & Hornbeck, M. (n.d.). *Reinvesting in teachers: Aligning district professional development spending to support a comprehensive school reform strategy*. Arlington, VA: New American Schools.

National Center for Education Statistics (2000, January 13). *Reference and reporting guide for preparing state and institutional reports on the quality of teacher preparation. Title II, Higher Education Act.* Washington, DC: Author.

National Center for Education Statistics (2001, October). *Characteristics of the 100 largest public elementary and secondary school districts in the United States: 2000–2001.* Washington, DC: Author.

National Center for Education Statistics (2002, May). *Revenue and expenditures for elementary and secondary education: School year 1999–2000.* Washington, DC: Author.

Odden, A. (1997). *How to rethink school budgets to support school transformation.* Arlington, VA: New American Schools.

Odden, A. (1998, January). *District Issues Brief—How to rethink school budgets to support school transformation.* Arlington, VA: New American Schools. Available: New American Schools Web site, www.naschools.org/uploadedfiles/oddenbud.pdf

Odden, A., Wohlstetter, P., & Odden, E. (1995, May). Key issues in effective site-based management. *School Business Affairs,* 61(5), 4–12, 14, 16.

Payzant, T. W., & Durkin, P. (n.d.). Unified student services in Boston Public Schools: Building a continuum of services through standards-based reform. Paper sponsored by the Center for Program Improvement (University of Colorado at Denver), Center for Research Synthesis and Product Development (University of Oregon), and the Education Development Center, Inc.

Purnell, S., & Hill, P. (1992). *Time for reform.* Santa Monica, CA: RAND Corporation, R-4234-EMC.

Rothstein, R., & Miles, K. H. (1995). *Where's the money gone?: Changes in the level and composition of education spending.* Washington, DC: Economic Policy Institute.

Wohlstetter, P., & Van Kirk, A. (1995, April). School-based budgeting: Organizing for high performance. Paper presented at the annual American Educational Research Association Conference, San Francisco. (ERIC Document Reproduction Service No. ED384953).

NOTES

1. We use the NAS designs because there are a lot of cost data available for them. Our use of these models, however, does not imply that there are no other models available to create systemic school improvement.

2. Instead of using the NAS designs, a real-life school district might have some other ideas that it would like to use to redesign the district. The NAS designs are used here only as an example.

3. Although we use a per-school per-year unit of analysis that creates a somewhat arbitrary standard with which to make our calculations, we think it is helpful.

4. U.S. Department of Education FY2002 budget, which includes FY2000 figures. The calculations were made based on the combined budget for Office of Elementary and Secondary Education, Office of English Language Acquisition, Language Enhancement, Academic Achievement for Limited English Proficient Students, and Office of Special Education and Rehabilitative Services.

5. According to the U.S. Department of Education Web site, federal funding in education includes allocations from the Education, Health, and Human Services and Agriculture Departments. Education Department spending alone represents less than 7 percent of federal education dollars.

6. See the Public Education Network Web site at www.publiceducation.org.

7. Massachusetts Department of Education, Grants and Other Financial Assistance Programs: FY2002—Bay State Readers.

8. California Department of Education, Immediate Intervention Underperforming Schools Program, Awards for Cohorts 1 and 2, FY2001–2002.

9. Survey of ten state Web sites for budgetary information, including Massachusetts, New York, Maryland, Texas, California, Illinois, Missouri, Ohio, Michigan, and Florida.

10. Total education expenditures for FY2000 were $372 billion according to "Early Estimates of Public Elementary and Secondary Education Statistics: School Year 2001–2002" (Washington, DC: National Center for Education Statistics, 2002). The state share of that spending was 48.4 percent, according to "Digest of Education Statistics: 2000" (Washington, DC: National Center for Education Statistics), or $180.5 billion.

Epilogue

They said they didn't have *time* for this sort of thing. Get back to them, they said, when we could tell them *what to do about it on Monday*. That's where their accountabilities connected them and they couldn't "let go." . . . For practitioners, parents and policy makers there is only "Monday"! It's their "kids," right now. Wherever a future vision is "supposed to" take them, the trip has to start where they are . . . on "Monday."

—Lewis A. Rhodes,
Putting Unions and Management out of Business

WHAT DO WE DO ON MONDAY?

When it comes right down to it, all that you and your colleagues can do is work in the present. Collectively, you have around 185 days of real responsibilities for real kids in real classrooms in real schools. Yet, if you truly want to create and sustain whole-district improvements, you have to let go of some of what you're doing so you can create something new.

Back in chapter 4, Ed Hampton and I used the metaphor of digging a hole to make space for a new azalea bush. If you want that new azalea bush to grow and prosper, you have to remove old, preexisting patterns (the grass and dirt) to create an empty space for the new bush to grow. If you just set the bush's root ball on top of the ground, it will soon die. In the same way, if you just pancake new reforms on top of current practices, year after year, those reforms will wither and die, too, or the current practices will suffer. You have to get rid of some of the old to make room for the new.

But then there is Monday to worry about, isn't there? Puzzling, isn't it? What a conundrum. You can't stop what you're doing to create what you don't have. And yet you must. Believe me, I do not have any easy solutions to this puzzle. Each district will have its unique solutions. However, I would like to share some thoughts with you that might trigger some creative thinking on your part.

You've got all of these "Monday responsibilities." You want to lead your district through whole-system change. You know what's required. You know you have irrevocable responsibilities and accountabilities. What can you do on Monday to get the ball rolling? Here are some ideas.

- While driving to work on Monday morning, make mental and emotional space for this thing called systemic school improvement (remember, you have to dig a hole for the azalea to grow; the same thing applies to your mental model for doing your job and for leading systemic change—you have to create space for the idea if you want it to prosper).

- Talk with two or three trusted colleagues first thing Monday morning about what you have in mind. Listen to their responses. Pay particular attention to their objections.

- Call or visit the president of your school board and the president of your teachers union, if you trust them. If you do not have trust in either of these people, talk with a trusted member of the board and the teachers union. Chat with them about your idea. Listen to their responses and pay close attention to their objections.

- Call one or two superintendent colleagues who are engaged in whole-district change or who have tried to lead whole-district change. Listen to what they have to say. Make notes.

- Given what you hear and what you "see" (i.e., what you see in your colleagues' nonverbal behaviors), make a decision whether to proceed with this idea you have for transforming your entire school system.

- If you decide to proceed, write a summary of everything you learned from your Monday morning conversations and plan on using this information as the "seed" for your district's new vision—the one that you will be collaboratively developing later.

- Then, at the right moment (not on Monday), move into the prelaunch phase of Step-Up-To-Excellence as described in chapter 6. Spend sufficient time in that phase because it needs to be done right if you want to succeed.
- Others may object to the direction you want to take by saying, "We don't have *time* for this sort of thing. Get back to us when you can tell us *what to do about it on Monday*." You need to have a response to this objection because it is valid and predictable. I cannot tell you what to say. You have to figure this one out for yourself.

We have come to the end of our journey together. I have given you an overview of the great abyss called "The Canyon of Systemic Improvement" and the territory called "The Land of High Performance." I have provided you with a map, compass, and other tools to make the crossing. It is my hope that you will take this information and use it to improve the overall performance of your school district—its central office and its clusters, schools, and classrooms. And so it is I leave you with the same question that I asked at the end of the prologue: "Do you have the courage, passion, and vision to lead your entire school system toward higher levels of performance, thereby, as Glickman says, 'unleashing the power of student learning'?" I think you do, and I know you can!

REFERENCES

Rhodes, L. A. (1999, December). *Putting unions and management out of business*. Unpublished draft of a manuscript published later in an abridged version in *The School Administrator*, 56(11), 20–21.

Index

making into a useful tool, 70; relationship to new mental models for change-leadership, 70; using productively, 70, 73; why change-leaders should care about, 66

characteristics of effective change-leaders, 115; new mental models for, 76; Stakeholder Management Model, 76, 87

class, social, 128; impact on school systems, 133; shaping expectations of children, 130; shaping personal expectations, 136

clinical supervision, xxii

Cluster Engagement Conferences, 186, 214

Cluster Improvement Teams, 186, 221

collaboration, 9, 31

commitment, 9, 26; as a consequence of leadership, 26; relationship to motivation, 26; revamping reward system to promote, 27

communication: "binding frame," 74–75; need for effective, 74

communities of practice, 191

Community Engagement Conference, 75, 179, 220

compliance, 9

control, locus of, 69

cost: counting "extra" money, 252; federal education spending, 254; federal title and nontitle monies, 244–45; fundamental principles for funding, 261; local education spending, 255; of design services, 241; of specialized personnel,

241; of teacher time, 240; of training materials and conferences, 241; of whole-district change, estimating, 238; out-of-pocket costs versus total costs, 242; private sector education spending, 255; resource reallocation, 244, 259; resources required for, 239; rethinking dollars, 260; rethinking staff assignments, 259; state education spending, 256

disequilibrium, 64

dissipative structures, 89; leadership as, 89

District 2, New York City, 106

District Engagement Conference, 75, 185, 214, 220; four major outcomes of, 185

Education Commission of the States, 238

effectiveness: balanced approaches to measuring, 204–8; competing values approach to measuring, 206; contingency approaches to measuring, 201; goal approach to measuring, 202; human relations model of, 207; internal process approach to measuring, 202–3; internal process model of, 207; open systems model of, 207; organizational, 201; rational goal model of, 207; resource-based approach to measuring, 202, 204; stakeholder approach to measuring, 205

efficiency, organizational, 203

empowerment, 69, 220

About the Author

Francis M. Duffy is a professor of education administration and supervision at Gallaudet University in Washington, D.C., where he teaches five graduate-level courses all focusing on organization improvement. He also founded the Alliance for Systems Knowledge, a Maryland-based "community of learners" studying large-system approaches to school improvement.

He was an honorary faculty member (an Associate in Education) in the Harvard Graduate School of Education during the 1980–1981 academic year. Sponsored by Professor Chris Argyris, he studied Argyris and Schön's views on organization learning. He served as the 1997–1998 president of the Council of Professors of Instructional Supervision (COPIS), which includes members such as Carl Glickman, Thomas Sergiovanni, Ben Harris, Robert Anderson, Ed Pajak, and Gerald Firth. He is a current member of the board of directors of the Association of Supervision and Curriculum Development (ASCD) and serves as the chairman of an ASCD task force and as a member of the ASCD Issues Committee. Frank is also the "founding" series editor for the new series on leading systemic school improvement, published by Scarecrow Press.